Time and Life Cycle
in Talmud and Midrash

JUDAISM AND
JEWISH LIFE

TIME AND LIFE CYCLE
IN TALMUD
AND MIDRASH

SOCIO-ANTHROPOLOGICAL
PERSPECTIVES

NISSAN RUBIN

Academic Studies Press
Boston
2010

ISBN 978-1-936235-03-2 (paperback)

Book design by Yuri Alexandrov

Published by Academic Studies Press in 2010
28 Montfern Avenue
Brighton, MA 02135, USA
press@academicstudiespress.com
www.academicstudiespress.com

CONTENTS

PREFACE AND ACKNOWLEDGEMENTS

The collection of essays in this book presents my research efforts in interpreting early rabbinic literature by means of socio-anthropological methods. By those methods I try to develop an interdisciplinary field connecting Judaic Studies and Social Studies, mainly sociology and anthropology.

The articles chosen for the present volume deal with two basic social issues: First, time in rabbinical perception; and secondly, various issues in rites of passage accompanying individual's life cycle. The idea in most of the essays is that long-term changes in social structure have an impact on the structure and meaning of the life cycle rituals.

Chapter one is mainly methodological. The main question this article addresses has to do with the systematic extraction of scientific insights from the textual sources, replacing the traditional historical-philological inductive approach with a deductive one. In other words, to develop research questions from a theoretical structure that may be validated or dismissed, I try to expose the hidden structures of texts using socio-cultural deductive methods, in order to understand the halakhah and the praxis inherent in these texts.

Chapter two (with Admiel Kosman) on the clothing of the primordial Adam, deals with perception of time of Talmudic sages. Their perception of time is regarded by some scholars as a-historical and non-developmental. Nevertheless, the sages gave much weight to remembrance. They formed a Jewish collective memory which is mythological rather than historical. What is remembered is not exactly what happened in the real world.

Chapter three on *brith milah* is on the drawing down of the prepuce and the incision of the foreskin (*periah*). Sources from the Hasmonean Revolt to Bar Kokhbah Revolt report about Jewish males who disguised their circumcision by drawing down their prepuce in order not to be identified as Jews. The paper presents evidence of a different circumcision process that was practiced until

Bar Kokhbah revolt in which the drawing down of the prepuce was possible. The rabbis devised a radical surgical innovation that thwarted this crossing of the community border. The rabbis camouflaged the change by attributing *periah* to the Torah commandement.

Chapter four on value of *pidyon ha'ben* (the redemption of the first born son) payment discusses the changes in the true value of five *shekalim* given to a *kohen*. It was at first a relatively large sum for a day laborer. The development of the *halakhah* shows that alternate methods were found which enabled every father to redeem his son in a way that did not represent an economic burden. In this paper I demonstrate how the rabbis interpreted the Bible and the *halakha* in an era of change. To deal with changing reality, they reinterpreted the text which in principle is unchangeable.

Chapter five "Rites of birth and marriage: A critical reading in rabbinic sources," discusses the deprived status of women as reflected in those rites. In a patriarchal and patrilineal society a woman, once married, changes her father's lineage identity to her husband's. Her children belong exclusively to her husband's lineage. A divorced woman or a widow returns to her father's identity. If she remarries she again changes her identity. This social instability is reflected in the *niddah* rituals so that their status oscillates between fertility and infertility during menstrual period. While menstruating she is impure and temporarily removed from home and community, both symbolically and practically. After purification in a ritual bath she may return to her home and community. Female's deprived status is also reflected in the absence of rites of births for girls. Paradoxically, she is very elevated during her wedding and marriage procession, makeup is applied, she is dressed specially, adorned with jewelry and carried in a palanquin along the bridal procession. All these are not for her own sake, since they symbolize her father's lineage standing that uses the bride as an icon. (The reader will find in this chapter repetitions of some ideas he read already in chapter one. It is due to the fact that they were originally published as separated articles).

Chapter six "On the sages' conception of body and soul," demonstrates the connection between social structure and cosmology. In the generations of the early Tannaitic scholars we find that the rabbis maintained a monistic view of the body-soul relationship. After the turmoil and social changes in the wake of Bar Kokhbah's Revolt there was a turn in rabbis' cosmology towards a dualistic view of body and soul relationship. They were considered as two different entities.

Chapter seven address the question of how the boundaries between life and death are reflected in the treatment of the dead body. According to the rabbis orientation death is determined at the moment of physiological death and dying is not a liminal state. The category *gosses* (dying) is meaningful in a physiological and not sociological sense. Two principles serve to blur the liminal stage and the sharpness of the transition from life to death, the principles of gradation and continuity, carrying polysemic symbols of opposed meanings of continuity and separation.

Chapter eight on *birkat avelim* (The "Blessing of the Mourners") discusses one of the ancient Talmudic practices of condolence, which gradually disappeared from Jewish life. The Sages introduced blessings for the mourners and the drinking of ten cups of wine in the house of mourning during the mourners' meal. The paper explains that the loss of the customs happened because elaborate mourning rites with special meals on each of the days of mourning, require an appropriate social setting. Such customs are possible when the community is composed of extended families. But as society becomes less integrated due to political and economical changes and families tend more toward a nuclear type, it is less likely that the daily meals could be carried out.

I am indebted to many colleagues and friends with whom I discussed the topics and issues in this collection of articles, but I cannot hope to thank all of those who were ready to listen and advice. Therefore I will mention by name only two people whose help made this book possible. Dr. Sam Cooper, of Bar Ilan University, Department of Sociology and Anthropology, who is an original thinker in the field of Anthropology of *Halakhah*, with whom I spend many hours of discussions. His work and mine are parallel in many ways with some differences of opinion regarding some issues.

I acknowledge the interest and encouragement of Dr. Simcha Fishbane of Touro College and thank him for his support in producing this book. Dr. Fishbane was the major organizing force behind the Canada-Israel Conferences on the Social Scientific Study of Judaism. These conferences led to the production of a number of serious papers on the subject, including some of the material presented here.

I gratefully acknowledge the following publications in which this essays appeared:

Chapter one, "The Sociology and Anthropology of Talmudic texts," in: Avi Ravitzki and Avinoam Roznek (eds.). Halacha and *Metahalacha: An Interdisciplinary Approach.* Jerusalem: Magnes Press. (forthcoming).

Chapter two, "The Clothing of the Primordial Adam as a Symbol of Apocalyptic Time in the Midrashic Sources," *Harvard Theological Review,* 90: 155–174, 1997 (with Admiel Kosman).

Chapter three, "*Brit Milah*: A Study of Change in Customs," in: Elizabeth Wyner Mark (ed.). *The Covenant of Circumcision: New Perspectives on an Ancient Jewish Rite*. Boston: University Press of New England and Brandeis University Press, 2003, pp. 87–97.

Chapter four, "Coping with the Value of *Pidyon Ha'ben* Payment in Rabbinical Literature: An Example of a Social Change Process." *Jewish History*, 10: 1–23, 1996.

Chapter five, "Rites of Birth and Marriage: A Critical Reading in Rabbinic Sources," in: Avi Ravitzki and Avinoam Roznek (eds.). *New Approaches to the Philosophy of Halacha*. Jerusalem: Magnes Press and Van Leer Institute, 2008, pp. 491–519.

Chapter six, "The Sages' conception of Body and Soul," in: Jack Lightstone and Simchah Fishbane (eds.). *Essays in the Social Scientific Study of Judaism and Jewish Society* (vol. I). Montreal: Concordia University Press, 1990, pp. 47–103.

Chapter seven, "From Corpse to Corpus: The Body of the Dead as a Text in Talmudic Literature," in: Jan Assman, Guy Stroumsa and Albert Baumgarten (eds.). *Self, Soul and Body in Religious Experiences*. Baltimore, MD: Numan, 1998, pp. 171–183.

Chapter eight, "The Blessing of Mourners: Ritual Aspects of Social Change," in: Herb W. Basser and Simchah Fishbane (eds.). *Approaches to Ancient Judaism*. Atlanta, Georgia: Scholars Press, 1993, 119–141.

Nissan Rubin
Department of Sociology and Anthropology
Bar Ilan University

PART ONE  INTRODUCTION

Chapter 1. THE SOCIOLOGY AND ANTHROPOLOGY OF TALMUDIC TEXTS

There has been a rapprochement in recent years between Jewish studies and social sciences. Barriers remain, probably the result of methodological issues between the disciplines. In this book I attempt to demonstrate ways and means of application of social and cultural theory to the Rabbinic sources. In this introductory chapter I discuss the meta-halakhic conception of the Rabbis, as reflected in the Rabbinical literature. Later I will show how meta-halakhic perceptions of the Rabbis are reflected in the development of rites of passage. Originally I presented this material in my work on Jewish rites of passage including birth ceremonies, circumcision, and redemption of the firstborn; betrothal and marriage; as well as burial and mourning rites.[1] The discussion of these rites employs sociological and anthropological theory and method. Here I examine the nature of these methods and their application in the study of Talmudic texts. At the end of this methodological statement I provide examples from my work on rites of betrothal and marriage.

The Treatment of the Sources

Researchers of the Rabbinic literature are faced with a codex of sources extending from the third century BC Jewish society in the Land of Israel, until the time of late Babylonian Jewry. Although there was a good deal of similarity between the two societies there were serious differences as well. Despite their being traditional societies, over the course of time they gradually underwent change. Internally, they were not necessarily culturally homogeneous, even within the same geographical area. Within the same

---

[1]   See Rubin, 1995; Rubin, 2004; Rubin, 1997.

expanse we find cultural diversity, such as the differences in the Land of Israel between Judea and Galilee. Different theological or ideological schools emerge such as the Pharisees, the Sadducees, and the various sectarians. Traces of all these appear in different texts: in the Talmuds (Palestinian and Babylonian) and the Midrash, in apocalyptic and apocryphal books, the Judean Desert scrolls, the books by Philo, the Gospels, the writings of Jewish and Gentile historians, and more. Within this vast collection scholar wishing to research a specific topic must tease out bits of material and lay them side by side, as in a jigsaw puzzle thereby fashioning a thesis that is meant to put some order into these sources, as it distinguishes between early and late, identifies different versions, and the like.

The study of the sources with scientific tools raises the question of the use of methodological instruments that are invasive of the Rabbinic halakhic and aggadic literature, and seek to interpret texts without utilizing the internal halakhic apparatus. The use of extra-halakhic tools in textual research is not new; for example scholars have applied philological-historical tools to examine language, version, and historical background. These are positivistic tools used for an inquiry into the overt textual stratum.

Philological methodology suggests a cautious approach to the sources. Every source is suspect until all its appended strata are investigated supplying a kind of archaeological dimension examining each piece of the puzzle closely until all suspicious residues have been removed. Philology is considered a "hard" science, objective and positivistic, and will become the basis for all succeeding scholarly activity. It is generally accompanied by historical research.[2] These two disciplines enable us to shift from the text to its historical background and the ideas and worldviews that scholars say it might represent. Eliezer Samson Rosenthal directed philological-historical interpretation "to the version, the language, and the literary and realistic historical context taken together."[3] This work is intuitive, based on streams of associations difficult to duplicate, and with one source leading to another. When it appears that all the sources within a certain realm have been collected, and organized, the researcher tries to generate an historical insight inductively and thereby shed light on the society under discussion.[4]

---

[2]   The philological-historical method of Talmudic research was established mainly by Jacob Nahum Epstein. See Sussman, 1997. The leading proponents of this school were Saul Lieberman (e.g., Lieberman, 1942; Lieberman, 1950; Lieberman, 1991) and Ephraim E. Urbach (e.g., Urbach, 1998; Urbach, 2002).

[3]   Rosenthal, 1963.

[4]   For a critique of this methodology, see, e.g., Halbertal, 2001: 18–19.

This modern approach began to change with the spread of the post-modern perception that is not satisfied with this approach, which relates to the questions of "what," and seeks to answer questions of "why" and "what for," allowing for a more interpretive method. This approach was progressively accepted by the scholarly world, and is expressed in Jewish studies in universities and other academic institutions.[5] This methodology incorporates a synchronic approach to the sources along with a diachronic one, and therefore is capable of observing the changes that occur over a protracted time span.[6] In this context, we should cite Bruno Latour, in his essay on the contemporary scientific discourse:

> Our intellectual life is out of kilter. Epistemology, the social sciences, the sciences of texts—all have their privileged vantage point, provided that they remain separate. If the creatures we are pursuing cross all three spaces, we are no longer understood.[7]

It is not surprising that the study of texts from the interpretive and structural perspective of the social sciences is still questioned by advocates of the positivistic philological-historical approach.

The Deductive Approach and Meta-Halakhah

Justifying the use of an "external" methodology requires a discussion of the concept of meta-halakhah, a prominent subject in the philosophy of halakhah.[8] This concept is multifaceted, and I will not relate to nuances of meanings given by scholars with different approaches. What they share is a negative formulation: metah-halakhah is not concerned with halakhic discourse per se, but with different extra-halakhic factors, both visible and

---

[5] To mention only a few studies: Halbertal, 2001; Rosenak, 2005, and nn. 113, 116 (p. 546), with references to Gili Zivan, Eliezer Goldman, and Menachem Elon; Seidler, 2005.

[6] In 1936 Louis Finkelstein sought to demonstrate, in his book on R. Akiva, how cultural-economic positions and class differences influenced the formulation and development of the halakhah. In the absence, however, of a sufficient theoretical and empirical infrastructure, this attempt was premature. Gedalyahu Alon rightly criticized Finkelstein's attempt. See Alon, 1958.

[7] Latour, 1993: 5.

[8] See the sources in n. 5, above. Halbertal, 2001: 19–20, observes that in the Shalom Hartman Institute the halakhah is studied from the hermeneutical aspect, as is the case in Beit Morasha College in Jerusalem.

implicit, that seek to explain the nature of halakhic discourse. Following Rosenak,[9] who extensively analyzed the nature of meta-halakhic research, I note two approaches in this realm: one, inner meta-halakhah, which is formalistic and positivistic, like the philological method; and the other, external meta-halakhah, that tries to reveal worldviews and schools in the background of halakhic policy. I subscribe to the latter approach, which relates to the halakhah as the philosophy of science relates to science, that is, in the discovery of the assumptions at the basis of scientific research. The scholar who desires to formulate a theory about human society is faced with the dilemma of how to connect the facts by means of a theory. To this end he must use a "road map," or a para scientific theoretical paradigm. This paradigm is our basic image of the society that guides our thought and research. Different scholars are likely to employ opposing paradigms to resolve the same problem. It is currently accepted that answers to the same problem can be given from different perspectives.[10] Consequently, just as the philosophy of science examines the paradigms on which research is based and the methodologies that suit this research, so, too, the external meta-halakhah seeks to uncover the paradigms, cosmologies, and intellectual models of the halakhists.

The main question this article addresses has to do with the systematic extraction of scientific insights from the textual sources, replacing the traditional inductive approach with a deductive one. In other words, to develop research questions from a theoretical structure that may be validated or dismissed.[11] We already mentioned that for some years Rabbinic literature has been studied using sociological and anthropological methods[12] consistent with

---

[9]   See Rosenak, in press; see his references to the literature on the question of meta-halakhah.

[10]   E.g., a sociologist can adopt a Marxist conflict perspective, which originated with Karl Marx, or a structural-functional-liberal view, that began with Auguste Comte. Both theories are "correct," but explain the same reality from different perspectives.

[11]   For quite a while scholars have sought to go beyond the philological-historical method, and deviations from it often arouse stormy reactions. As episodic of this, we should note that a controversy arose over this issue years ago, in the *Ha'aretz* newspaper, in the wake of Idel, 1993. Joseph Dan and Yehuda Liebes defined his book as the "metaphysics of interpretation." Itamar Gruenwald viewed the abandonment of the philological-historical method that emphasizes the formal aspect of the text, as a dramatic turning point, in order to raise the intellectual issue, namely, the nature of the messages in these texts. See Liebes, 1993; Dan, 1993; Gruenwald, 1993. On the entrenchment of methods from the field of cultural studies in the study of the Rabbinic literature, see Rosen-Zvi, 2004: 6–7.

[12]   Above, n. 5.

those of cultural studies and based on the writings of Michel Foucault.[13] While this is an advance in method,[14] we are still unable to explain social processes and changes using both synchronic and diachronic tools, in order to reveal the meta-halakhic principles in the Rabbinic sources.

In my studies I expose the hidden structures of texts using socio-cultural deductive method, in order to understand the halakhah and the praxis inherent in these texts. This seems to run parallel with Carl Hempel's analytical-synchronic approach,[15] Karl Popper's analytical-diachronic approach,[16] and the position of Thomas Kuhn,[17] regarding the need of a paradigm that is accepted by the scientific community.[18]

Much of modern anthropological research is inductive, especially the collection of ethnographic data in a field where knowledge is lacking. One must dive into a sea of facts achieve competence in a way that will allow for the discovery of new structures. These will allow for generation of hypotheses to continue the research.

Alternately, it is also possible to do ethnography based on theory generated from existing ethnography. The theory enables a controlled comparison, a-historic, between the object of research and already existing ethnographic knowledge.

Textual research does not require the creation of a database, as in ethnographic fieldwork, because the corpus of data already exists. From within this preexisting corpus, the researcher must locate the sources from which the new knowledge is to be formulated. In order to "create" new knowledge, the scientist requires an external "instrument" to derive this knowledge from the data within the texts. This device is the theory in the researcher's

---

13 See, e.g., Storey, 1996. See Foucault, 1965; Foucault, 1972; Foucault, 1980.

14 Neusner, 1979 is noteworthy among the first studies. The following are a number of studies of Rabbinic literature that employ social sciences methods: Deshen, 1978; Fishbane and Lightstone, 1990; Fishbane and Lightstone, 1992; Goldberg, 1987; Hoffman, 1987; Hoffman, 1996; Lightstone, 1988; Basser & Fishbane, 1993; Boyarin, 1993.

15 Hempel, 1959; Hempel and Oppenheim, 1953. See Rubin, 1997: 14–16, for the application of Hempel's methodology in my work.

16 Popper, 1945; Popper, 1959.

17 Kuhn, 1970.

18 The acceptance of a paradigm still does not mean that it is capable of explaining all the known facts in the field. From this aspect, according to Kuhn, science is subjective: one among a number of theories is "victorious," and its subjectivity becomes universally accepted. If the theory withstands empirical tests, then, according to Hempel and Popper, the paradigm will likely lead to objective knowledge. See Kuhn, 1970: 15.

mind[19] which channels the collection and classification of data by means of classification categories. The theory facilitates the discovery of the links between the categories, and provides the frame within which to fit the puzzle pieces.

Theory as a Device

A critical reading of a text must be both synchronic and diachronic.[20] A reading is synchronic, in the sense that the text is read in connection with nearby texts as well as in connection with texts with similar subjects. A reading is synchronic, also in the sense that anthropological interpretation compares the phenomena to similar phenomena in similarly structured cultures even where there is no temporal or geographic connection. In this respect, the comparison is a-historical. It is diachronic, when it is based on the assumption that every society, even the most conservative, undergoes change. Reality demands normative change even in traditional societies based on unchanging text. In other words, in these societies, tension exists between the fixed text and the changing context. Change is slow, and extends over a long period of time, as Braudel puts it,[21] and receives post factum value and justification.[22] This approach presupposes the relationship of external factors that influence the halakhah. The traditional commentary presents change as "noninnovative," a shift, or the discovery of the existent in the sources.[23]

We must now answer the methodological question: what is the source of the researcher's confidence that he indeed explains what he presumes to explain? In other words, what is the validity of the explanation, that is, are the sources collected by the researcher actually consistent with the theory?

---

[19] Indeed, Halbertal, 2001 speaks of the need for a theoretical background when dealing with halakhic and midrashic issues; so also Rosenak, 2005: 308. But it seems, however, that they still have not assessed the power of theory in explaining social change (see below).

[20] See Hauptman, 2001.

[21] In contrast with the positivistic historians whose subject matter is the short-term span of time, Fernand Braudel and the members of the Annales school argued that patterns of change of some historical events and social institutions are sometimes extremely slow, and are likely to extend for hundreds of years. They suggest therefore to regard also to long-term analysis See Braudel, 1977; Braudel, 1969.

[22] Mary Douglas showed how structural changes in society refocus the cosmologies that explain human existence. See Douglas, 1973.

[23] Katz, 1993. See the discussion by Tamar Ross (2005: esp. 408–9); Stollman, 2005.

Is there no possibility of explaining the facts by means of another theoretical framework? The answer to the first question is that the study is valid when it meets the conditions of construct validity. According to Cronbach and Meehl,[24] "construct validity" is the potential for explanation inherent in the theoretical structure. This potential exists when the empirical data that were collected "behave" as anticipated by the theoretical structure that they are supposed to represent.[25] Data that do not behave as expected are likely to contradict and invalidate the theory, but they may also indicate a way to expand it so that it will also include the "deviant" data. Another possibility is that the "deviant" data belong to another universe of content, and are not meant to be incorporated in the present structure. In examination of texts, the "empirical" data are the pieces of texts collected by the researcher from which he fashions his hypothesis. Bruno Latour depicted scientific work as differentiating between the basic categories that the hybrid reality combines, and scientists act to "purify" and separate the intermingled categories. He defined this as "creating order out of disorder."[26] The theory therefore determines which data will be selected and which rejected. As regards the second question, it is definitely possible that another theory will provide a different explanation; any other explanation is legitimate, provided the alternative theory is internally coherent and explains a majority of the cases that were examined.

It should also be stated that the scientific object, or the scientific product, that results from the study, is not only a technical product of the "laboratory" in the researcher's mind, it is also a symbolic, social, and political product. In attaining goals of a research, the researcher's involvement does not end with the material before him, his involvement also extends to the social-cultural world. Whether he wills it or not, ideologies, religious worldviews, cosmologies, and social norms penetrate the scientific activity—and every scientific product is socio-cultural. This is the realm of meta-science.[27]

---

24   Cronbach & Meehl, 1955.

25   The concept of "validity" is central in natural sciences and in empirical social sciences, with a distinction between "external validity," "internal validity," and "construct validity." But as for the study of texts, only "construct validity" is meaningful. On validity see, e.g., Krausz, Miller and Rubin, 1983: 26–31; Beyth-Marom, 1990: 31–43.

26   Latour, 1993: 5; Latour & Woolgar, 1979: 245–52.

27   Studies in sociology of science examined the process of constructing scientific knowledge within laboratories. They proved their assumptions that this knowledge, as well, is not objective. The scientific knowledge is created within interactions that also include personal, economic, and political considerations. See Latour and Woolgar (1979); Knorr-Cetina, 1981; Knorr-Cetina, 1999; and a recent Ph.D. dissertation by Nuni-Weiss, 2006.

A Sociological and Socio-anthropological Approach

One of the methods that I employ examines texts from a structural stand-point.[28] This is a sociological and a social anthropological approach[29] which is based on Claude Levi-Strauss's structural paradigm that point at the compositional power of a model: findings can be ordered and interpreted by means of the model. According to this paradigm, the text's meaning is derived from social structure, and the interpreter must therefore find the model most proximate to the structure. The ability to arrive at such a model is dependent on the degree of identity between the researcher's thought structure and the thought structure of the creators of the text, or of its readers, since they all are conditioned by that same structure. Levi-Strauss argues that the structural methodology provides an "objective" tool that aids the researcher to somewhat escape the subjectivity we indicated above, that is, the influence of the relationship between the researcher and the field of research. This methodology allows the meta-structural cultural system to be revealed. We may state that the assumption of the external meta-halakhic conception sits well with Levi-Strauss. The explanation for human behavior and social and cultural phenomena is also to be sought in the unconscious stratum of human thought. In the final analysis, this conditions visible human behavior and dictates social relations and cultural symbols.[30]

Notwithstanding this, Geertz observes, in his remarks on Levi-Strauss,[31] that Levi-Strauss himself is bothered by his inability to objectively enter the world of the subjects of his research. But Geertz himself is not troubled by the influence of the researcher's subjectivity upon his interpretation. Geertz writes:

> In short, anthropological writings are themselves interpretations, and second and third ones to boot. [...] the line between mode of representation and substantive content is as undrawable in cultural analysis as it is in painting; and that fact in turn seems to threaten the objective status of

---

28 See e.g. ch. 5 in this volume.
29 Modern anthropology is divided into two main research realms: cultural anthropology and social anthropology. The former examines the basic elements characteristic of culture, cultural uniqueness, and cultural processes, and studies how social and cultural phenomena reflect the culture in which they are embedded. Social anthropology examines the structural conditions for the existence of the phenomenon, and the conditions that create differences that lead to its change.
30 Levi-Strauss, 1962; Levi-Strauss, 1969b. For his structural conception, see Rossi, 1974.
31 Geertz, 1973: 345–48.

anthropological knowledge by suggesting that its source is not social reality but scholarly artifice.

It does threaten it, but the threat is hollow. The claim to attention of an ethnographic account does not rest on its author's ability to capture primitive facts in faraway places and carry them home like a mask or a carving, but on the degree to which he is able to clarify what goes on in such places [...] It is not against a body of uninterpreted data, radically thinned descriptions, that we must measure the cogency of our explications, but against the power of the scientific imagination to bring us into touch with the lives of strangers.[32]

He later asks:

Must the anthropologist despair? [...] No, because there is another avenue of approach to their [the savages'] world [...] the construction out of the particles and fragments of debris it is still possible to collect (or which have already been collected) of a theoretical model of society which, though it corresponds to none which can be observed in reality will nonetheless help us towards an understanding of the basic foundations of human existence. [...] The mind of man is, at bottom, everywhere the same [...] It is by intellectually reconstituting the shape of that life out of its [...] "archaeological" remains, reconstructing the conceptual systems that, from deep beneath its surface, animated it and gave it form.[33]

Geertz nevertheless demands that the researcher's interpretation be close to the world of the subjects under study and to the way they apply it to their experience. He also stresses the importance of examining the processes of change in the social structure and in the symbol system. According to his view, symbols explain the reality, but the constant search for meaning in changing social systems creates the changes in the symbolic systems and the content ascribed to them. Social tensions arise when the social system changes at a rate faster than that of the symbolic system. That is, Geertz asserts that a dimension of diachronic analysis must be included in discussing society and culture, in order to observe the parallel change of the social system and the cultural system. Merging Geertz's approach in that of Levi-Strauss thus enables the incorporation of synchronic and diachronic discussions.[34]

Geertz's insight could also be directed to the study of ancient texts. The researcher of such texts obviously cannot directly observe the society under study, but he must "ask" the texts the questions that he would have put to the

---

32 Geertz, 1973: 15–16.
33 Geertz, 1973: 350–51.
34 See the analysis of this methodology in Silman (2006).

members of that society, if he could have spoken with them. The structure from which he comes enables him to ask the relevant questions.

Levi-Strauss continues the structural tradition begun by Durkheim and Weber[35] which isolates the elements of the social structure and examines the degree of suitability between the structure's components, and the parallel changing of these components over time. For example, if observation for a prolonged period of time, according to the conception of Braudel,[36] reveals that change occurred in the economic structure, which is part of the social structure, does the family structure, the political structure, or the social stratification structure as well, undergo modification, paralleling this change; or do all the parts of the structure change one by one? This method's primary tool is the model, or Weber's "ideal type," by means of which we compose a theoretical constructs whose components are taken from within the social-historical reality, while the type itself is not the actual reality. Moreover, the ideal types not even suitable to serve as a scheme for a unique situation or action. It has the meaning of a pure and ideal[37] limiting concept, while for the researcher, it functions as a valid measuring instrument to which he compares the actual reality, in order to examine the degree of the latter's consistency with the ideal type.[38] This a-historical method is validated by comparing the model to historical reality. In the study of Rabbinic texts, this model could serve as a theoretical framework in which the sources could be incorporated as in a mosaic. Without a model, the researcher is liable to enter a maze of trial and error.[39]

---

[35] Weber, 1949; Durkheim, 1938.

[36] See above, n. 21.

[37] Ideal, in the sense of something that is an idea, and does not necessarily exist in the reality; ideal in the logical sense, and not in the moral sense of what "must" be. See Weber, 1949: 91–92; Burger, 1976: 155–56. Geertz (1974: 93–94) renamed the Weberian ideal type as a **model-for**, as distinct from a mere **model-of**. The model-of is iterative; model-for is transitive, able to create a theoretical construct for explaining reality.

[38] Weber, 1949: 93. Weber sought to clarify the logic of terms that appear in historical writings, such as "state," "city," "bureaucracy," or "charismatic authority." He argued that in order to define them use must be made of "a mental construct for the scrutiny and systematic characterization of individual concrete patterns which are significant in their uniqueness" (Weber, 1949: 92, 100).

[39] Jacob Katz was the trailblazer of this method in Jewish Studies. His book (1974), e.g., does not describe a specific historical society, but an ideal type of community with its social institutions. He constructed this type from the reality, but the community depicted in his book is not the historical reality. It can, however, be compared to any community in the historical reality. See also Katz, 1993.

A Cultural-Anthropological Approach[40]

Another methodology that I employ is the interpretive approach for cultural symbols, which attempts to understand the implicit meaning of the symbolic system under study, as a set within the culture's whole symbolic system. This approach calls for the deconstruction of symbols, which are to be read as alphabetical letters, and their combination and deconstruction enable us to understand how cultural symbols are incorporated into a single system. This tradition comes from the schools of Clifford Geertz, Roland Barthes, Victor Turner, and others, who maintain that the symbols are not part of a complex and fixed system, coherent, logical, and whole. The symbolic system is a dynamic system which may become separated from one system, and join the symbols in another.[41] Symbols are therefore multivocal, vague, and subject to manipulations.[42] Obviously, the symbols lend themselves to alternative interpretations, just as any text is open to different understandings. Every legitimate interpretation will be valid if its symbols relate to each other coherently.

The Use of Theory to Confirm Hypotheses

I will now attempt to show how we can establish the veracity of hypotheses using a sociological or anthropological theoretical structure. I examine the connection between social or cultural structure and a number of concepts related to the process of marriage, with examples drawn from my study of betrothal and marriage (Rubin, 2004). In order to avoid unnecessarily burdening the reader, I will not cite all the sources. I will refer to sources only occasionally in the notes. The sources in their entirety are cited in my book.

---

[40] See above, n. 29.

[41] Geertz, 1973: 345–48; Barthes, 1972; Firth, 1973: 15–30; Leach, 1976; Turner, 1967.

[42] E.g., Joseph Trumpeldor became a posthumous symbol for the socialist Zionist youth movement, on the one hand, and, on the other, for the nationalist, right-wing youth movement, that even changed the Hebrew spelling of his family name (from a *tet* to a *taf*), so that it would suit the initials of its Betar movement (*Berit Trumpeldor*), in addition to the historical significance of the city of Betar, that fell during the Bar Kokhba rebellion.

Age at Marriage[43]

In the discussion of age at marriage I use a structural method that connects the socioeconomic stratification with age at marriage and explain gender differences between the marriage of a male minor and a girl minor. In the course of my inquiry, I coined the concepts of "first minority" and "second minority."

One of the intriguing questions discussed in the study of the Rabbinic literature is the age at marriage for women and men, and the gap in the age at marriage between them. Some scholars give an early age for both, others set a later age for both, and yet other scholars give an early age for one sex. All these views are substantially based on the same sources. As I noted above, in this article I will not set forth the various opinions and sources, which I presented at length in my books, but rather the sociological and anthropological pattern of marriage age, which I will use to explain the significance of the sources relating to this question. I will do so by connecting marriage age with the socioeconomic and family structures, as is accepted in structural analysis.[44] This pattern also explains the way in which a spouse is chosen, either by an arranged marriage or by personal choice, and several additional issues.

Our starting assumption is that the family structure in a pastoral society differs from that in an agricultural society, and both are different from the family structure in a traditional urban society, or in a modern urban society.[45] Consequently, the age of marriage differs in various social structures. The Biblical family was usually one of herders, or of independent farmers or sharecroppers. The family in the Sages' sources ordinarily worked the land, from independent peasants to agricultural day laborers, or was a traditional urban family. Breakdown by social class might explain differences in marriageable age and the age gap between bride and groom.

The "market theory" of spouse selection is a sociological theory that explains the way of choosing a spouse in a given society and the differences in the ages of marriage.[46] According to this theory, people engage in bargaining, and the future spouses were evaluated according to a scale of values that impacted on the match, as Jacob Katz explained.[47] Men possessed economic

---

[43] Rubin, 2004: 35–72.
[44] See the classic book: Murdock, 1949; see also Keesing, 1975; Collins, 1988.
[45] On the connection between the economic and family structures, see Rubin, 1997: 15–18.
[46] Collins, 1988: 218–34.
[47] Katz, 1974: 139–42.

worth, prestige, and power; and the women, the values of beauty, sexual attractiveness, and domestic skills. These resources change with age: the man's assets increase as his economic standing becomes more established; while those of the woman decrease as she becomes worn with age. The men's increased assets are matched by their ability to marry younger women. Such conditions furthered the age differences between grooms and brides. (The marketplace theory is still valid in contemporary society: as the woman's standing becomes increasingly equivalent to that of the man, her marriage age rises, and the age difference between groom and bride decreases. The greater the husband's resources, the younger his wife. The very rich marry beautiful young women; and, the other side of the coin: very rich women marry younger pretty boys.) For many years it was accepted among scholars that, until the Industrial Revolution, the rural agricultural society in Europe, as well, was composed of extended families with many children who married at an early age. It transpires, however, that in agricultural England in the eighteenth and nineteenth centuries, brides wed at the ages of 24–27, and grooms, between the ages of 27–30. These were nuclear families, with a small number of children. According to the inheritance laws, the agricultural holding was passed down to only one of the sons, due to the inability of the farm economy to support all the married sons in the parent's family. Sons and daughters who did not inherit had to leave their parents' home once they became adults and find their livelihood as wage earners or as craftsmen in the city or village. Young people worked until a relatively advanced age in order to amass the means to establish a family. The late marriage age resulted in a small number of children (2–3 per family). Among the minor nobility with means, in contrast, grooms married from the age of 19, taking wives 19–20 years old. The upper nobility betrothed its daughters even at the age of nine.[48]

This teaches of the linkage between class and economic conditions, on the one hand, and age at marriage on the other. A similar phenomenon can be found in analogous social structures in different historical periods, and similarly in the Land of Israel in late antiquity.[49] We cannot speak of a marriage age dictated by the halakhah, even though it contains recommendations for the preferable marriage age for men and women. The marriage age for each of the sexes, and the age difference between the two, was likely to change in different classes and under different living conditions. Until the first century CE—and among the wealthy landowners even in the first part of the second century— the couple could have been included in the household of the groom's father.

---

[48]   Anderson, 1994.
[49]   On this connection, see also Baron, 1966: vol. 2, 220–21.

Grooms could marry at the age of 18–20 (or older) with a young girl, twelve years old, who had "reached puberty." This pattern could have existed in a later period as well, in the Land of Israel and in Babylonia, if economic conditions permitting. After the Great Jewish Revolt (70 CE) and especially after the Bar Kokhba revolt (132–135 CE), the numbers of independent farmers waned, with a corresponding increase in day-laborer farming families, or those of urban laborers and craftsmen. In these families, the couple had to stand on its own economically, without the option of reliance upon the parents' means.[50] Marriages were therefore postponed until the bride and groom were older. Some men married even towards the age of thirty, and women remained unmarried even after the age of twenty. The age gap between groom and bride apparently decreased. The ideal was to marry off girls while still minors, since they constituted an economic burden, for girls in an urban society did not contribute to the family income; moreover, they had to be provided with a dowry for their marriage. It was also feared that they would not maintain their virginity. In consequence, those who were capable of doing so would marry off their daughters "close to their reaching puberty." Marriages at an early age were more frequent in Babylonia, because of the economic structure that facilitated the existence of households with extended families that could absorb young families.[51]

The **actual** age at marriage differed between men and women, in accordance with class and economic situation. Women married earlier than men. Another issue is the minimal age at which a father could marry off his sons and daughters, that is, the halakhically **proper** age for marriage. The halakhic nature of this discussion provides us with another aspect of how the Rabbis perceived the question of gender. We learn that sexuality and the associated social obligations differed by gender. For **girls**, the period of **first minority** was established, from birth to the age of three, in which a girl was not fit to be married, and the father could not betroth her.[52] From the age of three to twelve was the period of **second minority**, in which her father could betroth her without her consent.[53] If her father had died, and her brothers or mother betrothed her, then she could refuse such a match. The period from birth to

---

[50]   On the economic situation in these centuries, see Safrai, 1994; Rubin, 1997: 92–93 and the additional literature in the nn.

[51]   Because of the diverse and complex nature of the sources on this topic, I refer the reader to my book (2004: 58–69).

[52]   M Ketubot 1:3; *Midrash Tannaim* on Deuteronomy (ed. Hoffmann, *Der Midrasch Tannaim zum Deuteronoium*, 1909), 142; JT Ketubot 1:3, 25b.

[53]   M Kiddushin 2:1; Niddah 5:4; BT Niddah 45a.

the age of nine was established as a **boy's first minority**, in which the father could not arrange his betrothal, nor could the son do so by himself.[54] In the period of **second minority**, from the age of nine to thirteen, the boy was not entitled to betroth, but if he engaged in sexual relations, this act acquired the girl and betrothed her.[55]

Why does this gender distinction exist? The difference between the boy's position and that of the girl apparently ensued from the fact that the girl remains dependent even as an adult. She therefore is perceived as passive,[56] and is capable only of a negative act, that of refusal to the proposed match when she is a minor,[57] but not a positive measure such as accepting the betrothal.[58] According to our structural approach, this is quite understandable: even if she were to be taken in marriage while an adult, she still would not be independent socially and legally, for she would be subservient to her husband (as we shall see below, concerning the status of the *na'arah*) and could not determine her fate. Consequently, she may be betrothed by her father without her consent. In contrast, when the boy becomes an adult, he would enjoy full social rights, including the ability to determine his social status; accordingly, his fate is not to be determined in advance by marrying him off without his consent.

The Status of **Na'arah**[59]

The structural approach we have set forth enables us to clarify an additional question for which scholarly research has yet to provide a satisfactory answer. Why was the special status of *na'arah* (a period of six months from the age of twelve years and one day), between "minor" and "adult," established for girls, but not for boys?[60] I will add a symbolic interpretation to a structural approach.

---

54 See above, n. 52.
55 M Yevamot 10:6–9; JT Kiddushin 1:2, 59c; BT Yevamot 96b.
56 BT Sanhedrin 74b; the thought behind the analogy is that of the passivity of the woman, like soil that is tilled.
57 M Yevamot 2:10; 13:1–2; T Yevamot 13:1.
58 E.g., T Kiddushin 1:1.
59 Rubin, 2004: 56–58.
60 Neubauer, 1994: 114–15 discusses this issue. He mentions the absence of a period of *na'arut* for boys, but ascribes no legal significance to this fact. Neubauer forces himself to prove that there is no fundamental difference between the legal competency of boys and girls. This is an apologetic attitude, because the halakhah patently takes a different stand regarding gender. See further on the legal distinction between "*ketanah*" (female minor), "*na'arah*," and "*bogeret*" (female adult): Bamberger, 1961.

Due to the socioeconomic structure of the Jewish society, woman's status was not stable. Until her marriage, she bore the identity of her father's household and lineage. Once she married, she assumed the identity of her husband's lineage. And if she was widowed or divorced, she returns to her father's lineage; if she remarried, she acquires the identity of new husband lineage. Her sons will continue the lineage of her husband, while her daughters will change their identity, following the lineage into which they will marry.[61] This instability is symbolically represented by the *na'arah* age category, between minority and adulthood. Torah law does not afford any special significance to the category of *na'arah*, which is similar to her male counterpart, the *na'ar* (a boy from puberty to the age of marriage). The Rabbis, however, gave the *na'arah* halakhic significance in the context of marriage and the annulment of vows, while refraining from investing the *na'ar* with similar meaning.[62] The transition from minor to adult and the instability of the transitional period were given symbolic meaning by the Rabbis in the woman's body, and the state of her breasts within her physical development also symbolizes social change. Her breasts are compared to a fig: a minor girl without breasts is a "*pagah*" (literally, unripe fruit); a *na'arah*, who has begun to develop physically, is a "*bohal*" (that originally denoted an interim stage in the development of the fig); and an adult woman is a "*tzemel*" (the last stage in the fig's growth).[63] The *bohel* is the interim phase, neither here nor there, but also both here and there. The same is true of her social standing in this period: if she is married, she is under the authority of both her husband and her father. While the female minor is subservient to her father, and the married adult woman, to her husband, the betrothed or married *na'arah* is answerable to both: in both worlds, as it were. This interim condition might have been the culture's solution for a situation that was potentially traumatic for the girl. Close to becoming an adult, she is taken out of her home to become part of her husband's household, which is foreign to her. Her new home was frequently distant from her parent's home and daily contact with them. The joint authority of her father and her husband enabled a certain moderation of the crisis, since she knew that she still had a protector in her father's home.[64] The male minor, in contrast, whose identity is unchanging during his entire life, and retains his lineage, does not

---

61   For a detailed discussion of the wife's identity, see Rubin, 1995: 17–19.
62   M Nedarim 10:1–2; BT Nedarim 62a.
63   M Niddah 5:7.
64   In my book (2004: 225–28) I showed that the role of the wife's *shushvinim* (relatives from her lineage) was to mediate between her lineage and that of her husband during disputes, and to defend her in her husband's home from unfair treatment by members of his lineage.See also ch. 5 in this book regarding *shushvin*.

undergo the phase of *naʾarut*, neither physically nor in his social status, and so his transition from minor to adult is direct.[65]

Arranged Marriages[66]

The discussion of arranged marriages, as well, will employ a structural approach that ties the choice of a spouse with social stratification. One conclusion from this discussion enables us to understand the issue of the Fifteenth of Av celebrations (if they actually existed), that presents the possibility of personal choice, as opposed to arranged marriages.

It is almost axiomatic accepted that in a traditional society parents arrange marriages for their children, while a modern society allows for the possibility of personal, romantic, choice. Parental matchmaking, however, is not self-understood, and is a function of the ownership of resources. In simple societies, like foragers, where amassing of property is not possible, the spousal selection is conducted by courting, as it is also in modern society, in which the spouses have resources of their own, such as education, profession, and perhaps independent capital, a family could be established without parental support. Thus, in most cases, spousal choice is personal. In, however, a society in which the extended family acts as a corporation, as in agricultural families and pastoral families, in which the accumulation of property is a collective effort, and is passed on to the next generation by male lineage (or, by female lineage, in a matrilineal society), the situation is different. Families arrange matches between themselves in order to maintain or increase their resources. The accumulated property is not solely economic; it also comprises social assets that include, *inter alia*, political power, prestige, knowledge, and family status. This is why the families do not permit personal choice based on romantic love, which might not correspond to the family's interests. Consequently, the parents insist on separation between the sexes and marry their children off at an early age. They thereby prevent encounters that lead to romantic love. Those without means, however, must postpone the age of marriage in order to build an economic foundation. Widowers with means, or young people who are not dependent on their parents, will likely choose their spouse on their own initiative, but in most cases, even if the marriage is the result of personal choice, it is masked as if a matchmaker was employed, so as not to harm the social norms and clash with public opinion.

---

[65] Halbertal, 1997: 69–93, argues that by adding the category of *naʾarah*, the rabbis improved her standing; I am not convinced of this. See Rubin, 2004: 112–113, where I explain why I have a different opinion.

[66] Rubin, 2004: 73–102.

Arranged marriages were influenced by the socioeconomic status of the family and the age of the (male of female) party to the match. Even a relatively older male who, either willingly or unwillingly, is dependent on his household resources, may well be under family supervision, and cannot freely choose a spouse. Notwithstanding this, even in the instances in which the father was without means and his children were adults, the Rabbis preferred that the marriage be arranged,[67] so as not to harm the existing order.[68] Attempts were made to marry girls at a young age, even those from families without economic means, lest they lose their virginity. A woman did not have the possibility of economic independence, and at every age needed the family's protection. She was always tied to the household, even if sufficiently adult, and therefore was subject to closer supervision.[69]

It seems that for young men and women who were "not good matches," in a certain period Jerusalem was the site of the celebrations held on Yom Kippur and the Fifteenth of Av,

> when the daughters of Jerusalem would go forth in white garments [...] to dance in the vineyards. And what did they say? "Young man, lift up your eyes and see what you would choose for yourself [...]."[70]

---

[67] The father's obligation to his children is to marry them off: M Kiddushin 1:7; T Kiddushin 1:11. The ideal of the Rabbinic elite in the Land of Israel and in Babylonia was for their sons to engage in Torah study until their early or mid-twenties (BT Kiddushin 30a), which continued their dependency upon the father and, obviously, the capability of supervising the chose of a wife. We learn from the narrative of the late marriage of R. Eliezer ben Hyrcanus that wealthy but uneducated farmers did not regard Torah study as an ideal, and urged their sons to marry at a young age (*Avot de-Rabbi Nathan*, Version A, chap. 13; Version B, chap. 13).

[68] The Bible tells that Shechem son of Hamor asked his father: "Get me this girl as a wife" (Gen. 34;4), even though he had already engaged in sexual relations with her; and that Samson asked his parents to take a wife for him from among the Philistines, after he had fallen in love with her (Jud. 14:1:9). Samson's actions unquestionably teach of his independence, but he nevertheless requested his parents to act as intermediaries. Naturally, we also hear of the arrangements made by parents from the outset: Abraham's servant is sent to his master's family of origin to bring a wife for his son Isaac (Gen. 24:1–67); Judith is married to a man from her father's lineage (*Judith* 8:2), and more. These episodes teach that the marriage was usually arranged by the parents. See Albeck, 1961, and his proofs from Philo and Josephus. We may conclude that this was most likely the practice in later periods as well, if the social structure was similar.

[69] On the marriage of young people under parental supervision in other cultures, see Goode, 1959 Hildred Geertz reported from Java that girls are married close to the time when they reveal an interest in men: Geertz, 1961: 56.

[70] M Taanit 4:8; JT Taanit 4:11, 69c; BT Taanit 31a.

These puzzling sources, of a romantic nature, attest to the possibility of the free choice of a spouse, without supervision and without needing the services of a matchmaker. This event was in contrast to the normative world of the Rabbis, who insisted on separation between the sexes and on marriages arranged by an intermediary. Many scholars raised various hypotheses, which we cannot expand upon here.[71]. I imagine that the Rabbis related to these celebrations as a ceremonial representation, which related that "once," in the distant past, men came to choose wives. If such dance festivals occurred, they were meant, in my opinion, for young men and women who were not from the social elites, and who had not succeeded in finding spouses in a large and anonymous city like Jerusalem. It may reasonably be assumed that a large heterogeneous city, unlike a small and homogeneous community, would contain many people without the suitable connections for finding a spouse in the accepted fashion. R. Aaron ha-Kohen of Narbonne (thirteenth century) therefore spoke a sociological truth:

Some wonder: how could the Rabbis have approved of this practice, which a man would snatch his wife and, Heaven forbid, it would seem as if the daughters of Israel were free for the taking? But this is not puzzling: for you should know that anyone with the wherewithal to marry off his daughter would not send her there. For if she were a minor, of what avail would be her being taken, for she is not betrothed without her father's consent? And if she were a na'arah or an adult, if he feared this [that she would be seized], he would not permit her to go forth; and if he permitted her to do so, he would warn her to be betrothed only to one who was fitting for her, and it is well-known that a woman may be betrothed only with her consent. This practice, however, was for those girls whose fathers did not possess the means to marry them off, and they would sit [i.e, remain spinsters] until the hair of their head would turn white, if it were not for this practice.[72]

Betrothal Effected by Means of Money, a Writ, or Sexual Relations[73]

I will use the long-duration analytical method of Braudel[74] to discuss the change that took place in the methods of effecting betrothal: from the legitimacy of betrothal by engaging in sexual relations to the use of money for this purpose. The man betroths the wife in the erusin ceremony. The halakhic

---

71   See the extensive discussion: Rubin, 2004: 94–100 and the list of literature.
72   Kol bo, para. 62.
73   Rubin, 2004: 107–29.
74   Above, n. 21.

sources discuss three modes of effecting betrothal: sexual relations, a writ, and money.[75] The question that arises after a study of the sources is whether these are three alternative methods that were in practice in different times, or different situations, or were these three methods employed contemporaneously over the course of a certain period, and at some point in time the monetary payment gained exclusivity?[76]

Sociological logic would dictate that if there were three betrothal methods, there would also have been three corresponding diverse social systems. If not, only a single method would have sufficed, just as there is only a single method for divorce. Indeed, the Tannaitic sources indicate that they did not think of these three betrothal methods as alternates that were in practice at the same time.[77] We may reasonably assume that each method corresponded to a different system of social organization. This can be understood if we examine a long-term historical process.

Betrothal effected by sexual relations has meaning in an agricultural society, that is based on lineage and the extended family, with each such unit being a corporation with political and economic interests. The couple's sexual act symbolically links the corporations, and represents a pact that was "sealed" between them that consists mainly of the rights that the husband's lineage receives over the offspring that will be born to the woman. The tie is finalized only when the couple have children (preferably males), for the child represents the pact between the groups. If the wife does not give birth, this, as we know from different cultures, might justify divorce. We know from societies of similar structure that in such a situation the wife's father, or brothers, must return the bride-price, or to give in exchange the wife's sister or some other woman from his family.[78] Within such a social structure, disagreements are settled within the framework of the lineage, in the presence of the heads of these units, and they have no need for documents attesting to the existence of agreements, or of courts to confirm them. We do not find all of these elements in the Jewish halakhah, but it is similar in several aspects.

---

[75]   M Kiddushin 1:1; T Kiddushin 1–3.

[76]   This is the opinion of Abraham Freimann (1945); and of Chanokh Albeck (1944: 17–18, esp. n. 18). Albeck vigorously rejected the argument by Louis M. Epstein (1927) that the intent of the Mishnah is that money, a writ, and sexual relations acquire together.

[77]   The Tannaitic literature establishes the halakhah that betrothal is effected "by money, by a writ, or by sexual relations." See JT Kiddushin 1:1, 58b; *Mekhilta de-Rabbi Ishmael* (ed. Horovitz-Rabin: *Mekhilta d'Rabbi Ismael*, 1931: 256); *Sifrei* on Deuteronomy (ed. Finkelstein, 1940: 287).

[78]   See Kottak, 1974: 309–13; Levi-Strauss, 1969a.

In traditional societies that are not composed of independent farmers or herders, but of urban dwellers, sharecroppers, agricultural laborers, and artisans, marriage can also be an agreement between individuals, and not only between lineages. Marriage agreements, however, are usually drawn up between the couple's parents, or between custodians. In these societies, among families that are not extended corporative families, an act of sexual relations does not establish or confirm a linkage between two groups. The children born to the couple do not belong to the father's lineage, but to the parents alone. In order to create a valid marital union in the Jewish society, a document must be written and delivered in the presence of two witnesses. Writs, however, are meaningful only within a stable social order, and when there is a court or another legal system that can confirm the writ. If so, then it is the witnesses and the court that make a pact—represented in the writ—between the couple and the community, that grants the former the right to procreate. The writ therefore creates a verifiable official social fact.

A writ is meaningless without a legal system capable of confirming it. A monetary transaction, in contrast, may be conducted between the parties anywhere, without public supervision. Money is a neutral means, lacking identity, by means of which transactions can be conducted as it passes from hand to hand. The exchange of an object for money, or one object for another, creates a fact. Monetary betrothal is therefore an uncomplicated means for the transfer of rights and obligations. Since, however, the real value of the rights and obligations that are transferred in betrothal cannot be assessed; the money (the sum required by the halakhah) is no more than a technical-symbolic means. Nonetheless, monetary betrothal, like betrothal with a writ, requires witnesses to confirm the act on the public's behalf, since betrothal is not a solely private matter; it is of great interest to the public, which demands supervision in this realm. This oversight is necessary, for example, to prevent incestuous and other forbidden unions, and other negative phenomena.

The witnesses, who represent the public, give the halakhic and ethical sanction to marriage. A woman may be betrothed with money or a writ by an agent and witnesses, without the groom being present. Among the third generation of Babylonian Amoraim we find the view that, at times, the practice or public opinion are the witnesses that an act has been done. They use the term "we bear witness," even when there are no actual witnesses. As in the case of a *yevamah* (the widow of a brother who died childless) and whose brother-in-law (whom she is to marry) is afflicted with boils, the initial argument raised is that she be exempted from marrying him without the usual *halitzah* ceremony of release, "for surely she would not have agreed to betroth herself upon this understanding." This view is rejected, because "we bear witness that this was amenable for her, following the view of Resh Lakish, for Resh Lakish said: 'It is better to dwell as two than to dwell as a widow.'"[79] Following this, some *Rishonim* (medieval Jewish authorities) ruled that custom can serve as a witness. For example, in a place where the custom was to send *sivlonot* (presents) to the bride, and the man sent her these gifts, it is presumed that there was an act of betrothal, for "we bear witness that he betrothed her."[80]

The three modes of betrothal therefore correspond to three different forms of social organization. The inclusion of a new mode does not totally cancel the previous modes, but weakens them. They can be found partially overlapping one another over the course of a lengthy period. Betrothal by sexual intercourse gradually disappeared due to structural change, to be replaced by monetary and writ betrothal. Monetary betrothal is more common, because of its flexibility. As time progressed, betrothal by sexual intercourse was prohibited, and came to be regarded as a licentious act.[81]

It might seem paradoxical that betrothal by sexual intercourse was legitimized specifically in a society in which the couple were under a strict supervisory system that did not allow for the free choice of one's spouse. It should be understood, however, that effective supervision of women in an agricultural society was possibly only in the relatively higher classes, whose daughters did not work outside the home; and in an urban society, only in "decent" residential quarters, for only the wealthy could imprison their daughters at home. In small farms, in contrast, women had to do their share of work in the household, or outside. Women from the lower classes therefore had more opportunities for unsupervised meetings with men. When, however, poor rural families succeeded in raising their economic and social standing, they, too, tended to confine their daughters to the home. In the Biblical society, that was a pastoral society for part of the time and in some localities, the supervision over girls could not be complete. A case such as "but if the man comes upon the betrothed girl in the field"[82] related to the everyday reality, since women worked in the fields. Sleeping in the field, as in the case of Ruth and Boaz,[83] could not be prevented, which explains the atmosphere in the Song of Songs.[84] In the post-Biblical agricultural society in the Land of Israel, as well, the girls who left their homes for their labors could not be supervised all the time. Instances of premarital sexual relations should

---

[79]   BT Bava Kamma 110b–111a.
[80]   Isaac ben Moses of Vienna, *Or zarua*, vol. 1, Responsa, para. 760.
[81]   BT Yevamot 32a; Kiddushin 12b.
[82]   Deut. 22:25.
[83]   Ruth 3:1–15.
[84]   1:8.

therefore come as no surprise.[85] The way to solve this problem, even if only after the fact, was to legitimize sexual-relations betrothal, although the Rabbis sought to preclude such betrothals whenever the lineage could supervise its sons and daughters.

Thus, daughters could be supervised by limiting their movement outside the home in the urban middle class environment, in which women did not work outside the home, and among the daughters of the rich, whether in the city or in the village. In, however, a rural environment in which women worked outside the home, such supervision was not easy. The Amoraim attempted to invalidate sexual-relations betrothals and thereby increase supervision, but it seems from the narratives in the Talmud that attest to complaints by husbands that their wives were not virgins[86] that the phenomenon could not be totally averted. Patently, without an effective system of supervision, sexual-relations betrothal posed a threat to the traditional family structure, out of fear that fathers would lose their authority.

In the final analysis, sexual-relations betrothals suited a patriarchal agricultural society, in which the wife was absorbed in her husband's family. Betrothal by writ were fitting for a society undergoing urbanization, with a stable judicial system that could enforce law and confirm writs. This method was replaced by monetary betrothal, which could function well in an unstable society, as well. It could easily be implemented, and did not require a court to confirm the betrothal. There were periods of overlap between the methods, before the final adoption of monetary betrothal.

Summary

It is clear that a theoretical framework can "create order out of disorder" in the sources. Order does not ensue solely from historical interpretation, it emerges from a theoretical structure as well. This structure is not historical, but is supported by historical data evolved from long-term examination. The halakhic system of the Rabbis had to respond to the changing social reality, while being chained to sacred and immutable texts. The liberties they took in reinterpreting the text when the context changed, by means of *midrash halakhah* and *midrash aggadah*, originated, whether consciously or not, in the infrastructures that evolved over time. The implicit foundation of

---

[85]   M Ketubot 1:5; *Sifrei* on Deuteronomy (ed. Finkelstein: 271); *Midrash Tannaim* on Deuteronomy (ed. Hoffmann: 155), and more.

[86]   E.g., BT Ketubot 10a-b.

the halakhic system responds to reality by means of response rules that are embedded within the system. For example, we understand that age at marriage was not determined solely by halakhic considerations of sexual purity, but was strongly influenced by social processes. Halakhic reasoning accompanied the change in the real world and evolved.

The theory of family structure enabled us to ask questions those at times evaded scholars: Why was the category of "na'arah" added, but not the corresponding male "na'ar"? Why was a matchmaking apparatus put into operation, with free choice not permitted. Why do the sources list three methods of betrothal? Along with additional questions that I did not raise in this article. The possibility of ordering various sources that relate to a diversity of topics from the same universe of content by employing a single theory strengthens the "construct validity" of the explanation. In this view theory and reality have a reciprocal relation feeding back into one another to generate understanding.

PART TWO  TIME

Chapter 2. THE CLOTHING OF
THE PRIMORDIAL ADAM AS
A SYMBOL OF APOCALYPTIC
TIME IN THE MIDRASHIC
SOURCES

Nissan Rubin and Admiel Kosman

The Perception of Time in the Bible and
in the Rabbinic Sources

One relates to existential reality through the lenses that one's culture supplies.[1] The culture of each society, in turn, includes the way it relates to time and, as a result, to history.[2] Time as a physical quantity would appear to be a neutral concept, but its measurement is arbitrary. Time is certainly not neutral in any culture. It assumes various qualities, depending on the symbolic meaning that persons attribute to it.[3] One therefore find different approaches to history or to the writing of history in different cultures. The Greeks in the classical and Hellenist eras and the Romans in the ancient world attempted to write history for its own sake and to satisfy intellectual curiosity. On the other hand, the Assyrians, Babylonians, and Egyptians wrote chronographies, but not history in the western sense. Ancient Israel lies between these: one finds historiography in the Bible, but not history for its own sake.[4] The Bible presents a view of Divine Providence in history,

---

[1]   On the link between culture and the perception of reality, see Douglas (1973).

[2]   On time as linked to the social structure and as therefore changing from one culture to another, see Bloch (1977). See also Rubin (1987). A great deal of literature has been written about the classification of time: Leach (1981: 124–136), which differentiates between linear time and cyclical time, secular time and sanctified time; Evans-Pritchard (1940: 94–138) differentiates between ecological time and structural time; Levi-Strauss (1966), differentiates between historical time and totemic time. Gell (1992) differentiates between social time and cognitive time; On the perception of time in the Jewish society, see also Rubin (1997: 77–83); Deshen (1978).

[3]   For a discussion about the views of anthropologists (Durkheim, Evans-Prichard, Levi-Strauss, Leach and others), see (Gell 1992).

[4]   See Herr (1977). See notes 2–5 for bibliography of the historiography of the cultures mentioned here and elsewhere; see also Herr (1983).

with God's essence being visible through historical deeds.[5] Great importance thus attaches to remembrance through various rituals, in prayers and in celebration on the Shabbat, festive days, and mourning and fast days.[6] These do not require those doing the remembering to be historians. On the contrary, a society that molds its members in accordance with unequivocal memory patterns does not permit them to examine its history in a critical fashion; it constructs in them a collective memory, which transmits a single incontestable message.

The rabbinic literature is different from the Bible in that, while it does offer some evidence of historical events (scattered legends in the Talmud and Midrash, *Seder Olam, Megilat Ta'anit*), it does not imitate the Bible's attempts at historiography.[7] No Jewish historian lived between the time of Flavius Josephus (late first century) and the eighteenth century.[8] The Sages sanctified the Biblical era as a mythological one,[9] an ideal paradigm for all future generations, and they accordingly read the present in the lenses of the Bible as they understood it. The view of linear time that predominates in the Bible underwent a change, and the rabbinic writings evince what Levi-Strauss refers to as a totemic time view.[10] The Rabbinic corpus expresses causal explanation of different events in mythological and eschatological terms: day-to-day events of life attain significance in reference to ideologies and myths of the formative era, and they lead to a preordained eschatological world. Humanity's life in this world is but a transitory interlude between the world from which it came to the world to which it is going.[11] In such a world, both contemporary time and the past time exist simultaneously. In reality, there is no such thing as an independent present, for the present draws on a past that, in turn, demands clearly defined behavior in order to attain the utopian future.[12]

---

5   Yerushalmi (1982); Rubin (1987: 8).
6   This find expression also in the Torah's different positive commandments to remember "six reminiscences": the exodus from Egypt, the giving of the Torah on Mount Sinai, the extermination of Amalek, the case of Miriam, the Sabbath, and the way God was angered in the desert—all of which are recited in the morning after the morning prayer.
7   See, Herr (1977); Rubin (1987) and Urbach (1978).
8   Yerushalmi (1982: introduction n. 5 and ch. 2); Paine (1983).
9   On the significance of mythological time, see, for example, Garber-Talmon (1952).
10   Levi-Strauss (1968: 233–234).
11   On the concept of liminality, see, Turner (1967: 93–111); Rubin (1987: 11–12).
12   Neusner (1975: 110).

It is not history, as a historian reconstructs it, that shapes the worldview of the Jewish culture of the Sages, but the collective memory of a society, constructed of a combination of past memories of individuals and groups, that transforms and combines these memories into a continuum with significant meaning. This process constitutes that society as a remembering community.[13] Of course, a collective memory exists in both modern and traditional societies, both in societies that are aware of history and those that are not. The difference is in the nature of this memory; this collective memory is either historical or a-historical, depending on whether or not a given society is aware of history's continuance. In a society that values its history, the historical story develops in a progressive causal line from past to future, even though individual events may acquire a mythical dimension in the process. Conversely, a society that is unaware of its history perceives time as continuously cyclical, expressesing the permanent, the stable, the unchanging.[14] The memory of those events that have attained a mythical dimension becomes permanent through routinization, and the use of ceremonies within traditional formats; time thus becomes eternal. The collective Jewish memory, for example, recognizes the pattern of the fast days upon which one says penitential prayers. This has have a fixed format: A Prologue (*Lekha Adonai ha'tzedakah* ["yours, O Lord, is righteousness"]), an opening hymn, a penitential hymn, a refrain (*Zekhor rahamekha* ["Remember your mercies"), Confession *(Mi she'anah* ["who responded"]) and supplication (*Tahanun*) in the Ashkenazic ritual. The content of the hymns and refrains varies according to the event being commemorated.[15] In reality, though, the historical content means nothing to the majority of those reciting the prayers. These hymns—with a specific historical significance—are in an abstruse poetic form that very few members of the community can understand. The importance of the penitential prayers lies is in the act of memorial, in the plea

---

[13] The first methodical investigation of the formulation of the collective memory come from Halbwachs (1980; 1941) and Mead (1929: 235–242), both scholars adopt a radical position whereby the perception of the past varies in accordance with the interests of the present. A more conservative view, that allows for continuity in the present's perception of the past is that of Durkheim (1965: 415, 420), and Shils (1981: 31–32). A third approach, according to which both change and continuity coexist side by side in society, is that of Schwartz. See, for example (Schwartz, 1991). See also Nora (1988).

[14] On the perception of cyclical time in ancient societies, see Garber-Talmon (1952); Rubin(1987).

[15] See, for example Goldshmidt (1965).

to God, and the request for absolution; the melody, atmosphere and time are all substantive parts of the ritual that shape and transmit the memory.

The change in the treatment of time from the view of the biblical literature and that of the rabbinic literature was a transition from a collective historical memory to a collective ahistorical memory. The perception of biblical time is a linear historical one, emphasizing a transition to the future. The Hebrew Bible regards the body and soul of the individual as a single psychophysical entity, whose reward and punishment are in this world (for example, "Honor your father and mother, that your days may be prolonged upon the land")[16]. The community as a whole, too, receives its reward and punishment on this world (for example, "If you follow in My statutes… I will give you rain in its season… and if you reject My statutes… I will visit confusion upon you…"). One must rectify one's sins in this world.[17] This is perception of time which is optimistic in nature, because it permits the rectification of wrongs within the realm of history (for example, social evils are rectified by means of the Sabbatical and Jubilee years).[18] It does not generally foresee a catastrophe in the world to come, because wrongs can be rectified. This is as opposed to the view of the Dead Sea sects, for example, which, while still optimistic, is such only for the chosen group, whereas all others will meet a catastrophic fate.[19]

In the Sages' perception of time, there are no such things as earlier and later periods. Time is static, non-developmental phenomenon. This perception of static time took root and developed in a society lacking territory and an autonomous political framework.[20] Its troubles annulled the view that reward and punishment are possible in this world and transferred these to the world to come. That this view is also optimistic by nature and not catastrophic, however, is because the extramundane reward comes to everyone deserving it. This shift is coincides with the transition to a dualistic worldview that envisions a separation between body and soul. This world is temporary and sits between two worlds: the world from which we came and the world to which we are going. One must live properly in this world, while the reward and punishment are for the future, in the world to come.[21]

---

[16] Exod. 20:12.

[17] Lev. 26:3–15. Cf. Urbach (1975: 214–218); Rubin (1990).

[18] On optimism in the Jewish perception of time, see Handelman and Katz (1990).

[19] See, for example, 2 Enoch 8:1–2; 9:1; 10:1–6; 40:12; 42:1–3; 4 Ezra 4:41–42; 7:80–88; 2 Baruch 21–22. See also, Martens (1990). On the discussion, see, Licht (1970).

[20] See, Rubin (1987); Neusner (1975: 111); and Paine (1983: 20).

[21] See a discussion in length in Rubin, 1990, and chapter four in this volume.

Time and Social Structure

We believe as Douglas formulated it,[22] that changes in the perception of time in terms of changing symbolic patterns indicates a link with the pattern of social boundaries. By this, we wish to say that human existential experience within different social boundaries produces different cosmologies to explain the meaning of existence. Any changes in the perception of the society's boundaries correspond to the change in life experience of individual and society. According to Mary Douglas, one can classify a society's boundaries with a typology based on two criteria. The first deals with the dimension of membership in a society or group. This involves the the more or less rigid conditions requisite for entering into the society, as well as how much loyalty (to the tribe, forefathers, church, sect or military unit) its members must show. The second deals with the ability of the society to control individuals, that is, the degree of freedom that the society grants to individuals. Following this scheme, Douglas outlined a typology of for basic social structures (along with intermediate types as well): individualistic, obedient, hierarchical, and fractional (or sectorial) societies. In an individualistic society the obligations of individuals to the society is weak, and supervision and direction by the society over individuals are also minimal. This is characteristic of modern democratic society, for example. The most prominent factor in such a social structure is the autonomy of the individual. The individual's selfhood does not depend upon the community, and his mind is free. There are no forbidden thoughts in this society. The next is the obedient society, in which the obligations of the members toward the society's institutions are weak, while the supervision by the institutions of the society's members is maximal. This is characteristic of feudal society, for example, in that individuals in such a society are powerless and defenseless, in the face of those with power. The third is the hierarchical society, in which the obligations of the individuals to the society are considerable, and the society's direction and control over its members is maximal. The individual knows his or her place in the group, a place subject to elite whose authority is exercised capriciously. These characteristics are typical of a very ideological or totalitarian society. Finally, there is the fractional (or sectorial) society members have a great deal of obligation to

---

[22] Douglas (1973: 54–84). See also her later books, in which she developed the concept and introduced changes into it: Douglas (1978; 1982: 3–8; 1987; Douglas and Wildavsky (1982: 138–151).

the general society, whose boundaries are clear but whose ability to supervise individuals is limited. The individual can negotiate status.

Whereas in the first type a separation exists between the individual self and the collective, in the other three types the individual is subordinate to the collective. The community is the source of authority and rewards. The private opinions of individuals are liable to appear as serious violations and as potential heretical. Such heretical thought, If it becomes public, can bring about punishment, or, even when private, can result in a loss of rewards in the world to come ("one who denies the revival of the dead has no place in the world to come").[23] In a hierarchical society or a fractional society, the self-identity of the person stems only from his or her being part of a society characterized by collective responsibility. The individual and the community become inextricably fused. In an obedient society as well, the mind of the selfhood of the individual are subordinate to the group, but out of fear, not out of identification with the community.

In very general terms, it is possible to say that from the Biblical times until the first generations of the Tannaim (Sages active from the mid-first to the end of the second centuries),[24] the part of Jewish society that followed the Sages was a hierarchical society. The commandments of the Torah, and afterwards their interpretation by the Sages shaped a society with clear categories of behavior. It supplied its members with a uniform worldview and behavior patterns. After the loss of political independence, the Sages, through their spiritual authority, still had the power to control social behavior. Until the time of the Bar Kokhba rebellion (132–135 CE), there was a relatively stable society with a central leadership, a monistic egalitarian body/soul worldview, and a conviction that reward and punishment came in this world.[25] A positive appreciation of life in this world, with a concomitant clear system of predictable reward and punishment dominated the Sages' perceptions. According to this view, history is not threatening but flows in a clear line to a future which is not catastrophic.

A social and political earthquake shook Israel as a result of the decrees of Hadrian and the Bar Kokhba revolt. When punishments were the result one's

---

[23] Cf., for example, M Sanhedrin 10:1.

[24] On the variety of facets of Biblical society, see Knohl (1995).

[25] An ancient Mishnah in *Kiddushin* states, "If a man performs but a single commandment, it shall be well with him and he shall have length of days and shall inherit the Land; but if he neglects a single commandment it shall be ill with him and he shall not have length of days and shall not inherit the land" (M. *Kiddushin* 1:6). See also, Urbach (1960).

observance of the commandments, a crisis of faith arose,[26] and the traditional belief in reward and punishment in this world became untenable. Accordingly Rabbi Akiva turned things upside down: death and suffering were not a punishment but a reward. Sanctions became rewards. From that point on, rewards are not for this world, but for the world to come.[27] A martyr's death is the became the highest honor possible, because the individual has offered his life for the community, in order for it to allow its survival. The rewards for deeds were, henceforth, in the world to come.[28]

Jewish social structure began to move toward the sectorial (fractional) model. While the authority of the Sages persisted, a competing center began to arise in Babylon. The Sages felt compelled to adopt means to ensure that individuals remain subject to their authority. They did this by redeveloping the theory of reward and punishment into one in which rewards and the core of existence shifted from this world to the world to come. The present world becomes but a passageway, a liminal world, and only by behaving properly in this world could one open the doors to the world to come.[29] Here the view of history undergoes a major change: in the Midrashim time stops moving. In order for the past to serve as a model for present-day behavior, it must resemble the ideal behavior in the present. If, for example, the actions of the heroes of the past did not correspond to the ideal behavior of the present, they might serve as a model for improper

---

[26] On reward and punishment in the Biblical perception and in that of the Sages, and on the change in the perception of the Sages, see, Rubin, (1990: 73–79) and chapter six in this volume. On the crisis atmosphere we read in the following source, dating from the decrees of Hadrian: "R. Nathan says, 'Of them that love Me and keep My commandments' (Ex. 20:5) refers to those who dwell in the Land of Israel and risk their lives for the sake of the commandments. 'Why are you being led out to be decapitated?' 'Because I circumcised my son to be an Israelite.' 'Why are you being led out to be burned?' 'Because I read the Torah.' 'Why are you being led out to be crucified?' 'Because I ate the unleavened bread.' 'Why are you getting a hundred lashes?' 'Because I performed the ceremony of the Lulab' " (*Mekhilta de-Rabbi Ishmael*, Tractate *Bahodesh*, 6, p. 227. See also, Hoshen (1991).

[27] See, Urbach (1975: 443–444); see too, JT *Berakhot* 9:7, 14b; JT *Sotah* 5:7, 23b.

[28] On the special reward reserved for those who gave their lives on behalf of the community, see the analysis of Levi-Strauss (1975).

[29] An example of this is the statement by R. Tarfon: "Know the reward given to the righteous in the Future to Come" (M *Avot* 2:17); or the words of R. Yaakov: " 'That it shall be good for you' (Deut. 22:7), in the world that is totally good." The conclusion of the Talmud is that "there is no reward in this world for performing commandments" (BT *Hullin* 142a). For a detailed discussion of this, see Rubin (1990: 78–79 and chapter six in this volume).

behavior.[30] This exlains the existence of Midrashim arguing that the Patriarchs, and even the antediluvians observed all the Torah. Shem, son of Noah, thus already had an academy called "the Beth Midrash ("house of study) of Shem and Eber,"[31] The Sages thus annulled all historical development, because the Torah was available to all even before its promulgation at Sinai. That thought pattern has operated throughout Jewish history ever since. Even great tragedies were unable to change this thought pattern. Everything has become a function of God's grace, even the most terrible events. No room exists, therefore, for political or any other interpretation.

Clothing as Representative of a Perception of Time

In this cosmological framework are two basic axes in time and space: a vertical axis that connects the world above with the world below, and a horizontal axis linking the world of the past to the world to come. In the Biblical and postbiblical eras, with their linear-historical view of the world, the up/down axis predominated. In those eras featuring an ahistorical memory, this intersected a past/future axis.

One way of expressing those conceptions of time and space was through clothing metaphors. As a cultural item, clothing serve both the biblical writers and the Sages as a means of conveying their differing perceptions of time and space. The biblical and postbiblical world, an era of clearly delineated external boundaries, characteristically emphasizes the prohibition against wearing clothing made of a wool-linen mixture (sha'atnez), or garments of the other sex, so as to ensure a clear boundary between the sexes.[32] The boundaries between the priests and the rest of the nation also take visible form in the distinctive garments of the former. Clothing thus serve to preserve the boundaries among persons of different statuses.

---

[30] See, Rubin (1987: 12–13). See also, Potolski (1975).
[31] *Genesis Rabbah* 63:10. The Forefathers also observed the commandments of the Torah: Abraham in M *Kiddushin* 4:14 and T *Kiddushin* 5:21; Isaac in BT *Yoma* 58b; Jacob in *Genesis Rabbah* 63:10, which states that he studied in the *bet midrash* of Shem and Eber.
[32] On the cultural and social significance of clothing, see Kroeber (1919); Simmel (1904); Kuper (1973); Davis (1992). On the flexible and inflexible boundaries of culture, see Douglas(1966; 1973; 1978; 1982). See also, Cooper (1987).

Clothing as a Bridge Between
the World Above and the World Below

In addition to this role, clothing also helps to bridge the gap between the worlds above and below. At the very outset one should note that both the heavenly creatures and God appear in the Bible clothed, even if their garments are frequently metaphorical.[33] As was customary in the ancient East,[34] in Israel holy vestments featured prominently in the temple. God commanded Moses, "You shall make a holy garment for your brother Aaron," and the aim of this command is, "For respect and glory."[35] It would appear that donning the holy garments helps to sanctify the priest;[36] as Ex. 28:3 puts it, "They shall make the garments of Aaron to sanctify him." These clothes could not leave the holy precincts,[37] and the priests had to doff them before leaving there.

This clothing assumed special attributes of its own, independent of its wearer. Wearing regal clothing adds authority and a dimension of the regal.[38] The Bible also stressed the transfer of Aaron's priestly garments, to his son Eleazar.[39] There are also garments unique to prophets, such as Samuel's special coat[40]

---

[33] As in, e.g. "You are clothed in glory and majesty" (Ps. 104:1; cf. Job 40:10). In the vision of Daniel 7:9, However, the clothing of God (the "ancient of days") is as white snow, and is therefore not merely metaphorical. On angels being clothed, see, for example, Ezek. 9:2. The angels that appeared to humans were undoubtedly clothed. See, for example, Jud. 13:15; and regarding the "men" that appeared to Abraham, see Gen. 19:1. Incidentally humans also, occasionally wear metaphoric garments, as in, "I clothed myself in righteousness and it robed me; justice was my cloak and turban" (Job 29:14).

[34] See 2 Kgs 10:22: "He said to the man in charge of the wardrobe, 'Bring out the vestments for all the worshippers of Baal,' and he brought vestments out for them." Also see, Haran (1962).

[35] Exod 28:2; 28:4; 31:10; 35:19; 39:1, 41; 40:13; Lev. 16:4, 32.

[36] Wrapping oneself in the garment transfers the priest into the transcendent plane and connects him to the holy. See n. 82 on this below as well. The clothes themselves also need to be sanctified. See Lev. 8:30.

[37] Ezek 42:14; 44:19. See also, Lev. 6:4 regarding the high priest, and Haran (1962). See also, Lieberman, 1962, T *Kil* 5:27, p. 664.

[38] See Haran (1962: 1048) This is especially true of the garment of the king ("Which the king wore"—Esth 6:8) which bespeaks importance and power.

[39] Num 20:25–28.

[40] 1 Sam 15:27; 28:14. Also 1 Sam 2:18–19 makes a point of saying that even as a young man he served before God in a linen Ephod, and that his mother made him a small coat.

and Elijah's distinctive mantle.[41] The holy garments of the Bible thus help link the world above to that below. Here the garment does not function for personal territorial separation and defense of selfhood, but for linking the worlds. This special quality requires the wearer be ritually pure. Otherwise, the garment can have a deleterious effect. The garment represents the charisma of a formal position without a direct reference to the quality of the priest wearing it. As these garments denote a formal position, their design is also formal and unalterable. The garment of the prophet, too, links the worlds—for example, Elijah's garment, which continues to be miraculous even in Elisha's hands.

In the Midrashic world of the Sages, the mythic garment also made as a metaphor tying together past, present, and future. Whatever the world needs existed already in the formative era of the Torah time, and any subsequent event is merely a duplication of the past. "The deeds of the fathers are a paradigm for the children."[42] For example, as we will explain below, Nimrod stole the mythic garment of the primordial Adam only to lose it to Esau, from whom it went to Jacob, then Joseph. The fleeing Israelite then took this garment out of Egypt. Before the sin of the Golden Calf, the firstborn, that is the priests who served in the tabernacle, initially used it in their sacrifices, and thereafter it passed to priests as a group. This garment thus acts in both temporal and spatial dimensions. It connects past and future, so representing a society whose worldview is liminal, one which is between two worlds, and whose cosmology relates a story that one can only decode by understing that it sanctifies the liminal situation, with the garment as an expression of this view.

In the world of the Sages, this holy garment ceases to be the exclusive property of the priest and the prophet (as in the Bible) and goes through a process of democratization, after which everyone may wear it and thereby stand before God. This is the garment in which one enfolds oneself during prayer or in other activities in the realm of holiness. Avot de-Rabbi Nathan, for example, records a series of stories about individuals living at the time of the destruction of the Temple, quoting the story of Nicedemon ben Gurion, who borrowed from "a certain ruler" twelve water wells for pilgrims to Jerusalem and promised to pay for their use if rain did not fall by a specific date.[43]

---

[41] 1 Kgs 19:13. cf. 2 Kgs 1:8; 2:12–14; see also 1 Kgs 19:19.

[42] On the source of this expression, see the note by Frenkel (1991, vol. 2, p. 607, n. 59).

[43] *Avot de-Rabbi Nathan* (Shechter ed.) (A) 6, p. 32. For details on the realia of this *ituf* in those days, see n. 47 below, and Krauss (1945, 2/2: 173–204).

When that date came, he entered the *Beth Midrash*, "enfolded himself and stood in prayer, and he said to Him..." As the looming clouds darkened the, the ruler claimed that this darkening proved that night had fallen, and thus the rain that fell did so after the specified date. As a result, Nicedemon again entered the *Beth Midrash*, and again he "enfolded himself and stood in prayer, and he said to Him..." It is impossible to tell if this was the custom before the destruction of the temple or at the time of the anonymous source of the story, but sources bearing the name of Sages dating back to the first Amora'im (Sages active between the third and fifth centuries) prove that by their era this was an accepted sacred ritual. One can also note from this and other sources that this enfolding (*ituf*) was not an everyday event but was a rare expression of an individual's drawing closer to God at a time of distress. Thus, R. Levi said, "When Mordechai saw Haman coming toward him, his horse in hand...what did he do? He enfolded himself in his *talit* ("prayer shawl") and stood up to pray..."[44]

Persons enfolded themselves in a garment not only during prayer, but also for other actions in the realm of the sacred. For example Rabban Gamaliel of Yavneh, of the second generation of Tannaim, traveled to Kheziv, where a certain man asked him about a vow.

Since Rabban Gamaliel had drunk wine, he refused to tell the man how to gain release from his vow until the effects of the wine had worn off, whereupon "he dismounted the donkey and enfolded himself and sat down and annulled his vow..."[45] Similiary the first generation Tanna R. Yohanan ben Zakkai, when he wanted to hear his student, R. Elazar ben Arakh, expound on the mystical Chariot (i.e., discussing mysticism related to the creation of the world), "dismounted his donkey and enfolded himself in his *talit* and they both sat on a rock underneath an olive tree, and he

---

[44] *Pesikta de-Rav Kahana* (Mandelbaum, ed.) vol. 3, the Omer commandment, pp. 143–144. If this were Levi bar Sisi, he was a member of the transitional generation between the Tanna'im and the Amora'im, but it is more logical to assume that this was R. Levi, an Amora of the third generation living in Israel. See Albeck (1969: 153–155; 256–257). An especially dramatic description of this *ituf* is to be found in BT *Rosh Ha'sh.* 17b, in the name of R. Yohanan, in his exposition on the verse, "The Lord passed before his face and he called out" (Ex. 34:6): "Had the verse not stated so categorically, this could not have been said. This teaches us that the holy one, blessed be he wrapped himself like a cantor and showed Moses the order of prayer." This statement of R. Yohanan implies that at that time not every person who prayed wrapped himself, but only the cantor. See also on this, Ehrlich (1994: 153).

[45] T *Pes*, 2:19 (Liberman edition); and see also JT *Ned* 11:5, 42c, on R. Yose.

(the student) expounded to him."[46] One also enfolded oneself in a garment when studying Torah[47] or sitting in judgment.[48] Much later Rashi (1040–1105) explained this custom: "When one sits in judgment, one (enfolds oneself) out of fear for the Divine Presence. They should not turn their heads this way and that, and their minds should be composed."[49] Rashi understands this enfolding as a technical action whose aim was to enable one to concentrate on the matter at hand. This view appears, however, in an earlier Midras, where the person enfolding himself must include his hands as well. Thus we find in Pesikta Rabbati (ca. ninth century): "What does one enfold? If one's arm was bare, one covers it and recites the blessing, in order to perform the commandment with (the proper) awe."[50] Enfolding is thus not merely a technical means of concentrating one's thoughts, but reflects a worldview that demands that one submerge one's individuality into the dimension of holiness. The Jerusalem Talmud thus writes in regard to the grace after meals:

> If one ate while walking, one stands and recites the grace; if one ate while standing, one sits down and recites the grace; if one ate while sitting, one reclines and recites the grace; if one ate while reclining, one enfolds himself and recites the grace. If he did so (i.e., if he recited the grace while enfolded), he resembles the ministering angels. What is the reason? (It is as the verse:) 'With two (wings) he covered his face and with two his feet' (Isa. 6:2).[51]

46 BT *Hag.* 2a.
47 See also, *Avot de-Rabbi Nathan*, (A) 26, p. 82: "Men who are wrapped (*atuf*) in sheets," which appears to be a synonym for a group of people who study the Torah; cf. *Kohelet Rabbah* 1:7 (end). See also, JT *Nedarim* 3:8, 38a, in the name of R. Aha in the name of R. Honeh (of the fourth generation of the Amoraim in Israel), which describes the actions of Esau at the end of days, when he will "wrap himself in his *tallit* and sit with the righteous in the Garden of Eden… and the holy one, blessed be he will drag him and take him out of there." Regarding this sheet, see also Krauss (1945, 2/2: 108, n. 1 and 174).
48 Cf. *Sifrei* Deut. 13, p. 22: "'Known to your tribes' (Deut. 1:13)—that they should be known to you. If he wraps himself in his *tallit* and he comes to sit before me, I cannot tell from which tribe he is, but you know me…"
49 See Rashi to BT *Shabbat* 10a, s.v. "*dayanin mitatefin be'talitan.*"
50 *Pesikta Rabbati* 9: 31b (Ish-Shalom ed.).
51 JT *Berakhot* 7:5, 11d, quoting R. Ba the son of R. Hiya the son of Abba, of the third generation of Amoraim in Israel.

A similar notion appears in the Babylonian Talmud regarding visiting the sick.[52] The Sages also customarily enfolded themselves (*ituf*) as the time for welcoming in the Sabbath approached.[53]

What is this *ituf*? The poor at the time of the Sages would war only one garment, a plain undergarment-like piece known as a *haluk*. A person of some means might wear several of these.[54] In contrast to the simple *haluk*,[55] the *talit* was broad and had many folds.[56] In order to differentiate between the two types of garments, the former was sometimes referred to as *malbush* and the second as *atifah*.[57]

---

[52] See Rashi to BT *Shabbat* 12b: "We have learned… One who enters to visit a sick person should not sit on the bed nor on a chair, but should wrap himself and sit before him, because the divine presence is above the head of one who is ill" etc. There, too, *Rashi* explains it in similar terms ("*mitatef*"): "From awe of the divine presence, as a man who sits in fear and does not turn to the sides."

[53] BT *Shabbat* 25b, notes that "on eve of the Sabbath R. Yehudah bar Ila'i would take a basin of hot water, and he would wash his face, hands and feet, after which he would wrap himself in a fringed robe, and he resembled an angel of the Lord of hosts." The comparison to an angel also appears in BT *Nedarim* 20b: "Who are the ministering angels? (These are) the sages. And why are they referred to as ministering angels? Because they resemble the ministering angels in their fine clothing." Rashi explains, in his commentary to BT *Kiddushin* 72b (on the Talmudic claim that "R. Levi son of Sisi stated, 'Show me the Torah sages of Babylon, who resemble the ministering angels"— [s.v. "*domim*"]), "they are dressed in white and are wrapped as the ministering angels, as it states, (Ezek. 9:11), 'the man clothed in linen,'..." Rashi understands this as a clear proof that angels wear clothing! On the significance of *ituf* in white clothing, as opposed to black clothing, see JT *Rosh Ha'shanah* 1:3; 57b, "It is customary for a person who must appear in court to do so in black clothing and wrap himself in black and to grow his beard, because he does not know how the decision will go, but [the children of] Israel [on *Rosh Ha'shanah*] do not act that way, but dress in white and wrap themselves in white and shave their beards, and eat and drink and rejoice—they know that the holy one, blessed be he, performs miracles for them." See also M *Middot* 5:4. It appears that wrapping oneself in white had an element of holiness and of resembling the angels, whereas wrapping oneself in black was a symbolic act of mourning and of fear of the verdict (see also Rashi on *Kiddushin* s.v. *la'se'irim*). The color of the *tallit* (at least in Babylon) was generally white, but on occasion it was black or red. See Krauss, 1945 2/2: 205–206. Women's hair covering was also generally white (Krauss, 1945 2/2: 270).

[54] Thus, "A man may wear one garment on top of another—even though his money belt is tied on the outside, provided that he places the cord and ties it between his shoulders" (T *Kilayim* 5:15 [Liberman ed.], pp. 20–21).

[55] On the different views regarding use of the *haluk*, see Krauss, 1945 2/2: 181, n. 1.

[56] Krauss, 1945 2/2: 175. See also, Krauss, 1945 2/2: 205, for a discussion of the folds' decorative purposes.

[57] Thus, for example: "If he was dressed in a cloak and wrapped in a *tallit*" (T *Taharot* 8:13, Zuckermamdel ed. p. 669), and see, Krauss, 1945 2/2: 176.

As already noted, the Sages thought that *ituf* made one resemble an angel.[58] More interesting, however, is that the ceremonial expressions of standing before God were not unequivocal.[59] Thus BT *Shabbat* 10a reads:

> Rava bar Rav Huna put on stockings and prayed, saying, "Prepare to meet your God, O Israel"[60] (Amos 4:12). Rava removed his cloak, clasped his hands and prayed, saying: "This is like a slave before his master." Rav Ashi said: "I saw Rav Kahana when there was trouble in the world, remove his cloak, clasp his hands and pray, saying: 'I pray like a slave before his master.' When times were peaceful he would put it on, cover himself and enfold (*mitatef*) himself, and pray, saying: 'prepare to meet your God, O Israel'."

In these texts, then, two evaluations of the garment in man's standing before God emerge. One line of interpretation stresses human lowliness: one removes those garments denoting one's importance, reducing oneself to the level of a slave. This humbling posture, however, is balanced by the element of intimacy projected by the wearing of everyday clothes. The other possibility stresses the idea of the clothing as a barrier between the human being and God. In this instance, the garment of prayer must be a closely supervised, ensuring that every aspect of human corporeality, particularly those aspects of a sexual nature, remain concealed.

Clothing as Connecting the Past to the Future

Up to now, discussion has centered upon the vertical dimensions that clothing signifies. Also important, however, is the horizontal dimension that the holy garment signifies. According to the thesis, one who wears holy garments in the world of the Sages does not thereby become merely connected completely thereby to God, but he or she also take a place in the stream of human history. The garment in this case testifies to the ahistorical view of the Sages. The Darshan ("omilist") R. Yudan (first half of the fourth century CE) summarized

---

[58]   Hence the stress in a number of places on the color white, which is characteristic of the angels (see n. 53).

[59]   See Ehrlich (1994: 158–160), on the differences in ancient customs between the ancient Christian perception (which the Tannaim and Amoraim in the land Israel, apparently also accepted) that a fitting way to appear before God was with one's head uncovered, and the evidently diametrically opposite view in Babylon, whose teachers felt the fitting way was to have one's head covered. A similar difference existed with regard to *ituf*.

[60]   Amos 4:12.

this idea in a short sentence: "If a person wears the clothes of his father, he is like him."[61] Rabbinic literature often regards the clothes of an exceptional person as of eternal significance and as having ability to link matters in a way that exceeds the powers of the individual wearing them. For example, 1 Sam 2:19 notes the special cloak that Samuel's mother made for him, while 1 Sam 28:14 identifies him after his death because of his wearing this cloak at Saul's séance. For the Sages, this constituted clear proof of the permanence of the garment.[62] Not only that, but JT *Kilayim* 9:4, 34b asserts that in the world to come the person will arise in his or her earthly clothes.[63] Returning to the clothing of the Primordial Adam, Midrashic Aggadah dates sacred garment to the beginning of history and claims that Adam's first garment passed in an indirect line and with various changes through time. When the Messiah comes he will be wearing a similar garment.[64]

Aggadic texts describe the garment of Adam not as a functional garment, but as a mythical one. According to one view in the Babylonian Talmud, God created this garment during the liminal time of twilight just before the Sabbath.[65] As Victor Turner has argued, liminal time and liminal societies in general, permit the creation of miraculous items existing outside the realm of nature.[66] A late Midrash that reflects the viewpoint of more ancient Midrashim states:

---

[61]   *Genesis Rabbah* (Theodor-Albeck ed.) 74, p. 871. See also, Theodor's notes there to line 1.

[62]   See *Midrash Shmuel* (Buber ed.) 6:2, p. 64. The commentators imparted a great amount of significance to Samuel's coat in the Bible in JT (*Ta'anit* 2:7, 65d): "Samuel wore the clothing of all the people of Israel." See also, Krauss (1945, 2/2: 182), who states, "The meaning of this may be that the prophet identified himself with all of Israel."

[63]   "It was learned in the name of R. Nathan, a garment which goes down with the person to underworld (*she'ol*) comes with him (in the world to come)," etc. See also Tractate *Semahot* (Higger ed.) 9:3, p. 179, and Higger's notes there.

[64]   According to various Midrashim, God sometimes gives humanity, and sometimes the angels, (metaphoric) clothing (and see note 33). Thus, for example, *Exod. Rabbah* 16:26 reads, "The clothing of the holy one, blessed be he is glory and majesty, and He gave Solomon regal majesty, as it states (1 Chr. 29:25), 'He endowed him with regal majesty.'" So too Exod. Rabbah 38:3 in regard to Aaron, or 38:8 in the words of R. Yehoshua of Sikhnin in the name of R. Levi. Regarding the condition of the Israelites in the desert, the question is asked (*Song Rabbah* 4:23 [Dunski ed. pp. 119–120]); see also *Deuteronomy Rabbah*, Ki Tavo, 11 (Liberman ed. p. 113) as to where they obtained clothing throughout the long years they were in the desert (cf. Deut. 8:4). "R. Shimon ben Yose ben Lacunia answers there that the clothing they had were "those worn by the ministering angels."

[65]   BT Pesahim 54a.

[66]   Turner, 1967: 93–111; 1974: 231–271.

"For I was naked"[67] What was the garment of Adam? Skin of fingernail and the Cloud of Glory covering him. When he ate of the fruit of the tree, the fingernail skin fell of him, and he saw himself naked, while the Cloud of Glory departed from him.[68]

As this garment was from the mythical era and not from real time, the standard rules of time do not apply to it.[69] Adam's garment does not wear out, but imparts to succeeding generations miraculous powers.

Ancient Midrashim exhibit only a few allusions to this idea. These include Jerusalem Targum to Gen 48:22, regarding Jacob's blessing to Joseph, that read:

"I have given you an additional portion over your brothers, which I took from the Emorites with my sword and bow." "I have given you an additional portion over your brothers": the garment of the primordial Adam, which Abraham, the father of my father took from the hand of the evil Nimrod, and which he gave to Isaac my father, and Isaac my father gave this to Esau, and I took it from the hand of Esau my brother, not by my sword and my bow, but by right and by good deeds.

Semiliary the Tanna R. Yehudah bar Ila'i explained Gen 48:22: "This [the additional portion] is the right of the firstborn and the garment of the primordial Adam."[70] While it is possible that R. Yehudah knew the traditions that Adam's garment reached Jacob, this text does not say so.

A full description of this topic does not exist in the ancient Midrashim, but only in medieval ones. Genesis Rabbah 63 contains a much older (and anonymous) exposition that explains Esau's words to Jacob at the time of the sale of the former's birthright—"Behold, I am about to die, and what use is the birthright to me?"[71]—by saying "Nimrod wished to kill [Esau] because of that garment which had belonged to Adam, for at the time that Esau would put it on, all the animals and birds in the world would come and gather by him." Esau subverted the powers of the garment, which Adam had used to

---

67 Gen. 3:10.
68 *Pesikta d'Rabbi Eliezer*, 14 (Warsaw ed. 1852), with commentary by David Luria, p. 33b.
69 Garber-Talmon, 1951: 201–213.
70 *Genesis Rabbah, Parashah* 98:22 (Thedor-Albeck ed. p. 1249); and the comments by Theodor to line 3. See also, Kasher (1950, vol. 8, Section 136, p. 1768), he claimed that this magic garment was Joseph's striped coat given him by his father.
71 Gen 25:32.

bring peace and tranquility by calming down all the creatures in the world and caused them to gather about him without fear. One's in Esau's possession, however, a garment of peace became one of violence.

The Midrash, moreover, links the two individuals whom Genesis describes as hunters.[72] The same motif appears earlier in *Pesikta de-Rabbi Eliezer*:[73]

> R. Yehudah says: "The garment which the holy one, blessed be he, made for Adam and his wife was with them in the Ark; and when they left the Ark, Ham the son of Noah took it and bequeathed it to Nimrod, and when he would wear it all the domesticated and wild animals and all the birds would come and fall down before him, thinking that this was because of his valor, and they therefore made him their king."[74]

The text adds that the leather garments that God made for Adam and Eve by God were of the hide of the infamous snake.[75] A midrash in Numbers Rabbah, develops this idea, and claims that the firstborn who brought sacrifices in the desert wore the garment of Adam:

> "Know, that the firstborn would offer the sacrifices until the tribe of Levi arose. Look at the beginning of the creation of the world: Adam was the Firstborn of the World, and when he offered his sacrifice, [...] he put on the garments of the high priesthood, as it states, 'The Lord God made for Adam and his wife coats of skin and He dressed them.'[76] These were choice clothes, and the firstborn would use them."[77]

A shorter version of this Midrash, in Tanhuma explains how this ancient garment traveled in a circuitous way from Adam until the firstborn who sacrificed in the desert:

> What are "leather coats"? [These are the garments of] the high priesthood. The holy one, blessed be he, dressed Adam in the garments of the high

---

[72] See also, *Genesis Rabbah* 63 (Mirkin ed., vol. 3: 23). See also, *Genesis Rabbah,* 65:15, p. 27: " 'The coveted clothes of her older son, Esau'—that he coveted them from Nimrod and killed him and took them."

[73] *Pesikta de-Rabbi Eliezer* 24, p. 56b.

[74] See also, Dan 1986: 33–134; and also, Ginzberg, 1968, vol. 1, pp. 319–320, and nn. 39–44.

[75] *Pesikta de-Rabbi Eliezer* 20, p. 46a. Cf. 22, p. 50b which deals with this at length.

[76] Gen 3:21.

[77] Numbers Rabbah 4:8 (Mirkin ed., vol. 9: 71–72). It was certainly not earlier than the twelfth century, even though the editor has had access to ancient Midrashim. See Mack (1996).

priesthood, for he was the Firstborn of the World. Noah came [and transferred them to Shem, and Shem] transferred them to Abraham, and Abraham transferred them to Isaac, and Isaac transferred them to Esau, who was his firstborn. Esau saw that his wives were practicing idolatry and he entrusted them to his mother. When Jacob arose and took the birthright from Esau, Rebecca said, "As Jacob has taken the birthright from Esau, it is only just that he should wear these garments," as it states, "Rebecca took the beloved garments of her son Esau."[78] Jacob went in to his father and he smelled him, as it states,[79] "he smelled the smell of his garments and he blessed him."[80]

While no single text explicitly say so, the tradition seems to have been that the holy garment went from Jacob to Joseph, to the Israelites who left Egypt, and eventually to the priests of the tribe of Levi.[81]

Finally one asks, what happened to that remarkable garment? Pesikta de-Rav Kahana, deduces from the verse in Isaiah 61:10 ("As a groom puts on a diadem"), that God will dress the Messiah in the garment which

---

[78]   Gen 27:26.

[79]   Gen 27:27.

[80]   *Tanhuma*, Genesis (Buber ed.) *Toledot*, 12, p. 132–133. Also compare this to a discussion in *Zohar*, Bo 39a-b. On a similar description of the passing of an understanding of intercalation from God to Adam and from him on, until Ezra see *Pesikta d-Rabbi Eliezer* 7, pp. 18a–19b. A similar story concerns Moses' staff, which was owned by Adam and was passed down from one generation to the next until it reached Esau, who guarded it scrupulously until Jacob took it from him and fled with it to Haran, and when he died he bequeathed it to Joseph and thus, according to some versions it reached Jethro and from him it went to Moses. See, Ginzberg, 1968, vol. 2, p. 293 and n. 95. A late Midrash adds that the staff is at present hidden, but will be revealed at the time of the Messiah. See Eisenstein, 1928, vol. 1, p. 176. Also see regarding this, our comments below regarding the holy garment, which in a similar fashion cuts across all of history.

[81]   Regarding this garment, the Sages in the Babylonian Talmud state that just wearing it is sufficient to atone for one's sins: "The priestly garments atone" (BT *Zevahim* 88b; *Arakhin* 16b; *Moed Katan* 28a); See also the words of R. Elazar ben Pedat in BT Moed Katan 28a: "Just as the priestly garments atone, the death of the righteous atones." Because of its importance, it was even included in oaths: "The garment worn by my father" (T *Hallah*, 1:10, Liberman ed., p. 277. *Tanhuma*, Noah 15 explains Lev. 10:5, which the sages interpreted to mean that vestments of Nadab and Abihu were not burned when they were, as follows: "How did God repay Shem [for his refined behavior when his father Noah became drunk and was uncovered in his tent (Gen. 9:23)]? When the sons of Aaron went in to offer sacrifices … their garments were not burned, but only the soul was burned and not the body, as it states, 'them' but not their bodies." Here, too, is an indication of the intertextual context linking the holy garment to Shem—through whom it was passed on to the priests. See also, Kasher, 1992: 5–7[12].

will shine from one end of the world to the other…and the Jews will use its light and say to the Messiah, "Blessed is the hour in which the Messiah was created… because from his lips comes blessing and peace and his speech is pleasantness and majesty, and from his lips come blessing and peace and his speech is pleasantness and majesty, and his clothing is majestic…"[82]

The clothing in which God will dress the Messiah marks the latter's recruitment for his tasks. One Midrash, accordingly, understands Ps 21:6—"Honor and majesty do you lay upon him"—to refer to the Messiah and to be a parallel to Ps. 104:1, which says of God, "You are clothed in honor and majesty." The Midrash surmises from this that the Messiah's clothing will come from God's wardrobe collection.[83]

Conclusion: The Apocalyptic Garment

One might ask at this point, if the role of the mythic garment is to annul the the distinction between past and future time, why do Midrashic texts not note that the same garment that passed through the generations throughout history will belong to the Messiah? It would appear that the answer to this relates to the special dialectic of the mythic garment. On the one hand, it is the same garment that bridges all of the generations, which by its very existence denies change. On the other hand, the Midrashim do not stop at so simple a view, but relates the garment's various adventures. It thus comes to the evil Nimrod one in an unscrupulous fashion; from him, Esau steals it, only to loose it through the "trickery" of Jacob and his mother, Rebecca. Their trickery, however, serves to place it back to the right hands, and even afterwards there is the danger that it will be lost by Joseph and Israelites, who almost succumbed to the ritual impurity of Egypt. Even though this is a garment that will annul any deleterious course of action, movement, or change in time, it is nevertheless unable to escape entirely the vicissitudes of time, even if after every "descent" there is an "ascent."

By making Adam's vestment "the garment of the Messiah," the texts we have examined emphasize the total and absolute annulment of time. This is a process of total rectification and an ultimate return to Edening innocence. It was, therefore, impossible for the Sages to develop ideas about the garment

---

[82] *Pesikta de-Rav Kahana* (appendices) 6, *Sos asis*, p. 470. See also, *Pesikta Rabbati*, 37, p. 164a.

[83] See *Tanhuma* (Buber ed.), *Beha'lotekha*, 15, p. 51.

in a normal linear progression and to say unequivocally that the garment, bearing as it does the "stains" of history and time, is the garment as that which the Messiah will wear. Their solution to this problem was to suggest that, with the arrival of Messiah God would create a new garment, albeit one like Adam's.

Here we confronted the two axes that we noted at the beginning of this article. In the Messiah's garment what is prominent is the vertical line, because it belong to God, who will enfold the Messiah in it. But this garment is also the final completion of the horizontal axis, for it signifies the end of the vicissitudes suffered by the mythic garment, whose starting point was Adam. The end thus relates to the beginning: the ritual purity of the Messiah's garment corresponds to that of Adam's.

PART THREE   BIRTH AND
                   MARRIAGE

CHAPTER 3. *BRIT MILAH*: A STUDY OF CHANGE IN CUSTOM

In traditional Jewish society two criteria determine the affiliation of males to the congregation of Israel: birth to a Jewish mother, and circumcision, which is a Torah obligation.[1] These set permanent and unequivocal bounds to the membership group of the Jewish people. A male who was not born to a Jewish mother may join Jewish society by conversion, during which he undergoes either circumcision or, if already circumcised, the ritual drawing of blood from his penis. Following this he is "like a newborn child,"[2] which means literally that he is to be regarded as one who was born a Jew.[3] A male who was born to a Jewish mother but was not circumcised, whether because of circumstances beyond control (such as illness, or other conditions that prevented his circumcision) or as a result of deliberate parental choice, is considered Jewish but is precluded from observing a small number of commandments.[4] This symbolically places him in a marginal position, a status that, according to Talmudic sources, is also the lot of one who was born circumcised (i.e. without a foreskin), in which case the halakhic question is whether he is to be regarded as an *arel* (uncircumcised), since the foreskin (*orlah*) was not

---

[1]   This research was supported by the Schnitzer Foundation for Research on the Israeli Economy and Society. Portions of this article appeared as "On Drawing Down the Prepuce and *Peri'ah*." *Zion* 54 (1989), pp. 105–117 (in Hebrew). My thanks go to Elizabeth Mark for her close reading and insightful comments, and to Samuel Cooper for his important comments. According to JT Yevamot 5:1, 6c; BT Yevamot 45b. See also: Rubin, 1995: 85.
[2]   BT Yevamot 22a.
[3]   For the process of conversion, see: Bialoblocki, 1964: 44–60; Samet, 1993. For the significance of conversion, see: Sagi and Zohar (1995a); Sagi and Zohar (1995b), pp. 1–13.
[4]   E.g., he may not circumcise another Jew (JT Yevamot 8:1, 8d) he is not permitted to offer the Paschal sacrifice (M Pesahim 5:3), and other restrictions. See: Rubin, 1995: 85 and 173.

removed, or as circumcised, since he has no foreskin.[5] A similar question addresses the status of one whose brothers died due to circumcision, and whose life would therefore be threatened if he were to undergo such a procedure. Should he be put at risk and circumcised?[6] In all these cases, the halakhah finally determined clear norms, so that every male can locate himself within the boundaries of these norms.

The question facing us in this essay is how the Talmudic sages related to a *mashukh,* a man who physically disguises his circumcision.[7] The practice of *meshikhat orlah*—the drawing down of the foreskin (in English, decircumcision or epispasm)—was known between the second century BCE and the second century CE. By stretching vestigial penile skin tissue to cover the glans penis, a man who desired to pass beyond Jewish communal boundaries to join non-Jewish society could remove the identifying mark of Jewish identity. The Rabbis discussed whether or not a repeated circumcision might offer him a way back, but they also took action to thwart this blatant transgression of the boundary. As this essay will show, until the middle of the second century CE the sanctioned method of circumcision allowed for the possibility of stretching and drawing down remaining foreskin tissue and thereby "crossing the border" of Jewish society, leaving no physical sign. I maintain that the requirement of *peri'ah,* (the splitting and peeling back of the mucosal membrane lining the foreskin, thus fully uncovering the glans penis) was instituted by the Rabbis following the Bar Kokhba Revolt for the purpose of sealing this breach. If so, this constitutes a striking example of change instituted in one of the most deeply rooted norms in Jewish law and society. After reviewing the evidence for the occurrence of this change, I will address the cultural mechanism that facilitates the process of change in a society closely guarding its textual foundations.

In the uncircumcised male, the foreskin that covers the glans penis (*atarah*) is actually a continuation of the skin covering the shaft of the penis. When foreskin tissue is excised by circumcision (*milah*), the membranous underlying tissue thereby exposed undergoes a process of epitheliazation, eventually taking on the character of an outer skin covering. Evidence from the recent foreskin restoration movement in the United States, involving numbers of men attempting to expand penile tissue in order to create pseudo-foreskins, shows that the more tissue that remains after circumcision, the more successful are

---

5   JT Yevamot 8:1:8d; BT Shabbat 135a; Yevamot 71a. For one born circumcised and his status, see: Rubin, (1988).

6   T Shabbat 15(16): 8; JT Yevamot 6:6, 7d; BT Yevamot 64b. See also: Rubin, 1995: 93.

7   See, e.g.: T Shabbat 15(16):9; JT Shabbat 19:2, 17a; BT Yevamot 72a.

the attempts to achieve the appearance of an intact foreskin. It is clear from numerous textual references that the Rabbis' introduction of *peri'ah* resulted in a change in surgical procedure that required a radical removal of tissue and the complete uncovering of the glans penis. The intention of the Rabbis was to make decircumcision no longer a feasible undertaking for Hellenizing Jews,[8] and the reports of present-day foreskin restorers support the inference that the Rabbis' halakhic intervention effectively served their goal. After a radical circumcision that removes the maximum outer skin and rolls back completely the inner membrane, the stretching of a sufficient amount of skin from the shaft of the penis to create a pseudo-foreskin would take years, according to reports from foreskin restoration groups, and the new covering might not remain in place without continued stretching. Such a lengthy time frame would hardly solve the circumcision problem facing the ancient world Jew.[9]

According to the extant sources, *meshikhat orlah,* the drawing down of the foreskin, has a long history in Israel, extending from the second century BCE to the second century CE.[10] To review the well-known ancient testimonies: the first is from the time of the Hellenists, during the rule of the Ptolemaids and the Seleucids in Judea. *I Maccabees* (1:11–15) tells of "wicked men" from Israel who "built a gymnasium in Jerusalem, in the heathen fashion, made themselves uncircumcised, renounced the holy covenant, intermingled among the heathen, and became the slaves of wrongdoing." The drawing down of the foreskin was done willingly, and was accepted among the Hellenists in Judea, who were under the influence of the Hellenist culture of the Ptolemaid-Seleucid period. There were those among the Jerusalem nobility, the priesthood, and the leadership strata who drew close to the non-Jews of equal standing, and who introduced Hellenist culture into the Jewish community. Jason the High Priest turned Jerusalem into a Greek *polis*, with the establishment of a gymnasium in which youths appeared nude. The circumcised who wished to participate in the games and were ashamed of their circumcisions drew down

---

[8]   On the process see Romberg (1982: 110–111); Denniston (1996); (http//faculty.Washington.edu/gcd/CIRCUMCISION). The first written testimony concerning the circumcision laws appears in *Kelalei ha-Milah* (The Rules of Circumcision) by R. Jacob ha-Gozer and his son R. Gershom ha-Gozer (thirteenth century). *Kelalei ha-Milah* was published in the book: *Sichron B'rith Larischonim* by Glassberg (1892). These rules are generally followed to the present, and certainly represent a long tradition.

[9]   For recent mechanical and surgical methods look at the websites under "foreskin restoration."

[10]   We do not know of any challenge raised against the practice of circumcision in Jewish society from the time of the Bar Kokhba Revolt to the era of the Enlightenment (*haskalah*). See Judd (2003) for the history of the nineteenth century circumcision debates in the German-speaking lands.

the foreskin.[11] A circumcised individual who appeared nude in public was undoubtedly subject to scorn and derision. For example, several generations later, Martailis (40–104 CE) ridiculed Jewish circumcision in general,[12] and in particular that athlete whose penis sheath (*fibula*) fell when he was on the sportsground, revealing to the surprise of his companions his circumcision. Even this athlete's close friends who bathed with him in the nude did not know that he was circumcised, because he constantly wore the penis sheath that was alleged to protect a man's voice by shielding him from sexual contact.[13] This episode plainly reveals how embarrassing it was to be circumcised, to the extent that such a fact was concealed even from those closest to the athlete.[14]

In the wake of the Hasmonean rebellion against Antiochus Epiphanes, the monarch imposed decrees against the inhabitants of Judea and, according to Josephus, "put pressure upon the Jews to violate the code of their country by leaving their infants uncircumcised and sacrificing swine upon the altar."[15] Anyone transgressing these decrees was punished, and Josephus even claimed that "they put to death the women who had circumcised their children, hanging the newborn babies around their necks; and they also put to death their families as well as those who had circumcised them."[16] Remarkably, we do not hear of instances of the drawing down of the foreskin as a result of these decrees against circumcision but only of assimilationists who did so of their own volition prior to the anti-circumcision edicts.[17] Thus, the author of the book of *Jubilees*, composed during the early Hasmonean period, predicts God's wrath upon the Jews because some have refused to circumcise their sons, adding: "they have made themselves like the Gentiles,"[18] a likely reference to *meshikhat orlah*.

---

[11] For the spread of Hellenism in this period, see: Tcherikover (1954; 1972); Stern (1976).

[12] Martialis, *Epigrammata* 7:55.

[13] Ibid., 7:82.

[14] See also Tacitus' opinion regarding circumcision: *Historia* 5:2–5; and also Levy (1960). See also the contempt exhibited by the Greek writers toward circumcision, and especially toward the Egyptians and the Phoenicians: Aristophanes, *Ornithes* 507; *Ploutos* 267; Strabo, *Geographical Sketches* 16:2:37; 17:2:5. Among the Roman satirists, see also Petronius, who mocks a wise servant who has only two drawbacks: he is circumcised, and he snores while sleeping (*Satyricon* 68:8).

[15] Josephus, *War* 1:34 (trans. H. St. J. Thackeray, *LCL*, vol. 1, p. 19); cf. *I Maccabees* 1:48. See Abusch (2003), for a discussion of the anti-circumcision campaign in the context of the Roman prohibition against genital mutilation.

[16] *I Maccabees* 1:60–61 (trans. S. Tedesche, *The First Book of Maccabees* [New York: Harper and Brothers, 1950], p. 79); cf. Josephus, *Ant.* 12:254.

[17] See: Alon (1984, 2: 586–587).

[18] *Jubilees* 15:33–34. *The Book of Jubilees* (trans. O. D. Wintermute, in J. H. Charlesworth [ed.], *The Old Testament Pseudepigrapha*, vol. 2 [Garden City: NY, 1985]).

The terseness of the textual references to the phenomenon of epispasm suggests that it was well known in the cultural context of the audience. No explanation was needed. For example, the Babylonian Talmud, reporting the story of an individual who had intercourse with the daughter of an idolater, matter-of-factly states that his foreskin was drawn down.[19] Various midrashim mention people who are held in low regard by the Rabbis; the drawing down of the foreskin is mentioned among their negative attributes, and the readers' comprehension was taken for granted. R. Judan b. Masparta (a second-generation Land of Israel Amora) says: "Achen was an epispastic."[20] R. Johanan, or other Amoraim, say of King Jehoiakim: "that he drew down his foreskin."[21] If *meshikhat orlah* had been remarkably uncommon, such laconic references would not have sufficed. Additionally, the New Testament provides clear evidence of the voluntary drawing down the foreskin as a familiar phenomenon of the period. As Saint Paul wrote to the Corinthians, "Was anyone at the time of his call already circumcised? Let him not seek to remove the marks of circumcision."[22]

The next source may allude to decircumcision among just such converts to Christianity. R. Eleazar ha-Moda'i pronounces in the Mishnah: "He who profanes the sacred things, and he who despises the festivals, and he who shames his fellow in public, and he who violates the covenant of our father Abraham (peace be upon him), and he who interprets the Torah not according to the halakhah [...] he has no portion in the world-to-come."[23] "Violates the covenant of our father Abraham" is a version of "violates the covenant in the flesh" found in *Avot de-Rabbi Nathan*.[24] The Palestinian Talmud is more explicit: " 'Violates the covenant in the flesh'—this refers to the one who draws down the foreskin."[25] Scholars have generally understood R. Eleazar

---

[19] BT Eruvin 19a; see *Dikdukei Soferim*.

[20] BT Sanhedrin 44a. For Esau drawing down his foreskin, see: Ruth Rabbah 1:13 (ed. M. B. Lerner, vol. 2, pp. 12–14); *Midrash Tanhuma*, Gen., *Toledot* 4; *Aggadat Bereshit*, *Noah* 4 (ed. Buber [Cracow: 1903], p. 119). See also: Ex. Rabbah 19:5: the Holy One, blessed be He, draws down the foreskin of the wicked after their death, so that they will enter Gehennom.

[21] Lev. Rabbah 19:6.

[22] 1 Cor. 7:18–19.

[23] M Avot 3:11.

[24] *Avot de-Rabbi Nathan* (A) 26.

[25] JT Peah 1:1, 16b. See also the parallel versions: JT Sanhedrin 10:1, 27c; *Sifrei*, Num., *Shelah* 112 (ed. H. S. Horovitz, p. 121); *Avot de-Rabbi Nathan*, ed. Schechter B. (44a); T Sanhedrin 12:15; BT Sanhedrin 99a. For a discussion of this subject and the version, see: Finkelstein, 1951: 72–74, 160–161; 1962: 632–633. See also: T Horayot 1:5: "The one who eats forbidden reptiles is an apostate [...] the one who eats the flesh of a swine, the one who drinks Gentile wine, the one who desecrates the Sabbath, and the one drawn down.

ha-Modai's dictum as directed against converts to Christianity, and especially against Paul, who abolished circumcision,[26] but he may also have had in mind another group of Jews: the wealthy, possessing Hellenistic education, who sought to attain Greek citizenship, either for themselves or for their offspring, in Hellenistic cities such as Alexandria, at the beginning of the Roman period. Education in an *ephebeion* and physical training in a gymnasium[27] constituted an essential condition for the acceptance of a youth to the body of citizens.[28] Tcherikover has already shown[29] that from the time of Augustus many Egyptian Jews, especially large numbers of the Jews of Alexandria, desired to receive municipal citizenship. Augustus distinguished between Greeks and other Egyptians; the former enjoyed various benefits and participated in the governmental institutions, while the Egyptians were regarded as subjects upon whom the burden of taxes was imposed. Augustus instituted a poll tax known in Egypt as the *Laographia*,[30] that was greatly humiliating and that proved to be extremely onerous for inhabitants who were not Greek citizens. This tax was doubly belittling for educated Jews who were steeped in Greek culture, since it attacked both their dignity and their pocketbook. According to the extant testimonies, the Jews made every effort to attain rights, one method of which was registering youths for the *ephebeion* and training in a gymnasium, with the completion of these studies granting civil rights. The struggle was difficult, and despite their efforts the successful applicants were immediately identifiable as Jews because of circumcision. They therefore had a powerful incentive to engage in decircumcision to preserve their right to attend the gymnasium.

Gedaliahu Alon interprets R. Eleazar ha-Moda'i's pronouncement as a reference to those who performed the act of decircumcision only because of the extreme anti-circumcision pressure of the Hadrianic persecutions.[31] However, its context in the mishnah and in parallel sources is not anti-Jewish oppression. Rather, the one "violating the covenant" in the sources is joined together with the one "who profanes the sacred things," and "he who despises the festivals," that are unrelated to the Hadrianic decrees, suggesting that this is a reference to individuals who engaged in decircumcision willingly in order to exit across the boundary of the Jewish community.

---

[26] See: Weiss, 1924: 131, n. 1; Bacher, 1922: 142, n. 3.

[27] In the Hellenistic period the *ephebion* was a cohort of youngsters aged 17–18, from the wealthy classes, who had their phisycal training in the gymnasium (literally: "school for naked exercise").

[28] See: Tcherikover, 1959: 162; Tcherikover and Fuks, 1957, 1: 38.

[29] Tcherikover, 1959: 310–326.

[30] See: Tcherikover, 1950: 179–207.

[31] Alon, 1980, 1: 75–76.

Another source, from the time of Bar Kokhba, reports a halakhic argument that might also be understood to imply that the drawing down of the foreskin was a reluctant action undertaken only in response to the persecutions:

> The one with a drawn down [foreskin] must undergo circumcision. R. Judah says: He is not required to undergo circumcision if he drew down, because this entails danger. They said: Many underwent circumcision in the time of Bar Kozeva (= Bar Kokhba), had children, and did not die.[32]

What emerges from this source is confirmation that in the period of the Bar Kokhba revolt there were individuals who had undergone decircumcision and who might have been subject to the death penalty if they chose to renew their circumcisions. The Rabbis obligated them nevertheless to undergo a second circumcision, despite the danger this posed. R. Judah alone exempted them, but the text seems to imply that were it not for the death penalty he too would have required a *mashukh* to undergo a second circumcision. The force of the Rabbis' negative attitude implies that they viewed decircumcision as a deliberate act of defection from the Jewish public, not justified by external duress. After all, the authorities had forbidden circumcision but had not required the physical reversal of circumcision. Possibly the statement "They said: Many underwent circumcision in the time of Bar Kozeva, had children, and did not die" teaches of a movement of "repentants" in the wake of the revolt and the fervor it aroused. One might understand this sentence as conveying the subjective impression of the "sayers" that there was a large movement of those who had undergone decircumcision, repented, and were circumcised a second time.

The Amoraim continued to deliberate this issue and clarified several points. They raised the question as to whether renewed circumcision for a *mashukh* was a Torah commandment or of Rabbinic force.[33] Is the "letting of the blood of circumcision" necessary?[34] May the one with a drawn down foreskin eat *terumah* [the priest's share of the offering], or is he forbidden to do so, as one who is not circumcised?[35] One Tannaitic midrash had already expressed the view that one "in whom the commandment of circumcision was fulfilled, even for a moment, even if the flesh returned and covered the *atarah* [glans penis], is not hindered from eating either the Paschal sacrifice

---

32 T Shabbat 16:9. The version in the JT Shabbat 19:2, 17a; JT Yevamot 8:1, 9a differs in its ending: "R. Yose said: There were many drawn down ones in the time of Bar Kozeva. They all underwent circumcision and lived, and had sons and daughters." See also: Gen. Rabbah 46:13; BT Yevamot 72a.

33 BT Yevamot 72a-b.

34 JT Shabbat 19:2, 17a.

35 T Yevamot 10:2; JT Yevamot 8:1, 8d; BT Yevamot 72a.

or *terumah*."[36] The *mashukhim* might have been included in this group, but the Amoraim do not relate to this Tannaitic midrash, perhaps because they rejected the idea that those who had chosen decircumcision deserved to be regarded as people "in whom the commandment of circumcision was fulfilled, even for a moment." All the sources reviewed above assume that the drawing down of the foreskin to disguise circumcision is technically possible. Indeed, the Tannaitic midrash just cited considers a spontaneous re-covering of the glans to be possible. There are other echoes of that view. For example, in the Amoraic discussion in the Palestinian Talmud, we find, "Either he drew down his foreskin, or it was drawn down by itself."[37] But a study of the Talmudic sources suggests that after the Rabbis included *peri'ah* in the act of circumcision the drawing down of the foreskin was no longer feasible. Accordingly, we may conclude that those who engaged in decircumcision did so in the period before the generalized adoption of *peri'ah*. Even after the institution of *peri'ah*, many years probably passed before it was accepted and firmly rooted, and therefore the phenomenon of decircumcision was known to the first generations of Amoraim, possibly also from first-hand knowledge, and not only on the basis of what they had heard.

M Shabbat (19:2) reports: "One may circumcise, and tear [the membrane], and suck[38], and put on it a bandage and cumin." According to this mishnah, circumcision and *peri'ah* are both part of a single process, in which the circumciser excises some or all of the foreskin and immediately afterwards performs *peri'ah*; that is, he splits the thin layer of mucosal membrane that is under the foreskin and rolls it downward, thus fully uncovering the head of the penis. In this method, circumcision and *peri'ah* are considered to be a single act.[39] The cutting of the foreskin was usually done with a knife,[40] while, according to late sources, there were two traditions regarding *peri'ah*: either with a fingernail or with a knife. The exact time when these methods were instituted has not been determined. A responsum of R. Hai Gaon teaches that there already was a tradition of *peri'ah* in Babylonia, either by hand or with an instrument.[41]

Notwithstanding that the mishnah explicitly requires circumcision and *peri'ah* at the same time, we find the sources warning that if one "circumcised but did not perform *peri'ah*, it is as if he did not circumcise."[42] If *peri'ah* had

---

[36]   *Mechilta de-Rabbi Ishmael*, ed. H. S. Horovitz and I. A. Rabin, *Bo* 15, p. 54.

[37]   JT Yevamot 8:1, 8d.

[38]   *Metzitzah*, the sucking of the wound (apparently for healing purposes).

[39]   See: *Kelalei ha-Milah*, in Glasssberg, 1892: 10, and the glosses of *Be'er Yaakov* ad loc.

[40]   M. Shabbat 19:1; JT Shabbat 19:1, 16d, and more.

[41]   *Teshuvot ha-Geonim Shaarei Tzedek* 1, 5 p. 10.

[42]   M Shabbat 19:6. See also: JT Shabbat 19:6, 17b; *Midrash Lekah Tov* on Genesis, *Lekh Lekha* 17:13; *Pirkei de-Rabbi Eliezer* 29.

been included from the outset in the circumcision process and universally practiced, it is unlikely that the sources would have related to it as a separate function that might be omitted. We can infer, therefore, that *peri'ah* was an innovation instituted over the course of time, most likely in response to the drawing down of the foreskin that was known from the time of the Hellenists and was still practiced during the time of the Hadrianic persecutions. The Rabbis sensed the need to reinforce their new ordinance both with warnings and by emphasizing the importance of *peri'ah*. Thus, the Palestinian Talmud adds to the mishnah that states "if one circumcised but did not perform *peri'ah*, it is as if he did not circumcise" the additional pronouncement that the punishment for omitting *peri'ah* is *karet* (being "cut off from one's kin"; see Gen. 17:14). In order to give even more force to this, the sages proved that the obligation of *peri'ah* is of Torah origin, and equated *peri'ah* with actual circumcision. Following the exegetical method of R. Akiva, they taught: "'*Himol yimol* [he must be circumcised—double wordings]' (Gen. 17:13)—from here you learn of two circumcisions, one [*himol*] for circumcision, and the other [*yimol*] for *peri'ah*." And according to the method of R. Ishmael, who did not learn out from double wordings, the supportive exegesis was: "'She [Zipporah, who circumcised her son] added: A bridegroom of bloods [*damim*, plural] of circumcision'" (Ex. 4:26). The use of plural implies two acts: one the blood of the actual circumcision and the other the blood of *peri'ah* incision.[43]

Proof that *peri'ah* is an innovative requirement is to be found as well in the tradition that the Patriarch Abraham did not practice it. According to Rav: "The commandment of *peri'ah* was not given to the Patriarch Abraham."[44] This tradition, accepted in midrash, enabled the exegetes to resolve a problem they faced; namely, how could the Israelites have received the Torah when they were uncircumcised, for they did not engage in circumcision while in Egypt: "For they [the Egyptians] were uncircumcised, and they [Israel] were uncircumcised."[45] Was it not inconceivable that the Israelites would stand at Mount Sinai uncircumcised to receive the Torah?[46] The response by the

---

[43] JT Shabbat 19:2, 17a. See also: JT Yevamot 8:6, 8d; JT Nedarim 3:14, 38b; Gen. Rabbah 46:17; *Midrash ha-Gadol*, Genesis, *Lekh Lekha* 17:13.

[44] BT Yevamot 71b. Gen. Rabbah 47:8: "Because he [Abraham] engaged in intercourse, he had no [fore]skin, and there was no need for *peri'ah*"; *Midrash Aggadah, Lekh Lekha* 17.

[45] Cant. Rabbah 2:6.

[46] See also: Ex. Rabbah 1:8; *Aggadat Bereshit* 17. This is despite the verse: "Now, whereas all the people who came out of Egypt had been circumcised" (Josh. 5:5). In contrast with these midrashim, others state that the commandment of circumcision was observed in Egypt (see: Kasher, 1992 on Ex. 1:8, p. 19, para. 86), or, alternately, that only the tribe of Levi practiced circumcision in Egypt (Num. Rabbah 3:6).

exegete is that they were circumcised both in Egypt and in the wilderness, but they had not undergone *peri'ah*, "and when they came to the Land of Israel [...] [Joshua] circumcised them a second time."[47]

All of these exegeses that speak of a distinction between circumcision (*milah*) and *peri'ah* reflect a specific reality in which circumcision without *peri'ah* had been practiced. When the requirement of *peri'ah* was instituted, we are witness to the addition of expositions in praise of Israel for fulfilling the commandment of circumcision with *peri'ah*. For example: "Ah, you are fair, my darling, ah, you are fair' [Cant. 1:15; 4:1]—you are fair in circumcision, you are fair in *peri'ah*"; "'How fair you are, how beautiful' [Cant. 7:7]—how fair you are in [observing] *neta reva'i* [the fourth year's fruits of a tree], and how beautiful you are in [observing] circumcision; how fair you are in [observing] *peri'ah*, and how beautiful you are in prayer."[48] Quite possibly, these expositions were intended to strengthen the faith of those who questioned *peri'ah* and support those who properly fulfilled the commandment.

Significantly, the institution of *peri'ah* was accompanied by the prohibition against leaving *tzitzin* (shreds of foreskin), thus emphasizing the Rabbis' intent to force the removal of as much tissue as possible, both foreskin and mucosal tissue, so as to preclude the stretching of vestigial tissue in a process of decircumcision. In the words of the Mishnah: "These shreds render the circumcision invalid [for if they are not removed, the infant is not considered circumcised]: the flesh that covers most of the *atarah*" (Shabbat 19:6). In such an instance, there is still sufficient skin ("flesh") to cover most of the glans penis. The Amoraim in both Talmuds were stricter, and established that not only skin that covers, that is, encompasses, most of the glans penis, is regarded as *tzitzin*, but also if it "covers the greater part of the height of the *atarah*," that is, in only one place, and not all around.[49] Clearly, a full and complete uncovering of the glans was the desired outcome.

The sages found support for the prohibition of *tzitzin*, and not just for *peri'ah*, from the Torah: "*Himol yimol* [he must be circumcised—double wordings]' (Gen. 17:13)—one [*himol*] for circumcision and one [*yimol*] for

---

47   *Pirkei de-Rabbi Eliezer* 29. According to some traditions, it is self-understood that circumcision was practiced in the wilderness. E.g., Num. Rabbah 12:8: "For if they were not circumcised, they could not gaze upon the Divine Presence." See also: Deut. Rabbah 11:3, the dialogue between Abraham and Moses. According to another tradition, circumcision was not practiced all the forty years in the wilderness because of the rigors of the journey, or because "the north wind did not blow on them" (BT Yevamot 71b–72a).

48   Cant. Rabbah 1:62; 17:12. See also: 4:1.

49   JT Shabbat 19:6, 17b; BT Shabbat 137b; BT Yevamot 47b; 71b.

tzitzin," according to the exegetical method of R. Akiva; and according to R. Ishmael: "She added: A bridegroom of bloods [*damim*, plural] of circumcision" (Ex. 4:26)—one [blood] for circumcision and one [blood] for *tzitzin*."[50] The Rabbis were so stringent regarding anyone who left shreds that "R. Judah says: One who does not remove [the shreds] is liable the death penalty,"[51] thus equating the removal of *tzitzin* with the circumcision itself.[52]

Additional support for the view that *peri'ah* was an innovation is to be found in the circumcision practices of the Samaritans. Historical studies of the Samaritans note their zealous observance of the commandment of circumcision, despite the decrees forbidding this act. The Jewish sources, which accuse the Samaritans on many counts, do not criticize them for the nonobservance of circumcision.[53] In the third century the Romans forbade the Samaritans to practice circumcision, as is attested by the Church Father Origen, in his book *Contra Celsum*.[54] The situation of the Samaritans worsened during the Byzantine persecutions, but then as well they continued to circumcise their sons, a practice they strictly observe to the present.[55]

The historical reports suggest that the Samaritan practices preserved early elements of the circumcision rite. *Peri'ah*, however, is absent from Samaritan circumcision.[56] The order of the Samaritan circumcision is as follows: the infant is always circumcised on the eighth day, with no possibility of postponement.[57] The day before the circumcision the infant is bathed in

---

[50] JT Shabbat 19:2, 17a and in the parallels: JT Yevamot 8:1, 8d; JT Nedarim 3:14, 38b; BT Yevamot 72a; Gen. Rabbah 46:12; *Midrash Lekah Tov*, Gen., *Lekh Lekha* 17:13.

[51] T Shabbat 15[16]:4.

[52] See also: JT Shabbat 19:6, 17b; BT Shabbat 133b.

[53] See: Pummer (1988: 6), who notes that even Josephus, who was one of their most forceful opponents, did not accuse them of neglecting circumcision.

[54] Origenes, *Contra Celsum* 2:13 [english edition: Chadwick (1953: 79)]. Antoninus Pius, who abrogated the prohibition of Jewish circumcision (see, Smallwood, 1959; 1961) maintained the prohibition regarding the Samaritans, who risked the death penalty for practicing circumcision.

[55] Avi-Yonah (1956); for additional bibliography, see: Pummer (1988: 6, n. 23). Also see: Jacob Son of Aaron (1908: 695–696).

[56] For the Samaritans and circumcision, see: Jacob Son of Aaron (1908: 649–710); Mills (1864); and recently: Pummer (1988: 6–10). See also: Kashani (1971). My thanks to Professor Alan D. Crown of University of Sydney, Australia, who directed me to some of the sources concerning the Samaritans.

[57] The version in the Samaritan Torah on Gen. 17:14 is: "And if any male who is uncircumcised fails to circumcise the flesh of his foreskin **on the eighth day**, that person shall be cut off from his kin; he has broken My covenant." The wording "on the eighth day" appears only in the Samaritan Torah, while the Jewish sources allow for a certain degree of flexibility in determining the day of the circumcision.

water (cf.: M Shabbat 19:3). His mother, or another woman, holds the baby during the ceremony.[58] The circumcision is preceded by a reading from the book of Genesis, from the beginning until the creation of Adam, along with other verses relating to the commandment of circumcision given to Abraham. Beginning in the fourth century, it was customary to chant a special hymn by the Samaritan *paytan* Marka that tells of the act of Germanus, the Bishop of Neapolis who, despite the standing prohibition, permitted the circumcision of Baba Rabbah.[59] During the recitation of this hymn, the priest (or someone else, in the absence of a priest who is capable of circumcising) circumcises the infant. The priest asks the child's father the name of the infant, which he then loudly announces. Refreshments are served to those present after the circumcision. The Samaritans emphasize that their circumcision does not include *peri'ah*, nor did it in the past. Jacob b. Aaron, a Samaritan High Priest at the beginning of the twentieth century, states that the Jews improperly add to the words of the Torah and require the tearing of the membrane, while the command is only for circumcision (*milah*) itself.[60]

The Jews and the Samaritans reject each other's circumcision. In the fourth generation of Tannaim, the students of R. Akiva, R. Yose, and R. Judah discuss whether a Cuthean (= Samaritan) may circumcise an Israelite, and whether an Israelite may circumcise a Cuthean,[61] with different opinions on this issue. The requirement of *peri'ah* might not have been definitively enacted in their time, thus allowing for the view that permitted circumcision

---

See: M Shabbat 19:5. They also permit the postponement of the circumcision due to illness. See, e.g.: T Shabbat 16(15):8; JT Yevamot 8:1, 15a. In later sources, beginning in the medieval period, the Samaritans contend with the Jews, who at times allow the postponement of the circumcision. For an eleventh century controversy, see: 'Abd al-'Al, 1957, 2: 689 (text); 530 (tr.). For a similar dispute in the sixteenth-eighteenth centuries, see: 'Abd al-'Al, 1957, 2: 690, 698 (text); 532, 541 (tr.). It should be noted that the fundamentalist approach of the Judean Desert sects, like the Samaritan approach, does not allow for any flexibility. See, e.g.: *Jubilees* 15:25.

58 The custom of the "*sandakit*" ("godfather," f.) or "*ba'alat ha-berit*" was also known in Jewish circumcision. Sperber (1983) has already shown that women functioned as "*ba'alat ha-berit*" until the thirteenth century, when the practice was prohibited by R. Meir of Rothenburg. see also: Kahana, (1960), para. 210, p. 262. The word *sandak* ("godfather") is first mentioned in *Midrash Tehillim* 38:10 ed. Buber (Vilna, 1891), 154b. The Talmudic literature is silent as to who held the infant during the circumcision, and how. In later sources the *sandak* is generally termed the "*ba'al berit*." See, e.g.: *Kelalei ha-Milah*, in Glassberg, 1892: 15, 59, 65–66.

59 Kirchheim (1851: 90). See also: Kashani (1971).

60 See: Jacob Son of Aaron (1908: 697); Mills (1864: 196); Pummer (1988: 9).

61 T Avodah Zarah 3(4):13. See also: JT Shabbat 19:2, 17a; JT Yevamot 8:1, 8d–9a; BT Avodah Zarah 27a.

by a Cuthean. On the other hand, we possess testimony from the late fourth century that the Samaritans rejected Jewish circumcision and required those who had undergone such circumcision to undergo a ritual re-circumcision. In his book *De Mensuris et Ponderibus,* Epiphanius of Salamis relates that both the Samaritans who converted to Judaism and the Jews who became Samaritans were, respectively, required to undergo a second circumcision,[62] thus attesting to the mutual negation of the other group's practice. This report is not supported by additional testimonies, but all the above sources together attest that the Samaritans scrupulously observed their method of circumcision, which differed from the Jewish procedure of circumcision-*peri'ah.*

We accordingly see that both Rabbinic and external sources point in the same direction: the obligation of *peri'ah* as well as the accompanying prohibition against leaving *tzitzin* was established after the Hadrianic persecutions, and following the process of assimilation in the Hellenistic cities where there were many instances of Jews engaging in decircumcision. This regulation was enacted for the purpose of ensuring that no tissue remained that might facilitate the successful accomplishment of *meshihat orlah.* The addition of *peri'ah* raised even further the barrier between Jew and Gentile. Pre-*peri'ah* circumcision, which was supposed to imprint an indelible mark, did not withstand the test. It could be annulled, enabling the individual to cross the boundaries, leave the Jewish community, and subsequently reenter it. The regulation of *peri'ah* put an end to this possibility, and after its enactment there are no further reports of drawing down the foreskin in Israel. Since the Rabbis wanted to seal this boundary breach firmly, they placed the obligation of *peri'ah* and the removal of the *tzitzin* on the same level as circumcision itself, so that a circumciser who did not tear and roll back the membrane or cut away all the remaining "shreds" did not perform his duty and the circumcision was considered ritually invalid.

The modification in the practice of circumcision thus instituted by the Rabbis represents their method of interpreting the halakhah during a time of change. In order to understand the interpretive process, we must discuss the anthropological question of the relationship between text and context. Jewish society is based on the written text, considered sacred and unchanging. The context, the social reality, however, is likely to change as a result of political and economic shifts. The text, which accompanies the society and serves as a source for its values and norms, must undergo an interpretive process in order to constitute a source of authority under new conditions as well. Classical anthropologists such as Robertson-Smith and Boas[63] who investigated societies

---

62   See: Dean (1935: 32); Pummer (1988: 9–10); see also: Duliere (1967).

63   Robertson-Smith (1927: 16–18); Boas (1896: 270–80).

lacking a written language, could not relate to the historical dimension in their analysis of the culture of these societies. They deliberately disregarded the interpretation of their customs by members of these societies, because they viewed this interpretation as subject to change in accordance with changing circumstances. These researchers therefore interpreted the practices from an external theoretical perspective. Goldberg[64] considers this long-established method unsuitable for the analysis of a society with a sophisticated and written culture, because this would ignore the historical dimension of the text and the custom, and the contribution that could be made by a diachronic approach to the interpretation. Goldberg maintains that we must also listen to the interpretation given by the members of the culture under study over the course of history in order to understand the interaction between the written interpretation set forth by the recognized interpretive authority and actual practice. In the final analysis, loyalty to the text, as perceived by the members of each generation, and as based on the authoritative-traditional interpretation, assures uniformity within the normative framework, even though contentual change has occurred.

This problematic nature of the connection between the halakhah and the reality was noted by Jacob Katz in his discussion of Jewish non-Jewish relations.[65] While the halakhah forbids contact between Jews and non-Jews, especially during the latter's holidays,[66] in practice everyday contact continued in medieval Germany, on non-Jewish festivals as well. Katz argues that the halakhah took care to maintain a balance between adaptation to contemporary conditions and concern for the preservation of Jewish identity. At times the halakhah was forced to find ways to adapt to the changing social conditions, but guarded the Jewish identity, finding *ex post facto* justification for such a course of action.[67] This same phenomenon explains how the halakhah managed the drastic change in circumcision practice instituted by the Rabbis. A means was found to introduce change in response to contemporary circumstances, but the rabbis camouflaged the change by attributing both *peri'ah* and the removal of the "shreds" to the Torah commandment. Thus, the received tradition continued to define the Jewish practice of circumcision as an unchanging ancient rite dating back to God's command to the first patriarch while at the same time accommodating an innovation in praxis that effectively addressed a contemporary challenge perceived as threatening to community survival.

---

[64]   Goldberg (1987).

[65]   Katz (1961: 24–47).

[66]   M Avodah Zarah 1.

[67]   A number of recently published studies examine the relationship between the halakhah and the actual practice. See, e.g.: Cooper (1987); Friedman (1992); Rubin (1993) and ch. 8 in this volume; Rubin (1996).

CHAPTER 4. COPING WITH THE VALUE OF THE *PIDYON HA'BEN* PAYMENT IN RABBINIC LITERATURE: AN EXAMPLE OF A SOCIAL CHANGE PROCESS

I

The development of the *halakhah* regarding *pidyon ha'ben*—the "redemption of the (firstborn) son"—is an interesting example of the change processes which take place in a traditional society. Such a society is, by definition, one which is not attuned to change because of the sanctity of its traditions, which the society perceives as immutable. But even a traditional society does not remain rooted in one place. Processes of change occur slowly over an extended period of time. In reality, these changes are not recognized as innovative, but rather as the correct interpretation of the text. Such an interpretation can only be given by those qualified to do so. These produce their interpretation based on interpretive rules which are themselves rooted in the tradition.[1]

In this article, we will deal with the change which took place in the real value of the amount paid for *pidyon ha'ben*: how the real amount which a father must pay to redeem his son, namely five *shekalim*, became a ceremonial sum without any economic or real value. The true value of five *shekalim*, as we see from the rabbinic sources, was at first a relatively large sum for a day laborer, amounting to as much as a full month's earnings. By analyzing the sources and their context, it appears that there were fathers—and it is the father who is responsible to redeem his firstborn son—who tended to delay the time of the redemption, simply because of the expense involved. It is possible that there were even fathers—because of the cost involved—who simply avoided the performance of this commandment. On the other hand, there were no doubt poor people who went to great lengths to fulfill the commandment in spite of the hardship entailed. There were two conditions which enabled those who wished to refrain from performing this commandment to do so. The first was that during the time of the Temple and that of the Tanna'im the redemption

---

[1] See Katz (1960).

was evidently not carried out in a public ceremony nor at a specific time[2] (we will yet discuss this below). The second is that only a small number of males who are born require *pidyon ha'ben* (demographic calculations show that only about a quarter of all males who are born require it[3]). A custom which has no specific place or time and is not carried out publicly, and which, in addition, does not apply to all people equally, is a relatively easy one to evade. One should note that the commandment to circumcise one's sons cannot be evaded, because all expect it on a specific day and it is carried out publicly and in a festive manner.[4] As opposed to this, one is able to evade *pidyon ha'ben* because the community does not necessarily know if any particular infant needs a *pidyon ha'ben* or not. First of all, many firstborn are exempt from the ceremony.[5] Furthermore, there is, as will be seen below, no specific day on which to expect the ceremony to take place. Our claim is that, in order to lessen the economic burden involved in performing this commandment and in order not to have considerable numbers of people evade their duty, alternate methods were found which enabled every person to redeem his son at the appropriate time and at a price which would not represent an economic burden.

II

In a number of places, the Torah commands that the firstborn be redeemed, i.e., that his inherent sanctification as a firstborn son be removed by redemption from a *kohen* (Ex. 13:2; Ex. 13:12–14; Num. 18:15–16),[6] but the Torah does not specify any further detail. One may hypothesize that the primary

---

[2]   On the *pidyon ha'ben* ceremony in detail, see Rubin (1995: 123–146).

[3]   According to the data of the *Israel Statistical Yearbook* (the Central Bureau of Statistics, Jerusalem 1994, Vol. 45, Table 3.18, p. 145), there were 78,442 live Jewish births in 1992. Of these, 22,447 were first births. As the birthrate is 1.06 males for every 1.0 females born, 41,574 males were born in 1992, of which about 12,000 were first births. If we deduct 20% from this to cover children whose fathers are *kohanim* or Levites or whose mothers are the daughters of *kohanim* or Levites or who were born after a miscarriage or by caesarean section (all of which are exempt from *pidyon ha'ben*), a total of about 9,600 males were born who require a *pidyon ha'ben*, that representing about 12% of all births and about 23% of all males.

[4]   On circumcision as a public ceremony, see Rubin (1995: 114–119).

[5]   See *supra*, n. 3.

[6]   On the firstborn in the Bible, see: Brin (1971; 1977; 1994); Rubin (1981: 155–176; 1995: 123–125).

focus in the redemption ceremony was the giving of five *shekalim* to a *kohen*, but we do not know if this was supposed to be in the child's presence or without him present; whether only the father and *kohen* were to be present or whether it was to be a public ceremony; whether there were specific blessings to be recited or none such. According to the literal meaning of the verse, "You shall redeem each firstborn of your sons and you shall not see My face emptyhanded" (Ex. 34:20), it appears that the one doing the redeeming— evidently the father—had to come to the Temple and give the money for the redemption there together with the other *matanot* (literally "gifts"—the various items that one was duty-bound to give to the *kohanim*) and sacrifices.[7] It is very possible that those who lived close to the Temple could bring their son with them, but for those living far away it was difficult to take an infant who was not much more than a month old on a long journey.[8] It appears that the redemption day was also not a fixed one, and it was possible to redeem one's firstborn any time from when he was a month old and thereafter ("His redemption from a month old you shall redeem," Num. 18:16),[9] just like other redemptions which do not have a fixed time.

Regarding the Second Temple era, we know of the covenant in Nehemiah 10:37, where we read the following undertaking: "The firstborn of our sons and cattle, as it states in the Torah, and the firstborn of our herds and flocks to bring to the house of our God, to the *kohanim* who serve in the house of our

---

[7]   Compare Ex. 27:15 and Deut. 15:19–20, that one should not attend the pilgrimage festival with empty hands. From this it would appear logical that one should bring the firstborn of one's cattle along with money for the *pidyon ha'ben*. *Rashi*, however (basing himself on the interpretation of the Sages, see below, n. 22) does not go along with the literal interpretation of the verse. According to him, "My face shall not be seen empty-handed" does not refer to the firstborn, because the commandment of *pidyon ha'ben* has nothing to do with the pilgrimage. Rather, the verse teaches us that each person should bring a sacrifice when he comes on the pilgrimage.

[8]   Hannah, too, did not bring her son Samuel to Shilo "until the child was weaned" (I Sam. 1:22).

[9]   According to the interpretation of the Sages, a firstborn human can be redeemed from the 31st day on and thereafter forever. See discussion and sources in Rubin (1995: 128–129). One might possibly say, taking the literal meaning of the text, that a firstborn son might be redeemed between the ages of one month to five years, as in the sum of estimation (*arakhin*) in Lev. 27:6, "And if it be from a month old even unto five years old, then your estimation of the male shall be five *shekels* of silver" (Lev. 27:6). See Ashley (1993: 95, 351). There is a view that the estimations in Lev. 27:2–8 represent the average price of male and female slaves in the ancient Near East, by age and sex. Five *shekalim* was the estimation of a male until the age of five. See: Wenham (1978: 264–265).

God." In other words, those present undertook to redeem their firstborn sons with the other *matanot* which are meant for the Temple. According to this covenant—if they indeed acted in accordance with it—the firstborn son was brought to the Temple. It appears that that was only possible in a community which lived close to the Temple, such as the Jewish community at the time of Nehemiah. Other people evidently added the amount needed for the redemption to the other *terumot* ("waive offerings") and *ma'asrot* ("tithes"), and brought all to the Temple during the three pilgrimage festivals. It is difficult to ascertain from the verses to what extent they made sure to bring the different offerings to the priests and Levites during the Second Temple era. From the verse in Neh. 12:44 ("And at that time some were appointed over the chambers for the treasures, for the offerings, for the firstfruits, and for the tithes, to gather into them out of the fields of the cities the portions of the Torah for the priests and Levites, for Judah rejoiced for the priests and for the Levites that waited"), it would appear that they did indeed fulfill their obligation and brought the *matanot* joyfully (compare Neh. 13:13). However there are scholars who believe that this was not a realistic picture, and it only corresponded to the emotional period when the Temple was consecrated. On a day to day basis, during those difficult times, it was a heavy burden to support the Temple and its many employees.[10]

Regarding the post-Biblical era, we learn from three sources about the *pidyon ha'ben* and its location. We have evidence from Philo about this era, to the effect that the money for the *pidyon ha'ben* was brought to the Temple,[11] as had been the custom at the beginning of the Second Temple era. Philo discusses *the matanot* to the *kohanim*, and among others he mentions the firstborn of cattle and of donkeys and the redemption money of the firstborn. After listing the different *matanot*, Philo writes, "And so that none of those who gives it would embarrass [the priests] who received it, [the Torah] commanded that they should first bring the gifts to the Temple and from there the *kohanim* would receive them later on."[12] This way, the *kohanim* avoided the embarrassment of receiving the *matanot* directly from people. Alon has already noted that Philo's words contradict Jewish law, which permits various kinds of *matanot* to the *kohanim* to be given in any place and to any *kohen*.[13]

---

[10]   See, for example, the views of Myers (1965: 205–207); Clines (1984: 234–235); Batten (1913; 283–284); Blenkinsopp (1989: 349–350); Fenshman (1982: 258–259). See also Malachi 3:8–10 on refraining from giving *ma'asrot*.

[11]   *De Specialibus Legibus I*, 132–142; see Alon (1957: 91).

[12]   *De Specialibus Legibus I*, 132–142; Alon's (1957:83) translation from Greek to Hebrew

[13]   Alon (1957: 83, n. 2).

The second source is in Luke 2:21–23, where we read, "And when eight days were over for the circumcising of the child, his name was called Jesus, as he was so named by the angel before he was conceived in the womb. And when the days of her purification were completed[14] according to the Torah of Moses,[15] they brought him to Jerusalem, to present him to the Lord;[16] as it is written in the Torah of the Lord, 'Every male that opens the womb shall be called holy to the Lord';[17] and to offer a sacrifice according to that which is said in the Torah of the Lord—two turtledoves or two young pigeons."[18] It is clear that these verses refer to the *pidyon ha'ben*, even though the five *shekalim* are not mentioned. From the words of Luke we see that Jesus was not redeemed on the thirtieth day after his birth as the Torah states in regard to the *pidyon ha'ben* (Num. 18:16), but on the fortieth day, because a woman who has given birth is forbidden to enter the Temple until forty days after she gave birth to a male have passed and she has brought a sacrifice to purify herself (Lev. 13:1–8). The methodological problem with the source in Luke is that the author could not have been a witness to the events, because he was a Christian non-Jew and not from Eretz Israel, and who wrote his work between 80–85 C.E., many years after the event; one may thus not be able to rely on his testimony.[19] In this regard, we can at least say that this source does not contradict others and is supported by the statement in Philo's work. This therefore evidently represents a tradition which had been received in regard to the *pidyon ha'ben*.

---

[14] In the correct Greek manuscripts the version is "their purification," as opposed to others where it is "her purification," which would seemingly be more appropriate, because the father has no obligation of *taharah*. That was why the copiers changed "their" to "her." See, Fitzmyer (1981: 418–427). There are those who say that both parents went up to Jerusalem, each for a different ceremony: the father to redeem his son and the mother to bring a sacrifice. The author wished to stress that both went up to the Temple, and it appears that way from Luke 2:27. See, *The Interpreter's One-Volume Commentary on the Bible* (Nashville and New York, 1971), 676.

[15] In accordance with Lev. 12:4.

[16] Luke stresses "to present him to the Lord"—in the Temple, and there is no clear source for this in either the Bible or in the Mishnah. See Fitzmyer (1981: 425).

[17] Luke notes that this refers to "a male who opens the womb," but the verse to which he alludes ("Sanctify for me every firstborn who opened the womb among the Children of Israel among man and animal it is mine" (Ex. 13:2) does not mention the gender. For a discussion about this, see, Michaelis (1981: 876–877).

[18] In accordance with Lev. 12:1–4.

[19] See, Fitzmyer (1981: 424). Regarding the date of authorship of Luke, see, for example, Aune, (1994: 62–65).

From a third source, from toward the end of the Second Temple era, it appears that they had stopped coming to Jerusalem for the *pidyon ha'ben* and they would redeem the firstborn in the *gevulin* (a term used to indicate all of Eretz Israel with the exception of Jerusalem). We find in *Tosefta*, "Twenty-four *matanot* of the *kehunah* ("priesthood") were given to Aaron and his descendants... ten in the Temple and four in Jerusalem and ten in the *gevulin*." Among the ten in the *gevulin* we find the commandment of the *pidyon ha'ben* (T *Hallah* 2:7–9; see also M *Hallah* 4:9). According to Alon, one can rely on Philo's tradition, he himself possibly having once made the pilgrimage to Jerusalem, and that does not contradict the tradition of the era of the return to Zion in Nehemiah's time. Alon proves from other sources that throughout most of the Second Temple era they would bring their *terumot* and *ma'asrot* to the Temple treasury, and the treasury would distribute these among the *kohanim*. It is possible that even though the Sages permitted certain *matanot* to be given in any place and to any *kohen* or levite, it was still preferable to bring them to Jerusalem. Regarding the *pidyon ha'ben*, Alon states there were certainly people who brought their firstborn to Jerusalem, as mentioned in Luke, and there were evidently those who were far from Jerusalem who sent the redemption money to Jerusalem, as testified to by Philo.

When did they stop bringing the *matanot* to Jerusalem and start giving them in the *gevulin*? Based on evidence from the end of the Second Temple era, as found in Josephus Flavius (*Antiquities of the Jews*, 20:181; 20:205–207; *Life*, 12), Alon shows[20] that wealthy and powerful *kohanim* would send their slaves to collect *ma'asrot*, while poor *kohanim* would die of hunger. This shows us that already at that time there were those who did not bring up their *ma'asrot* to Jerusalem. According to Alon, the turnabout came during the time of the dispute between Hyrcanos and Aristobolos (at the end of the 60s in the 1st century B.C.E.). Those who followed Aristobolos refused to bring their *matanot* to the Temple treasury controlled by Hyrcanos, and it was due to this fact that the law was amended to permit the giving of *matanot* in the *gevulin* as well, this including the *pidyon ha'ben*.[21] After the destruction of the

---

[20]   Alon (1957: 87–92).

[21]   According to a different interpretation of the sources, one can pre-date this dispute to the days of Yohanan Hyrcanos, who at the end of his life became a Sadducee. See Alon (1957: 91, n. 22). On p. 87, n. 15, Alon raises another hypothesis: that when the number of *kohanim* increased and they spread throughout the country, they divided into 24 shifts of *kohanim*, with each shift working two weeks a year and on the pilgrimage festivals. There were *kohanim* who had bought land and no longer supported themselves with the *matanot* received by the *kohanim*, and that might have been the reason why the method of giving *matanot* to the *kohanim* changed.

Second Temple, it was already obvious that the money for the *pidyon ha'ben* was given to the *kohanim* who lived in the *gevulin*. When the Talmud discusses in a *Beraita* (BT *Kiddushin* 29b) whether "one should redeem his son or ascend for the pilgrimage ceremony" if the person does not have the wherewithal to do both, that *Beraita* was no longer of any practical consequence, because there was no longer any ascent on the pilgrimage festivals. According to the first Tanna, the *pidyon ha'ben* comes first, whereas according to R. Yehudah going on the pilgrimage comes first. At the same time, it is clear that, according to both of them, the *pidyon ha'ben* was to be performed where one lived, and not in the Temple. In explaining the reason of the first Tanna, the Talmud does not use the literal meaning of the verse, "You shall redeem each firstborn of your sons and you shall not see My face emptyhanded" (Ex. 34:20). According to the literal meaning, one should come to the Temple along with the firstborn and the *matanot*, but the verse is interpreted as follows: " 'You shall redeem each firstborn of your sons,' and then 'you shall not see My face emptyhanded.' " The Tanna explains the two parts of the verse as referring to two separate cases: the first is the *pidyon ha'ben* without making the pilgrimage, and the second is a reference to making the pilgrimage without this being connected to the *pidyon ha'ben*. Thus the interpretation of the verse supplied legitimation to an existing situation.[22]

A few of the discussions about the *pidyon ha'ben* indicate economic distress. Later on we will see the value of the amount of the redemption and what percentage of a wage-earner's income it represented. But already now we can say that from the question posed by the Tanna'im, whether to redeem oneself or to redeem one's son where one cannot afford both, that there was economic hardship, either because the redemption cost was high or because the combination of the two was cause for economic hardship. According to one Tanna, "the person['s redemption] takes precedence over [that of] his son,"while according to R. Yehudah "his son['s redemption] takes precedence" (*Mekhilta de-Rabbi Shimon bar Yohai*, 43). The reason given for R. Yehudah's position is that "both the commandment for the father (to be redeemed) and the commandment of the son (to be redeemed) devolve upon [the father]" BT *Bekhorot* 49b; *Kiddushin* 29b). The final decision was only reached in the days of R. Yirmiyahu (an Eretz Israel Amora of the third and fourth generations), that according to all the father must first

---

22 See also, *Sifrei Korah* 118 (Horowitz edition, 1907: 138): "Just as with the firstborn of a human he is permitted to give it to a *kohen* in any place which he wishes." See also *Mekhilta de-Rabbi Yishmael, Masekhta de-Pis'ha* 16 (Epstein-Melamed edition, 1955: 58).

redeem himself while the son will then redeem himself when he Is able to. If is doubtful that such a question would have been asked had the amount of money been but symbolic. Here we hear of a situation, which may be no more than theoretical, where a second generation will also suffer economic hardship. The very discussion, even if it but hypothetical, indicates an awareness of economic distress.

We noted earlier that the verse, "His redemption from a month old you shall redeem" (Num. 18:16) teaches us that the redemption is only to take place after thirty days have passed, and is not to take place earlier,[23] because— according to the definition of R. Shimon ben Gamaliel—"Whoever has sur- vived for thirty days is no longer an aborted fetus" (BT Shabbat 135b). Various Amora'im add that even if the infant was healthy but "became terminal ill within thirty days, he is not redeemed"[24] and one does not argue that once thirty days have passed the obligation to redeem his son has devolved upon the father, as potentially this firstborn should have been redeemed after 30 days. This is what arises from a discussion in the Mishnah regarding an infant who had been redeemed but who died within thirty days. The question is whether the *kohen* is required to return the redemption money (M *Bekhorot* 8:5–8). The Baylonian Amora'im are divided about whether a child who was redeemed before he was 30 days old is considered to have been redeemed: "Rav said he is redeemed and Shmuel said his son is not redeemed." The conclusion of the Talmud is that the son is indeed redeemed unless the father stated at the time, "my son is redeemed from now" and the *kohen* did not use the money before the child was 30 days old. It appears that in the time of Rava the view was accepted that if one redeems his son before the time, the son is nevertheless redeemed (BT *Berakhot* 12b).[25]

If the father did not redeem his son at the right time, he can redeem him "forever" (BT *Bekhorot* 12b), and he is not penalized for doing so.[26] In *Tosefta* (*Bekhorot* 6:10) there is a view that under certain conditions one is able, at the

---

23   *Sifrei* (*supra*, n. 22), 139; BT *Bekhorot* 49a quotes an Amoraic interpretation which differs from that of the Tanna'im in *Sifrei*. See also BT *Bekhorot* 12b: "There is no estimation and *pidyon ha'ben*… less than thirty."

24   BT *Bava Kama* 11b and BT *Menahot* 37a. *Rashi* in *Bava Kama* explains that the firstborn had become terminally ill and had died. *Tosafot* s.v. *Bekhor she'nitraf*, dis- agree with *Rashi* and interpret this as referring to a firstborn who became terminally but did not die.

25   Rava interprets the *Beraita* in *Bekhorot* 12b (*supra*, n. 23) as referring to a case where he says "from now."

26   See *Rashi* on BT *Bekhorot* 12b, s.v., *Umosifin*. However in a responsum attributed to Rav Hai Gaon we are told that "one must add a fifth." See B. M. Levin, *Otzar ha'ge'onim*

very outset, to postpone the redemption. The question in *Tosefta* is whether "one should rather redeem himself or go up (to the Temple) on the pilgrimage festival,"where the person does not have enough money for both (In the *Beraita*, *Kiddushin* 29b, the question posed is whether "one is to redeem his son or to go up on the pilgrimage festival"). According to the first Tanna, his first duty is to redeem himself (or his son) and only then to make the pilgrimage, while R. Yehudah states, "He makes the pilgrimage and only then does he redeem himself, because this commandment (going up to Jerusalem on the pilgrimage festival) is one which lapses with time."

We thus see that the Tannaitic literature brings views that one can redeem a son before he is 30 days old and thereafter, but ideally this should took place on the child's 31st day. It is possible that the flexibility in this regard made it easier for those who found it difficult to meet this obligation. If they managed to obtain money before the days were up, they would be able to hasten and redeem their son (M *Bekhorot* 8:6), and if they were unable to obtain the money within 30 days, they could postpone the redemption (even their own redemption, if their father had not redeemed them) until such a time in the future as they were able to pay the amount.

It is possible to interpret these sources as being purely legal deliberations regarding principles, dealing with all types of theoretical situations without this being a reflection on any historical circumstances. That is too facile a rejection of the argument, because if we add to these sources those sources which indicate the high cost of the *pidyon ha'ben* as compared to the wages of a day-laborer, we can see that this was a not insignificant economic burden, even for those who wished with all their hearts to fulfill the commandment. The fact is that various regulations have been found which served to circumvent the provisions of the law, or that the real value of the amount needed for the redemption was not preserved. In terms of methodology, it is more logical to hypothesize that the *takkanot* ("regulations") and changes which we will discuss represented a concrete economic situation rather than to offer an alternative hypothesis that these were merely discussions in principle without any necessary connection to reality. Furthermore, these sources do not contradict one another and there is no dispute between them. Rather, they all flow in the same direction. Later, we will clarify the real value of the money paid for the *pidyon ha'ben* and the adjustment of this value to different places and different times.

---

li'fesahim (*Anthology of the Geonim on Pesahim*), 131. See there the note of the editor, that the source of this additional fifth is unknown.

III

According to Torah law, the redemption must be for "five *shekalim* of the holy *shekel*, this being twenty *gera*" (Num. 18:16). Indeed, the *shekel* was a common currency in the Near East and was used both as a unit of weight and as a unit of payment. In Eretz Israel, for many years the common currency was the Phoenician *shekel*, made of silver. At first this *shekel* was minted in Sidon and afterwards it was minted in Tyre. The Tyrian *shekel* was minted up to about 55–56 C.E. With the outbreak of the Great Revolt against Rome, the rebels minted silver coins of a *shekel*, half a *shekel* and a quarter of a *shekel*. During the Bar Kokhba rebellion, too, a new coin was minted, this being the *sela* or tetradrachma.[27]

The value of the *shekel* changed with the times, and the *shekel* of the Torah is not identical to that of the Mishnah.[28] During the time of the Mishnah they no longer redeemed the firstborn with five *shekels* of their time, because the value of their *shekel* was less than that of the Torah *shekel*. The Sages therefore decreed that the five *shekels* of the *pidyon ha'ben* would be based on the Tyrian *maneh*. In the language of the Mishnah, "Five *sela'im* of the son are in the Tyrian *maneh*" (M *Bekhorot* 8:7 and T *Bekhorot* 6:12). The *sela* substituted for the holy *shekel* for *pidyon ha'ben* purposes. The value of the coins, as reflected in the Talmudic literature during Tannaitic times and at the beginning of the Amoraic period was as follows:[29]

Maneh	Sela (Tetradrachmon)	Shekel	Dinar (Zuz)	Ma'ah
1	25	50	100	1000
	1	2	4	40
		1	2	20
			1	10
				1

---

27   The word *shekel* has the root letters of *shin, kuf, lammed*, which relates to weighing. In the Bible we find a gold *shekel* (Gen. 20:4, 22; *et al.*) as well as different systems of weights: of the holy (Ex. 32:24–26), the "monarchical" (2 Sam. 14:26). On the systems of weights and of coinage, see Frankel (1956); Sellers (1962); Ashley (1993).

28   On the value of the holy *shekel* in the Bible in terms of income, see Wenham (1981: 144); See also his article (Wenham, 1978). According to him, the cost of the *pidyon ha'ben* was equivalent to six months' wages.

29   The table is based on Sperber (1970: 236).

Thus we see that a *sela* was worth four silver *dinarim*[30] and five *sela'im* were 20 *dinarim*.[31] The weight of the *dinar* was 3.75 grams of silver, and the total needed for the *pidyon ha'ben* was 71.4 grams of silver.[32]

In order to determine whether this amount was considered a major or minor expense, we will compare it to the average wage of a day-laborer during the Tannaitic and early Amoraic period.[33] During this time period, the wage of a day-laborer was between 1 to 2 *dinarim* per day[34] and a loaf of bread weighing about 500 grams sold for a *pundion*, of which there were

---

[30]   During this era, gold *dinarim* were also in use, but then they are referred to clearly in the sources as a "gold *dinar.*" On the coins of the period, see, Sperber (1974: 31–24). One hundred gold *dinarim* were worth a *maneh. On the* maneh, see Sperber (1970a: 591–611).

[31]   Already in the 4th century C.E. do we find Rava quoting a *Beraita* which had been preserved by him but in no other source, whereby, "A silver *dinar* is a twenty-fifth part of a gold *dinar.*" Rava continues, "What practical significance is there to this? In regard to *pidyon ha'ben*" (BT *Bava Metzia* 44b). In other words, if the father handed a *kohen* a gold *dinar*, whose worth was 25 silver *dinarim*, for the *pidyon ha'ben*, which requires twenty silver *dinarim*, the *kohen* would have to return five silver *dinarim*. It appears that Rava had the continuation of a *Beraita*, whose beginning is in *Eduyot* 4:7. Other sources have the gold *dinar* as being worth 24 silver *dinarim* (M *Me'ilah* 6:4; JT *Kiddushin* 1:1, 58d). On the fluctuations in the value of the coins, see Sperber (1974: 76).

[32]   See Sperber (1966: 164–168).

[33]   We will relate here only to this era, because until the 3rd century C.E. there was a relatively stable economy in Eretz Israel. For hundreds of years, until the 3rd century, there were no sharp fluctuations of the value of the coinage. There are those who attribute this stability to the stability in the value of the Tyrian *shekel*, which had begun to be minted in 126–5 B.C.E. and ceased being minted in 55–6 C.E. The Tyrian *shekel* was legal tender until 135 C.E., and possibly even up to 170 C.E. In other words, it had a noticeable influence on the economy for about 300 years. See, Ben David (1974: 271–2). Ben David claims that there were about 600 years of economic stability, among others because of the Tyrian *shekel*, but it would appear that this *shekel* can only be said to have been influential for about 300 years.

[34]   On wages in the first century of the Common Era, see, for example, *Avot de-Rabbi Nathan*, Version B, 26 (Schechter edition, 1887: 27b), which relates that Hillel asked workers, "'How much are you going to earn today?' One answered, 'One *dinar*' and another answered 'two *dinarim.*'" Hillel himself earned a half *dinar* (a *tarapik*) per day (BT *Yoma* 35b). On wages in the 2nd century C.E., see BT *Avodah Zarah* 62a: "We have learned (in a Mishnah): One who says to a worker, 'Here is this *dinar* and for it gather for me vegetables today.'" R. Meir, who was a good scribe, earned 3 *sela'im* (12 *dinarim*) a week, or 2 *dinarim* per day (Eccl. Rabbah 2:17). In T *Bava Metzia* 6:15 we find that the daily wage for harvesting or threshing was between 1 *dinar* to 4 *dinarim*. See the list of wages and prices in Sperber (1974: 101–102). On the income of a worker, see also, in detail Heineman (1954); Ayali (1987).

12 to the *dinar*,[35] so that a person had to work between half an hour to an hour (based on a 12 hour day) to earn enough for a loaf of bread. Clothes were very expensive when compared to income, with a shirt or *tallit* for a man costing between 1 to 3 *sela'im* (4 to 12 *dinarim*) for an inexpensive or moderately priced garment, ranging up to 25 *dinarim* (or a single gold *dinar*) for an expensive garment.[36]

An examination of the *ketubah* which the groom pledged to his bride and of the dowry that the father pledged to his daughter shows similar findings. The *ketubah* of a virgin was 200 *zuz* (*dinarim*) and of a widow 100 *zuz* (M *Ketubot* 1:4, 4:7, *et passim.*; T *Ketubot* 1:2–3; 2:2, *et passim.*) The *ketubah* was meant to ensure an income for the woman should she be widowed or divorced. It appears that 200 *zuz* was an amount sufficient to support the woman for a year. Dividing this amount by 12 months yields somewhat under 17 *zuz* per month, that being a little more than 4 *sela'im*, an amount approaching the amount to be paid for the *pidyon ha'ben*, namely 5 *sela'im*. The minimal amount of a dowry was equivalent to about a month's wages, i.e., 25 *zuz* (six and a quarter *sela'im*) according to the *Tosefta* (*Ketubot* 6:4); or two months' wages, 50 *zuz*, according to the Mishnah (*Ketubot* 4:5). It would appear that to determine criteria for income, it is convenient to use units of a month and a year.

This data indicates a relatively low standard of living in Eretz Israel.[37] An agricultural laborer who worked an average of 20 days a month (excluding the Shabbat, festivals, and sick days) earned between 20 to 40 *dinarim* per month. Based on the data that we have brought, that allowed one to maintain only a low standard of living. The 20 *dinarim* that a father would have to pay for the *pidyon ha'ben* would represent the income of between half a month to a full month's labor, like the price of an expensive garment.

The ceremonial amount, 5 *shekalim*, cannot change, but the actual amount paid can change based on the exchange rate of the coin: it can become larger or smaller in accordance with the standard of living, as long as it maintains its relative value in accordance with the father's income. Indeed, we find that the

---

[35]   See Ben David (1974), who estimates that a standard loaf of bread weighed about 500 grams (1.1 lb.). On the price of bread in the 1st and 2nd centuries C.E., see M *Pe'ah* 8:7; *Shevi'it* 8:6; *Kelim* 17:1; T *Shevi'it* 6:21; and so too Sperber (1974: 103).

[36]   M *Me'ilah* 6:4; T *Bava Metzia* 3:14; *Arakhin* 4:3; *Bekhorot* 6:13; *Me'ilah* 2:10. See Sperber (1974: 103) and Ayali (1987: 82–96). Ayali discusses fluctuations in wages, but his conclusion is that generally the wage earned by laborers was very low.

[37]   On the standard of living in Eretz Israel, see Ben David (1974: ch. 6). For a comparison between the standard of living in Eretz Israel and that in Egypt, see Sperber (1974: chs. 17 and 30). See *infra*, n. 51, about the cost of food for the poor.

Sages discuss a varying exchange rate in regard to the coin for the redemption. Regarding the Mishnah of "Five *sela'im* of the son are in the Tyrian *maneh*" (*Bekhorot* 8:7), the Amora'im of Eretz Israel in the 3rd and 4th centuries C.E. discussed the issue. In BT *Bekhorot* 49b–50a) we read: "What is the Tyrian *maneh*? Rav Asi said, 'The *maneh* of Tyre.' Rav Ami said, 'The Arabian *dinar.*' R. Hanina said, 'A Syriac *istira*, eight of which are bought for a [gold] *dinar*, five of them are for *pidyon ha'ben.*' R. Yohanan said, 'A worn Hadrianic-Trajanic *dinar* which is sold for twenty-five *zuz*, subtract from them one-sixth and this (i.e., what is left) is for the *pidyon ha'ben.*'"[38]

R. Hanina (an Eretz Israel Amora of the 1st generation) compares the five *sela'im* to the Syriac *istira*, which was evidently the tetradrachma cistophorus coined in Asia Minor in the 2nd century C.E.: eight *istiras* were equivalent to a single gold *dinar* or 25 silver *dinarim*. One *istira* was therefore worth 3.225 silver *dinarim* and five *istiras* were equivalent to 16.125 silver *dinarim*[39] (60 grams of silver). R. Yohanan (an Eretz Israel Amora of the 2nd generation) states that the five *sela'im* of the Torah are 5/6 of an worn gold coin of Caesar Trajanus Hadrianus,[40] i.e., 20.8 silver *dinarim*[41] (78 grams of silver). Rav Asi (an Eretz Israel Amora of the 3rd generation) states that the basis is the Tyrian coin. The *sela* is evidently the Tyrian tetradrachma which we mentioned earlier[42] and 5 *sela'im* are 20 silver *dinarim* (75 grams of silver). According

---

[38]   The version here is according to the Munich ms.

[39]   See Sperber (1974: 225, n. 36; 230), and not as Safrai (1967: 257).

[40]   Sperber (1974: 229–230), offers an interesting interpretation. According to him, because of the monetary crisis in the 3rd century C.E., people stopped trusting silver coinage and went over to gold coins. There is evidence that people buried their coins in hidden places and later used them. It is to this that R. Yohanan alluded, at the end of the 3rd century C.E., when he spoke of a worn Hadrianic coin. This was a coin of the emperor Traianus Hadrianus of the previous century, and not as *Rashi* and *Tosafot* there, who regarded Traianus and Hadrianus as two different emperors. In the Munich ms. of the Babylonian Talmud, *Avodah Zarah* 52b, the version is "*dinara Traiana veHadriana*," and that refers to two people, but that is the only such source, especially as if, indeed, the reference was to two emperors, the text should have been, "*dinarei Traiana veHadraina*, which is the plural, "*dinarim*," and not the way it actually appears—*dinera*—which is in the singular. The order of the words in BT *Avodah Zarah* supports the proposal that this was a single person, because the full name of Hadrianus (Hadrian) was Traianus Hadrianus.

[41]   The gold *dinar* was worth 25 silver ones, and therefore $(25 \times 5)/6 = 20.83$ *dinarim* for the *pidyon ha'ben*. In the Munich ms. the conclusion of R. Yohanan's words is, "and these are twenty and two," i.e., the cost of the *pidyon ha'ben* was $^5/_6$ of a *dinar*, which is 22 silver *dinarim*, but this is not an exact number, because in reality they are loss than 21 *dinarim*. In the printed text and in other versions, this sentence is missing.

[42]   See *supra*, n. 30, and so too Sperber (1974: 230).

to Rav Ami (a contemporary of Rav Asi), it evidently refers to a Nabatean coin, possibly as opposed to the himyaritic coin, whose value was higher.[43] According to this source, it appears that in each era the Sages adjusted the value of the *pidyon ha'ben* to the value of the coins used in that era.

In Babylon, too, the Sages evaluated the cost of the *pidyon ha'ben* in accordance with the local currency. According to Rava, a *sela* of the Torah is 3⅓ *dinarim*, which is a lower exchange rate than the generally accepted value of 4 *dinarim* to the *sela*. It was this exchange rate which Rav Ashi (two generations after Rava) also used, when he sent Rav Aha bar Ravina 17 *zuzim* (*dinarim*) for the *pidyon ha'ben*. He based himself on 3⅓ *dinarim* to the *sela* and thus according to him 5 *sela'im* were equivalent to 16⅔ *dinarim*, and he asked Rav Aha to send him ⅓ *dinar* in change. Rav Aha, though, demanded the rate of 4 *dinarim* to a *sela*, and he therefore asked Rav Ashi to send him the additional amount needed to bring it up to 20 *dinarim* (BT *Bekhorot* 50a).

One may assume that in Babylon, too, the cost of the *pidyon ha'ben* in the period under discussion (between the 4th to the 6th centuries C.E.—from the generation of Rava to that of Rav Ashi) was relative high in comparison to the income of a day-laborer, but we do not have any clearcut information in these generations of the costs in relationship to wages in Babylon, and it is therefore difficult to make an unequivocal comparison between Babylon and Eretz Israel.[44]

IV

Based on the above data, it is quite clear that the cost of the *pidyon ha'ben* was a financial burden to those working as employees. This fact explains why we find discussions in the sources about fathers who did not redeem their sons, and of the obligation of the sons to redeem themselves once they grew up. This fact also explains the significance of the discussion of what takes precedence—one's own redemption or that of one's son; and what takes precedence—the redemption of one's son or attending the Temple at the pilgrimage festival; and why there was no insistence that the *pidyon ha'ben* must take place on precisely the 31st day. As noted earlier, it is easy to claim that all of these are simply theoretical discussions which did not necessarily reflect a concrete reality. But we have stated that if we set alongside these

---

[43]　See Sperber (1974).

[44]　See Sperber (1974: 145). Those interested in the entire question of relationships between prices should see ch. 20 there.

sources—which, whether they were real or merely theoretical, are certainly an index of economic inability to pay—the sources about the value of the redemption, it would be logical to assume that the sources combine to depict a certain socio-economic situation. This hypothesis is strengthened even further, as we will see below, by the actions taken by the Sages to enable the redemption to take place by decreasing the real value of the amount to be used for the redemption. Against this hypothesis, one can also claim that the sources about the cost of living and about the average wage during the centuries under discussion here[45] (the 1st to the 3rd centuries C.E.) are merely legends, which should not be taken to reflect historical reality. To counter this, one may state that as these are the only sources which we have and they do not contradict one another, and as at the same time they do not contradict the *halakhic* sources which deal with prices, they can be regarded as valid. In sociological methodology, the pragmatic approach is accepted which states that if there is congruence or an overlap between messages of sources, or of data, one tends to regard them as having construct validity,[46] even if there are no external criteria for validating them. This applies when the theoretical relationship indicates that the data are linked to one another; in such a case, when one variable in the data changes, one may hypothesize that the variable linked to it will change as well. Here we note economic changes and changes in prices, which are accompanied by changes in the value of the amount for the *pidyon ha'ben*. In the absence of sufficient data one cannot indicate—as a historian would wish to—an exact chronology of covariation, but in the long term the covariation takes place. Generally, technical changes do not cause immediate normative changes, the gap being closed over a period of time. There is thus great importance to the general tendency within the given events.

The large amount involved in the *pidyon ha'ben* can shed light on the words of the Mishnah, "One who set aside (the amount for) the *pidyon ha'ben* and it was lost" (*Bekhorot* 8:8). This refers to a person who saved up money in advance for the *pidyon ha'ben* in the event that a son would be born to him, because if the amount was only symbolic there would be no need to set aside the money in advance. One should note that while the amount involved might be a considerable expenditure for the father, it represented a sizable income for the *kohen*. This fact may help us to clarify the background for the discussions in the Mishnah and the *Tosefta* in which questions are discussed

---

[45]   See the story with Hillel the Elder in *Avot de-Rabbi Nathan* and midrashic sources, *supra*, n. 34.

[46]   On the construct validity, see, for example, Philips (1976: 140–141).

dealing with problems, such as when the father is exempt from paying for the *pidyon ha'ben* to the *kohen* and when the *kohen* is required to return the amount to the father.[47] It is possible that it was just because the amount involved was so high that it was determined that the amount might be distributed among a number of *kohanim* (*T Bekhorot* 6:14).

There were Sages who dealt with the question of the expense involved in the redemption and who sought solutions for the problem.

First, R. Tarfon, who was a *kohen*, was accustomed to return the amount tendered for the *pidyon ha'ben*: "This was the custom of R. Tarfon, who would take and return (the amount), and when the Sages heard about this they said, 'He has fulfilled this law.'"[48] R. Tarfon, who had been alive while the Temple was still in existence, may have had authentic traditions according to which he acted; it is also possible that it was he who introduced this practice, or, alternately, that that was the practice among upright *kohanim* of the time who were wealthy. R. Tarfon himself was known for his great wealth[49] and his charitable acts.[50] Such charitable acts made things considerably easier for poor Jews. The fact that the Sages praised R. Tarfon for his actions would indicate that he forwent a large sum of money, which would tend to corroborate our claim about the real value of the amount for the *pidyon ha'ben*. It is possible that this custom of his was the cause of the *halakhic* principle that if "he (the Jew) gave it to him (the *kohen*) and he went back and took it from him, his son is redeemed" (*T Bekhorot* 6:14). That was also the practice of R. Hanina (1st generation of Amora'im in Eretz Israel), but one time, when he saw that a father who had redeemed his son was waiting at his door for the money to be returned to him, R. Hanina did not return the money, because, according to him, the one who gives it must give it as a complete gift and not expect to have the money returned to him (BT *Bekhorot* 51b).[51]

---

47   Such as: if the father died before redeeming his son, is there a lien on his estate for the redemption, and is the obligation for redemption transferred to his heirs? Or, let us say a man has two firstborn sons from two wives, and before the thirtieth day he gave 10 *shekalim* to two *kohanim*, and then one of his sons died, must one of the *kohanim* return the 5 *shekalim*? See, M *Bekhorot* ch. 8; T *Bekhorot* ch. 6.

48   T *Bekhorot* 6:14, and BT *Bekhorot* 51b.

49   BT *Nedarim* 62a.

50   JT *Yevamot* 4:14, 6b; T *Ketubot* 5:1. See also the story with R. Akiva in Lev. Rabbah 34:16. Heiman (1964; 528), deduces from this that R. Tarfon appears from to have been miserly and he comes to his defense, but this is unnecessary.

51   R. Hanina, too, was known for his wealth (JT *Pe'ah* 7:4, 20a) and the accounts of his charity (BT *Ketubot* 67b). He would send a certain poor man 4 *dinarim* each Friday, i.e., an amount sufficient for a week if one lived frugally.

Second, one who did not have the cash available was permitted to redeem his son using chattels (but not land, promissory notes or slaves[52]). Indeed, if the father said to the *kohen*, "'This calf for five *sela'im* for the redemption of my son' or 'this *tallit* for five *sela'im* for the redemption of my son,' his son is redeemed" (*T Bekhorot* 6:13). We have already seen that the value of a *tallit* was close to that value, and the value of a calf, according to the sources, was about 20 *dinarim*,[53] i.e., five *sela'im*. Being able to pay in chattels rather than cash is no real reduction in the price, but has an advantage for a person who does not have the needed cash available. As will be clarified later, this *halakhah* of being able to pay in chattels enabled the payment of a reduced amount for the *pidyon ha'ben*.

In Babylon, a solution was proposed, evidently based on the idea in the *Tosefta*, but it was taken one step further: one is able to redemption one's firstborn son with an object rather than money, even if the object is not worth five *sela'im*, provided that the *kohen* is willing to accept it and to declare that in his eyes it is worth five *shekalim*: "As in the case of Rav Kahana [fifth generation of the Amora'im of Babylon], who took a scarf from the home of a *pidyon ha'ben*. He said to him, 'In my eyes it appears to be worth five *sela'im*'" (BT *Kiddushin* 8a). Rav Ashi, the disciple of Rav Kahana, rejected this method. Instead, he approved of a another method which R. Tarfon and R. Hanina had used in Eretz Israel: to return the money involved to the redeemer. In this, he implemented the words of Rava, that "a gift which given on the condition that it be returned is considered to be a (valid) gift" (BT *Kiddushin* 6b).

V

These are solutions which arose due to the circumstances and there is no way to date at what point they became established as the general custom. One can only see that Rav Ashi, who bases himself on the universal principle that "a gift which is given on the condition that it be returned is a gift," provides a normative solution for one of the alternatives which had already been in force in the Tannaitic period. It is possibly that once solutions such as these became

---

52   M *Bekhorot* 8:7–8, and so too, T *Bekhorot* 6:13. In *Sifrei Korah* 118 (Horowitz edition, 1907: 139), Rebbi permitted one to redeem his firstborn using any method except a promissory note.

53   See M *Menahot* 13:8, and T *Bava Metzia* 5:2, that a hundred calves were worth 100 gold *dinarim*, so that a single calf was worth 1 gold *dinar* or 25 silver ones.

more common, the ceremony began to be crystallized. We have already seen from a number of sources that the amount for the *pidyon ha'ben* was given to the *kohen* either before the thirtieth day or after it. If there is no insistence on a specific day, it does not appear that there would be any insistence on holding a specific ceremony. Obviously, a central part of such a ceremony is the handing over of the money to a *kohen*, but if the money is not given on a fixed date there is no reason to have a ceremony on a specific day without the major element—the giving of the money—being present. If it is possible to pay the amount without any ceremony and at any time which is convenient to the father, then, when the amount involved was very high in comparison to income, a breach was opened to avoid paying at all. The person who wished to avoid payment could claim that he had already paid the money to a *kohen*, even though he had not done so, something impossible to do where there is a fixed ceremony at a fixed time. We find the first hint of this being a festive occasion in the first generation of the Babylonian Amora'im: "Rav, Shmuel and Rav Asi happened to come to the home of the *shavua* of a son while others say it was the home of the *yeshua* of the son."[54] (BT *Bava Kama* 80b) "The home of the *yeshua* of the son" is evidently a reference to the *pidyon ha'ben* (*Rashi*: A feast made for the *pidyon ha'ben*—*yeshua* is translated as *purkan*, like redemption").[55] If all three of these great rabbis came to a home where there was the *pidyon ha'ben*—according to one of the versions of the story— it appears that it must have been a festive occasion and it might even have included a festive meal. To support this claim, we may note that we are told (BT *Hullin* 95b) that Rav never partook of a meal unless it was one which the person was obligated to partake. The very use of the word "home" in regard to the *pidyon ha'ben* (see also "Rav Kahana took a scarf from the home of a *pidyon ha'ben*"—BT *Kiddushin* 8a), would seem to indicate the institutionalization of this as a festive event, just like "the home of a circumcision" (BT *Ketubot* 8a).

---

[54] On *shavu'a ha'ben* and *yeshu'a ha'ben*, see Rubin (1995: 117–119).

[55] This is also the way how *Arukh* explained it. S.v. *"sheva,"* and see also *Tosafot*, where Rabbenu Tam disagrees with *Rashi* and explains that this refers to where a man had a son born to him, "and as he was born and there was parturition from his mother's womb... it used the term *yeshuah* (i.e., implying being saved) and they were accustomed to making a festive meal." According to him, this was a meal made on the day of birth. *Rashi's* interpretation appears more logical, because we have not found any other source for a meal on the birth date itself. Among the *Aharonim*, there is a dispute about whether a meal to celebrate the birth of a son is considered a *se'udat mitzvah* (i.e., a meal mandated by *halakhah*). Moharik Section 472, *Magen Avraham* Section 640 subsection 13 and others believe that this was a custom but not a religiously mandated meal. *Nahalat Shiva*, *Mehudashim* Section A, holds that this is indeed a *se'udat mitzvah*.

But this conclusion is not unequivocal. We have already mentioned the case in Babylon of the last generations of Amora'im there, that Rav Ashi sent Rav Aha bar Ravina 17 *zuzim* (*dinarim*) for the *pidyon ha'ben* (BT Bekhorot 50a). That resulted in a discussion between them, through an emissary, as to whether this was equivalent to 5 *sela'im*. From this source, it is clear that the money was sent to the *kohen* through an emissary, and it is therefore unclear whether there was any ceremony without the presence of the child. It is not clear by whom and at what time the blessings for the *pidyon ha'ben* were recited—or even if they were recited. One might be able to conclude that in Babylon there were different customs in different places, or that over the generations changes gradually took place. There were places, and times, in which a public ceremony was conducted, and there were places, and times, where the *pidyon ha'ben* took place by sending gifts to the *kohen* without any public ceremony.

In Eretz Israel we hear of Rav Simlai, of the 2nd generation of the Amora'im, who "happened to be at the home of a *pidyon ha'ben*"[56] (BT Pesahim 121b). From that source, the implication is that the *pidyon ha'ben* took place at a festive ceremony, but the text of the blessings had not been finalized, because Rav Simlai was asked, "(The blessing of) 'Concerning the *pidyon ha'ben*' is certainly recited by the father of the child, but (concerning the) *sheheheyanu* blessing, does the father of the child recite it, or does the *kohen* recite it, because he is the one who benefits from it?" Rav Simlai did not have an immediate answer and only after discussions in the *bet hamidrash* was it decided that the father recites both blessings.[57]

From this source we learn for the first time about the blessings at the ceremony—the blessing "concerning the *pidyon ha'ben*" and the *sheheheyanu* blessing. There was certainly a formula of what was said at the time of the *pidyon ha'ben*, when the father handed over money to the *kohen* and the *kohen* returned the child to his father. One can find an indirect hint to that effect from a *Beraita* in the Babylonian Talmud, in *Kiddushin* (8a): "'This calf for the redemption of my son' or 'this *tallit* for the redemption of my son,'— he has not said anything (i.e., the statement is worthless, and the child is not considered to be redeemed). 'This calf for five *sela'im* for the redemption of

---

56   The printed version is that "they happened to come to a *pidyon ha'ben*," but the Munich ms. rendered it, "they happened to come to the home of a *pidyon ha'ben*."

57   It appears strange that the *kohen* would pronounce the *sheheheyanu* blessing, whereas the father, who would only have one opportunity in his life to recite it, should not be the one to do so. Isn't it an ironic question, which criticizes the high cost of the *pidyon ha'ben*? For if indeed the *kohen* receives a large sum, it would indeed be appropriate for him to recite the *sheheheyanu* blessing...

my son' or 'this *tallit* for five *sela'im* for the redemption of my son,' his son is redeemed." It appears that at the time of redemption the father would say, "These five *sela'im* are for the redemption of my son," and when the payment was in chattels he would say, for example, "This calf for five *sela'im* for the redemption of my son."It appears that that text was recited by the father before the blessings.

Can we conclude from the silence of the sources until the time of the Amora'im that there was no *pidyon ha'ben* ceremony until their time? In terms of methodology, such an absolute statement would not be valid. But we cannot say definitely that there was such a ceremony up to the time of the Amora'im. The context of the sources tends more to a decision that the ceremony was formulated after the conditions for a ceremony had been created, i.e., the granting of an opportunity for every person to be able to redeem his firstborn son. The general tendency was of change in the way the redemption took place and the crystallization of the ceremony. Over the time the techniques of how the redemption was performed were improved upon.

VI

That is all we know from the Talmudic literature about the *pidyon ha'ben*. However, in 1974 some of the manuscripts of Margoliot's estate were published, including two sections from the genizah which portray the custom of Eretz Israel in the Byzantine era, before the Arab conquest, and may be reflecting even more ancient customs.[58] The two sections resemble one another in terms of content, and Margoliot hypothesizes that the author copied the information from two versions he had before him, or that he copied one version from the original before him and the other was an account of the practice of his time. This is the text of the first version:

> The *pidyon ha'ben*: He brings silver and gold and *follarin* (a type of coin) and asks the father: "This is your firstborn and you are redeeming him?" He answers, "Yes." And you—the *kohen*—say to the firstborn: "when you were in your mother's womb you were in the custody of your Creator and now you are in our custody and are holy... while these objects and the silver and the gold are profane. Your father has agreed to redeem you with them and with the five *shekalim* which the Torah stated... You have left our custody to the profane, to the custody of your fathers, and these objects with the five *sela'im* will enter in your place for your redemption into our custody, and this

---

[58]   Margoliot (1974: 15–31).

money will be profaned on that. Blessed are You O Lord of the Universe our God, King of the universe, who has sanctified us with His commandments and commanded us concerning the redemption of this firstborn son. If I redeemed properly that is good, and if not he is redeemed according to the Torah and the *halakhah* and in accordance with a skilled person in Israel and according to the conditions of the *bet din*."[59]

The second version is as follows:

The redeeming of the firstborn among people, this is the way: He brings gold and silver and whatever he finds and the representatives of the community, the *kohanim*, place gold and silver and five *sela'im* of *follarin* into a basket and they carry the infant and they say to this father of his: "Your son is holy to the Lord of the Universe and he belongs to the *kohanim*. Do you wish to redeem him?" He says, "Yes." And you (the *kohen*) say: "This firstborn son is holy... and this silver and gold is profane. Now his fathers have agreed to give to this son the objects and the silver and the gold as his redemption for five *sela'im* which the Torah stated... for his redemption and he will leave our custody for the custody of his father and his own custody for the profane, and the silver and the gold will enter in his place for his redemption into our custody and into the custody of the *kohanim* and will become holy." And this money is to profaned onto these objects and will complete the amount for the owner even if it is less than five *sela'im*. Blessed are You O Lord of the Universe our God, King of the universe, who has sanctified us with His commandments and commanded us concerning the redemption of this firstborn son..."

According to these two texts, the order of the redemption is as follows:
a) The *kohen* brings the silver and gold items and the coins.[60]
b) The *kohen* asks the father if he wishes to redeem his son.
c) The father's answer.
d) The blessing of the redemption recited by the *kohen*. In the first version, the opening is a long formula in the second person and is addressed to the child. In the second version, the formula is more concise and is in the third person.

---

[59]   The formula, "If I redeemed properly," is to be found at the end of other redemption ceremonies as well, as found by Margoliot in the *Genizah*: the redemption of *ma'aser sheni*, of *neta revai*, and evidently of a firstborn donkey (the manuscript is fragmentary). See Margoliot (1974: 18), and compare to similar language in JT *Pe'ah* 5:2, 18d; *Yevamot* 8a, 8d. Regarding the "condition of the *bet din*," see T *Tevul-Yom* 2:17; JT *Demai* 5:2, 24c. For discussion about this, see Margoliot (1974) and the appendix by Ta-Shma to Margoliot's book, pp. 32–38.

[60]   Ta-Shma (in Margoliot, 1974: 35) discusses this.

e) The conclusion, in a legal formula, about the successful completion of the ceremony in the first version. In the second version the end is missing, but it states how to divide up the money of the *pidyon ha'ben* among the *kohanim* and the poor.

When we compare this to the little we know about the *pidyon ha'ben* ceremony in the Talmud, we immediately see a major difference: here it is the *kohen* who recites the blessing—and not the father—and only a single blessing. Neither version mentions the *sheheyanu* blessing. It thus appears that the *kohen* is the one considered to be performing the commandment: it is he who brings the items for the redemption, he conducts the ceremony and he recites the blessing. This is the exact opposite of the story of R. Simlai (quoted at the end of BT *Pesahim*) and of the *halakhah* determined in accordance with that account, that it is the father who recites two blessings. The implication is that even during the Byzantine era there were various customs in Eretz Israel, and these were greatly different from the ceremonies of which we are aware in Babylon during Geonic times.[61]

What is interesting is that in this Eretz Israel version the redemption was performed in two stages: in the first stage, the child was redeemed against gold and silver, the sanctity of the child thus being transferred to the gold and silver, and then the sanctity of the gold and silver was transferred to the five *follarin*. The gold and silver thus reverted to their prior non-holy state, whereas the coins were given to the *kohanim*, who divided them up among themselves and among the poor. As the text is fragmentary, the way this division was performed is not clear.[62] The *follarin* is a coin already mentioned in the Talmud and the Midrashim,[63] its value being very little when compared to the original five *sela'im*. From this it appears clear that a severance had taken place between the ceremonial value of the five *sela'im* and their real value. According to this view, the commandment for the *pidyon ha'ben* was no longer an economic burden.

Margoliot explains the meaning of the double redemption as follows: "The actual value of five *sela'im* was not known for sure. As they were afraid the *sela* of the Torah had been greater than the *sela* used in their days, they tended to increase the amount for the *pidyon ha'ben*. In order to fulfill their obligation, those of Eretz Israel would first redeem (the child) using gold and silver objects which certainly were worth five *sela'im* according to all

---

[61] See, for example, the formulation for the *pidyon ha'ben* in *Siddur Rav Amram Gaon* and a discussion regarding the topic in Rubin (1995: 131–141).

[62] Margoliot (1974: 15).

[63] See Sperber (1974: 53–54) on this coin.

opinions."[64] It is possible in principle to accept the view of Margoliot, but it would seem that they acted this way not because they did not know what the exact value was of the 5 *sela'im*. Even if they knew it, it is possible that they sought a way to decrease the financial expense. In order to have the monetary value equal to the original real value, they would first redeem the child using gold and silver, which were certainly worth 5 *sela'im*, and afterwards they would transfer the sanctity of the gold and silver onto 5 *follarin*. What supports this view is the fact, noted by Ta-Shma in an appendix to the article by Margoliot, that the gold and silver objects were not brought by the father but by the *kohanim*, a fact which emphasizes the ceremonial significance of the 5 *shekalim*.

VII

The transformation undergone with the amount involved for the *pidyon ha'ben* is an example of the method employed by the Sages in interpreting the Bible and the *halakhah* in an era of change. Methodologically, we have before us an example of the anthropological problem of the relationship and link between the text and the context. Jewish culture is one of a written text, whose texts are considered to be sacrosanct and unchangeable. But the context, the social setting, changes as political and social living conditions change. The text which accompanies the society and which dictates its values and norms, must undergo a process of interpretation in order to continue to be relevant to it and to continue to be the guiding text. The classical anthropologists, such as Robertson-Smith (1927: 16–18) and Boas (1986: 270–280) who studied non-literate cultures, did not deal with a diachronic analysis and did not include a historical dimension in their analyses. They deliberately ignored the interpretations offered by the members of a society being studied gave for their customs, because they related to these as interpretations which were liable to change in accordance with the circumstances and is therefore transitory. Instead, they explained the texts and customs utilizing an external theoretical perspective. This view, according to Goldberg, is not appropriate for a society with an extensive literate culture. It ignores the historical dimension of the development of the customs and texts and the contribution that a diachronic approach would have to the interpretation. A historical view, which also relates to the interpretations given by the members of the society being studied, can explain the changes in customs based on the condition of the variable and

---

[64] Margoliot (1974: 30).

can illuminate the interaction between the written interpretation and actual behavior (Goldberg, 1987). By examining the written text, one can ascertain the reciprocal play between the text in practice and the official interpretation that the interpreting authority gives to the text. In the end, loyalty to the text ensures a great deal of uniformity within the normative framework, even though the content of the framework may change.

Jacob Katz was the first one to note the problem involved and its solution in his discussions about the question of the relationship between Jews and non-Jews. While the Torah and *halakhah* require a total separation between Jews and non-Jews, we find, in practice, that in medieval times in Germany there was a constant dialog between the two, even during Christian festive days.[65] The *halakhah*, says Katz, preserved the balance between the two forces: adaptation to conditions on the one hand, and the maintenance of Jewish identity on the other. *Halakhah* sometimes was forced to adapt to social changes, but it guarded its Jewish identity while at the same time *ex post facto* justifying these changes.[66] In this article, we have seen that reality forced solutions similar to those already found among the Sages of the Talmud: the way to deal with a changing reality was by means of an interpretation of the text which in principle remained unchanged.

The process was thus as follows: at first, the local currency was adjusted to be equal to the real value according to Torah law. This amount, which was high in comparison to laborers' wages, was evidently a burden on many fathers who were required to redeem their sons. There were certainly some who made every effort to fulfill the commandment, but there were also those who sought to avoid fulfilling it, or to postpone it to a time when they might be able to afford it. Of course that is not the proper way for one who wishes to fulfill the commandment. As a result, ways were found to bypass the requierment so that the normative system would accept them as having remained unchanged. The first was the payment in chattels of the equivalent value rather than in money. This payment in chattels made it easier for a person who had no cash available and might otherwise have needed to borrow money against his goods. The second was payment in chattels whose real worth was less than 5 *sela'im*, but the *kohen* receiving them would proclaim that he accepted them as being worth 5 *sela'im*. The third was the returning

---

[65] Katz (1961: 35–56). Katz notes that Ephraim Orbach was of the opinion that the purpose of the *Ba'alei Ha'tosafot* was to reconcile contradictions between the source of the *halakhah* and the customs of the time. See Orbach (1955: 523–574).

[66] Recently, other studies have been published which show the reciprocal relationship between *halakhah* and custom. See, for example, Cooper (1987); Friedman (1992); Rubin (2003) [chapter 3 in this volume].

of the money to the father. The *kohen* received the money as a gift which had been given on the condition that it be returned. The fourth was through a fictitious redemption: transferring the sanctity of the redemption money to coins of a much lesser value.

By accepting any of these alternatives, the basis *halakhah* which requires the *pidyon ha'ben* for 5 *sela'im* was not changed, but the *halakhah* was bypassed in a way which was not regarded as changing the *halakhah*. The case of the *pidyon ha'ben* again confirms the idea that in every traditional framework there is an internal mechanism which permits—in certain conditions and in accordance with certain basic principles—change and deviance.[67] The fictitious *pidyon ha'ben* had the best chance of being accepted as Jewish custom because of the *halakhic* precedent of a fictitious *pidyon*, for example, of tithes and *neta revai*.[68]

The other alternatives are less practical: *pidyon* using an object of equivalent value does not in reality solve the problem. Redemption with an object of lesser value is problematic because it does not determine a uniform norm: the assessment is dependent on the *kohen*, whereas the ceremony is based on uniform norms. Finally, the return of the money to the child's father is a private, non-stable solution. It depends on the goodwill of the *kohen* and one cannot always find a *kohen* who is willing to forgo such an income.

---

[67] For example, the principle of *davar ha'aveid*—a mourner is forbidden to engage in any work throughout the seven days of mourning, and others, too, are forbidden to work on his behalf, but if by failing to do so an irreperable loss will be suffered, it is permitted (*Semakhot* 5:2). Or the principle of *kavod ha'rabim*, which permits a *kohen* to defile himself to a dead body (*JT Berakhot* 3:1, 6b; *BT Berakhot* 19a; *Semakhot* 4:9), which permits a craftsman, such as a baker or barber, to perform work for the community even during the days of his mourning (*Semakhot* 8:7).

[68] For sources, *supra*, n. 59.

Chapter 5. BIRTH AND MARRIAGE RITUALS: WOMEN'S STATUS IN A CRITICAL READING OF THE TEXTS

Socio-Anthropological Aspect of Rabbinic Sources

On the Nature of Ritual

This article examines anthropological aspects of women's status in the Rabbinic sources, focusing on two important rites of passage: birth and marriage.[1] I discuss the sociology of those rituals by employing anthropological or sociological methods, and attempt to clarify a certain aspect of the rabbi's conception of women's status, as it emerges from a critical reading of the rabbinic sources.

It is important to clarify the connection between "ritual" and "halakhah." Anthropologists tend to define a religious ritual as a formal, stylized, and cyclical behavioral pattern that is generally accompanied by a verbal formula, song, and body movements, and directed to a transcendental entity.[2] A secular ritual, in contrast, neither draws its authority from the transcendental, nor addresses it. In secular ritual authority is immanent, eminating from society or the individual. Such are civil and national public rituals; rituals performed by individuals, such as birthday rituals; and personal definitional rites. Secular rituals are also present in societies that is generally governed by religious norms, just as religious rituals are to be found in societies that follow secular norms.[3]

---

[1]   A rite of passage is a concept defined by Arnold van Gennep as a ritual that accompanies a change in status, place, situation, and age. Individuals undergoe rites of passage from birth to death; in most known cultures, rites of passage mark the events of birth, maturity, marriage, and death. See van Gennep, 1960 (first published in French, in 1909). On rites of passage, see also Haviland, 1975: 317–19.

[2]   See, e.g., Turner, 1960; Turner, 1967.

[3]   On secular rituals, see Moore and Myerhoff, 1977; Handelman, 1990; Cheal, 1992. On personal definitional rites, see Rubin and Peer, 2000.

The society represented in the Rabbinic sources accordingly contains ritual elements that are not required by the halakhah, but are nevertheless deemed ritual. This is the case if we relate a commonly accepted broad definition of "ritual": "The performance by one or more persons of actions designed to express some range of meanings, these actions being permeated by symbolic content and highly constrained by the character of that content."[4] Some scholars distinguish between "ritual" and "ceremony."[5] The former refers to halakhik mandatory elements without which the act is invalid; while the intent of the latter is to a nonessential component that was appended to the ritual to give it additional force. In the following discussion of rituals, I identify those that are halakhically obligatory, such as the woman's immersion in a ritual bath after having given birth; as well as those that are mere "ceremonies," and not required by the halakhah, such as bringing a bride in a palanquin. In this way ritual breaches the bounds of the halakhah, by adding ceremonial units. The addition of elements that are not halakhically required is dependent, in great degree, upon the status of those undergoing the ritual and the community's economic and political standing. For example, during a period of anti-Jewish persecutions, the rabbis cancelled the bridal procession with a palanquin, and modified the bedecking of the bridal canopy and the finery of the bride and groom themselves.

Methodological Comments

Although studies that apply social science methods to the interpretation of the rabbinic literature have been published for a number of years,[6] this is still not common. I therefore proceed with a number of preliminary comments.

Structuralism and the Interpretation of Symbols

The first comment relates to the method. In order to validate hypotheses that arise during a reading of the sources from a sociological and anthropological perspective, I adopt two accepted social science methods: the structuralist

---

[4]   For this definition, see Wallis, 1983. I used this definition in my books on rites of passage in Jewish society. See Rubin, 1995; Rubin, 1997; Rubin, 2004.

[5]   On this distinction, see Pickering, 1974.

[6]   The following are a number of studies of rabbinic literature that employ social sciences methods: Fishbane and Lightstone, 1990; Goldberg, 1987; Hoffman, 1987; Hoffman, 1996; Lightstone, 1988; Basser and Fishbane, 1993. A number of works have been published in Hebrew, e.g.: Deshen, 1980; see also Rubin, 1995; 2004; 1997.

method connecting social phenomena whose linkages can be discerned, according to Braudel,[7] only in the long term (*longue durée*). The structural tradition, that was founded by Durkheim, Weber, Levi-Strauss, and others,[8] separates the components of social structure and examines the degree of compatibility between the structure's parts and the parallel change of these components over an extended period of time. For example, if there is long-term change in economic structure, that is a part of the overall social structure, is this matched by corresponding change in family, political, or social stratification structures? And, do all the parts of the structure change simultaneously, or sequentially? The main instrument of this methodology is the model, or Weber's "ideal type." This type enables us to compose a theoretical "structure," whose elements are assembled from the historical social reality. The type itself is not the actual reality. Rather it functions as a yardstick to compare to actual reality, and measure the degree of proximity or distance from the ideal type. This ahistorical method is validated by comparing the model to the historical reality. In the study of rabbinic texts, this model could likely serve as a theoretical framework in which the sources could be incorporated in a mosaic. Lacking a model, the researcher is liable to enter a trial-and-error maze.[9]

The second method is the interpretation of cultural symbols, which attempts to understand the hidden meaning of the symbolic system under study, as a set within the culture's whole system of symbols. This approach calls for the deconstruction of the symbols, which are to be read as letters of the alphabet; their combination and deconstruction enable us to understand how cultural symbols are incorporated into a single system. This tradition comes from the schools of Clifford Geertz, Roland Barth, Victor Turner, and others, who maintain that the symbols are not part of a fixed set that is complex, coherent, logical, and whole. The system of symbols is dynamic comprised of signifiers and the signified in which the latter are liable to change over time. They may be separated from one system, and join the symbols in another.[10] Symbols are multivocal, vague, and subject to mani-

---

[7] Braudel, 1972–1973; Braudel, 1977.

[8] Weber, 1949; Durkheim, 1938; Levi-Strauss, 1969b.

[9] Jacob Katz was the trailblazer of this method among the researchers of Jewish society. His book (1974), e.g., does not describe a specific historical society, but an ideal type of community with its social institutions. He constructed this type from the reality, but the community depicted in his book is not the historical reality. Any community in the historical reality, however, can be compared with it. See also Katz, 1993.

[10] Geertz, 1973; Barthes, 1972; Firth, 1973; Leach, 1976; Turner, 1967.

pulations.[11] Symbols lend themselves to alternative interpretations, just as a text is open to different understandings. Every legitimate interpretation is valid if its symbols relate to each other coherently.

The main difficulty that each of these methodologies poses comes from researchers' inability to interview the members of the society, or observe their actual activity in the field of research, as is accepted in sociological or anthropological research. Cultural research by means of texts can only ask itself what questions it would ask of the members of the society under scrutiny if the researcher would live everyday life together with them. The researcher formulates these questions based on his theoretical knowledge of social structures and of other cultures. This instrument will likely enable the researcher to reveal all the information hidden between the lines of the text.

Structure of Jewish Family

A second comment relates to the structure of the Jewish family. The structure of a family unit is mainly determined by society's strategy of adjustment to its environment. The patterns of adjustment to the physical surroundings in an agricultural or pastoral society are different from those in an industrial or postindustrial society. The family type characteristic of societies of the former sort is a cluster of families whose kinship is based on a lineage that can be traced back to a common ancestor. The lineage is a corporative unit for defence of shared property, such as grazing and water rights, supervises common property and cooperates in daily life. In such a framework, the nuclear family is protected through membership in a more complex entity. Organization within the descent group is based on extended families, including, in a patrilineal family, father's family and those of his married sons, who maintain a common household under father's control. Upon their marriage, generally daughters leave their lineage for the husband's household. Marriages are arranged: the family selects mates for its offspring of appropriate status. Society does not

criollo = 1st generation Spaniard born in Mexico

---

[11] E.g., Victor Turner analyzed the symbols used by Miguel Hidalgo, the leader of the first Mexican revolt against Spain in 1810. Hidalgo was a Creole and a Catholic priest, who adopted the image of the Aztec mother of god Guadaloupe, who also became the Catholic mother of god. This symbol became the focus for mestizo and Indian identity. The symbols of liberty, equality, and fraternity of the secular and atheistic French Revolution were joined to the icons of Guadaloupe, along with the added local Mexican meaning of land, fertility, maternity, and homeland. Hidalgo's movement created a melting pot of meanings from a diverse range of symbols. See also ch. 1, n. 42 in this volume.

leave such an important decision to the romantic inclinations of the young people themselves. From the Biblical period to the time of the Mishnah and Talmud, the most common family type was patriarchal, in which authority was held by the head of the patriarchial lineage. This family usually engaged in agriculture or herding.

The family type characteristic of industrial society is nuclear, consisting of parents and children who still live at home. An urban society could not maintain a shared extended family household, and therefore married children leave their family of origin and go to live separately as a nuclear family. Nuclear families are not linked by economic obligations to their descent groups or extended families; the choice of a spouse is relatively free from intervention by the family kinship system. Notwithstanding this, in traditional urban societies, such as the Jewish society in the Land of Israel in the late Tannaitic period, or the medieval urban Jewish society, father's authority over his children continued to be significant. Authority over the daughters after their marriage passed from her father to her husband.[12] Already at this juncture, I should mention that the gender relations within the family is a function of the family structure.

Nature-Culture

The third topic I wish to clarify is Claude Levi-Strauss's accepted distinction between nature and culture. He maintains that man dominates nature through culture, through which he transforms the former. Everything that passes from nature to the realm of culture goes from a "raw" (= natural) state to a "cooked" (= cultured) one, and becomes subservient to culture's principles and ideas.[13] In the Jewish context, the nature-culture distinction does not mean that "nature" is everything not controlled by culture, but rather refers to the realm that did not undergo a process of isolation and classification by the Jewish cognitive order.[14] Whatever is Jewish is within the sphere of "culture," and whatever is not, is within the realm of "nature."

---

[12]   On the patriarchal family, see Keesing, 1975; on the Biblical family, Bendor, 1996; on the patriarchal family in Jewish society in the time of the Mishnah and Talmud, see Rubin, 1997: 93–102; on women's status in a patriarchal society, see Paige and Paige, 1981.

[13]   Levi-Strauss, 1969c.

[14]   Ruth Gruber-Fredman already conducted a discussion of Jewish society in accordance with these concepts. See Gruber-Fredman, 1981: 20–21.

Cutting and Removal as Central Symbols in
the Jewish Rites of Passage

The forth topic I wish to clarify was already mentioned above: every system of symbols must be examined as a single set. I will exemplify this with the rites of passage of the Jewish culture. A rite of passage is a ritual that each individual undergoes during his life cycle when one of his master status changes.[15] In Jewish culture, as reflected in rabbinic literature, we find equivalent symbols in each of the individual's rites of passage (birth, marriage, and death),[16] that consist of breaking or cutting. These symbolize an irreversible separation from former situation: cutting the foreskin of the male in circumcision expresses his departure from the "uncircumcised" sphere and his entry to the Jewish world;[17] the breaking of the glass during a wedding signifies the end of bachelorhood, and also the end of the woman's virginity;[18] the rending of the mourner's garment express the finality of death.[19]

According to Cooper, cutting and removal express the passage or transformation from "not Jewish" to "Jewish,"[20] or from "nature" to "culture." Jewish culture "Judaizes" what is "non-Jewish," that is, it moves things from the non-Jewish outside, whose use is prohibited, to the Jewish inside that may be used, by the removal or cutting of a part. For example, the way to "Judaize" food and make it halakhically permitted is by removal. Priestly and Levitical gifts of various types must be brought: from fruits and vegetables—by bringing the firstfruits; from the grain—by setting aside the *terumah* (heave-offering); from dough for bread—by taking *hallah* (the portion of the dough originally given to a priest); from fruit-bearing trees—by removing *orlah*, the fruit that grows during the tree's first three years; from grain, wine, oil, the flock, and

---

[15] On status and master status, see Macionis and Plummer, 1997: 156–57.
[16] Coming of age rituals, such as the currently celebrated Bar or Bat Mitzvah, are not mentioned in the rabbinic literature.
[17] On circumcision as a rite of passage, see the discussion: Rubin, 1995: 28–29, where I also discuss why girls are not entitled to a rite of passage. See also my article (2003) [chapter 3 in this volume] that examines leaving Jewish society by drawing down the prepuce and, conversely, the incision of the foreskin, which prevented this act and thereby precluded departure from the Jewish community.
[18] On the significance of the breaking of the glass at a wedding, see the following studies: Lauterbach, 1925; Lerner, 1963; Davidovitch, 1977; Gladstein-Kestenberg, 1978; Villien, 1996; Goldberg, 1998. See also Rubin, 2004: 297–300.
[19] On the rending of the mourner's garment and the prohibition of mending the tear, see Rubin, 1997: 163–67.
[20] On this idea, see Cooper, 1987.

the herd—by setting aside tithes; the firstborn of animals fit to be sacrificed must be so offered, while other firstborn must be beheaded; human firstborn must be redeemed by the priest for five *shekalim*. Additionally, gifts must be set aside for the poor: *leket* (gleanings), *shikhehah* (the forgotten sheaves); *peah* (the "corner" of the field), *olelot* (small branch/single bunch gleanings), and poor man's tithe. After all these have been "removed," the food becomes potentially Jewish, but not always in practice; so that fit kosher animals may properly be eaten, they must undergo the additional "Judaization" process of ritual slaughter, which means "cutting." Then "removal": the sciatic nerve and certain internal parts must be removed from the animal, and its blood must be removed by soaking and salting. Insects that may not be eaten must be removed from fruits and vegetables. Only after all these removals, with care taken to separate meat and milk, and with blessings preceding and following the meal, is this food fit to be called "Jewish food."

The acts of separation in the rites of passage mentioned above are immediately followed by the symbolic acts of incorporation: after the cutting of the foreskin, the father recites the blessing: "to bring him into the covenant of our father Abraham";[21] after this, the infant is included in the chain of the generations by the calling of his name: "and his name in Israel shall be called so-and-so son of so-and-so." The breaking of the cup at the wedding, which is a symbol of separation, is performed under the wedding canopy, which symbolizes incorporation. The mourner rends his clothing—the symbol of separation, and immediately afterwards passes between the rows of consolers, in an act that expresses incorporation.

Contrasts

The last clarification pertains to Levi-Strauss's distinction,[22] which argues that human thought is built on binary contrasts that are at the basis of the implicit structure underlying the overt social structure. That is, a concept becomes comprehensible by means of its contrast. For example, the distinctions: black-white, life-death, bachelorhood-marriage, and others are perceived by contrasting one state against its opposite. Reality, however, is more complex, since it is a continuum, with interim states between its extremities: grey is between white and black; dying is between life and death; betrothal is

21 T Berakhot 7(6): 12–13 (ed. Lieberman, pp. 36–37); JT Berakhot 9:4, 14a; BT Shabbat 136b. On the circumcision blessings, see Rubin (1995: 106–10).
22 Levi-Strauss, 1962.

between bachelorhood and being married, and the like.[23] Thus, Cooper says, examining meaning of symbols requires a distinction between dichotomies. For example, in the world of Jewish symbols, the significance of the blessing recited by women for kindling of the Sabbath lights may be understood as a contrast to the blessing recited over the *Havdalah* candle marking the conclusion of the Sabbath, that is recited by men; while the woman recites the blessing over two (or more) Sabbath candles in the undefined time of twilight, which is a liminal time between secular weekday and sacred Sabbath, the man recites the blessing over a single *Havdalah* candle (that consists of a number of braided wicks) in the defined time of night, after the appearance of three stars. While the woman sanctifies the Sabbath with the blessing over the lights in the vague time of twilight, the man sanctifies the Sabbath over a cup of wine in the unequivocal time of night; the woman kindles lights that provide illumination and represent domestic peace and tranquility after the entrance of the Sabbath, a time with no labor, while he man recites *Havdalah* over a braided candle, that represents the fire of labor, in the mundane time of night. In other words, the rituals express the gender roles: the woman's place is in the home, while that of the man is outside, in the world of labor[24].

This distinction indicates the social status of man and woman in society as a whole: men are active in clearly defined domain, while women act in the twilight areas—which is a dangerous region, where evil spirits dwell. Indeed, we see that women, who is exempt from a large portion of the commandments, is exclusively responsible for three commandments that represent the twilight region: *niddah* (menstrual impurity), *hallah*, and the Sabbath candle-light. On this, the Mishnah declares: "For three transgressions women die at the time of their giving birth: for their not having been careful regarding *niddah*, regarding *hallah*, and regarding the kindling of the lamp"[25] (M Shabbat 2:6).[26] Women are commanded to separate *hallah* from the dough; and the dough, like the kindling of the lights at twilight, symbolizes an interim state of a continuing process: the preparation of the dough requires both cultural skill and the natural processes of fermentation. Until its baking, it rises and expands in a natural process. Control over the final product is only partial due to the fermentation, which is beyond human control. The fermentation continues

---

23   See Huntington and Metcalf, 1979: 8–11, who discuss combining the approaches of Levi-Strauss and van Gennep.
24   Cooper in an unpublished manuscript, has dealt with this in terms of symmetry. See Cooper (ND) "Symmetries in Jewish law and custom."
25   See also Cooper (NDa) "The three sins for which women die in childbirth."
26   See also JT Shabbat 2:4, 5b; BT Shabbat 32a.

"nature" after the action of "culture," and only baking stops the natural process. Consequently, when the woman separates *hallah* from the dough, she does so when the dough is in the twilight region, under the control of "nature." Similarly, the woman's monthly cycle is a process controlled by "nature," and not under human domination. In this period, during which she cannot conceive, the woman is a *niddah*, and is in an interim period.[27]

We could, of course, ask whether the Rabbis "meant" this interpretation, and what is its validity. Today, we do not know how the rituals were formulated, and whether they were fashioned in committees, or in some other fashion. Rituals usually emerge and are fashioned in the course of everyday life. If ritual symbols reflect social reality, they will be accepted by the community. If not, they will undergo modifications until they answer needs, or they gradually disappear or become irrevelavent.[28] If the interpretation of a group of symbols is consistent with the interpretation of the entire symbolic corpus, creating a coherent symbolic structure, then it may reasonably be assumed that the interpretation is valid. Nonetheless, coherent alternative interpretation that is also valid is obviously a possibility, just as there are different interpretive levels for the Torah or for any other text.

Distinction by gender is one of the fundamental symbols of any culture. Such distinction is not born as a theoretical abstraction, it rather is the consequence of experience. Mary Douglas[29] states that the shared existential experience of individuals in a group in everyday life fashions group's ideology. When existential experience changes, group ideology refocuses, like lenses in binoculars, giving new meaning to the reality. The perception of gender in contemporary Western society patently differs from that of the Rabbis; and is also dissimilar to the gender perception of contemporary halakhic Judaism. Modern Orthodoxy's perception seeks to draw close to the Western conception, and the process is still underway. This tension seeks to be resolved by the renewed interpretation of the text, that is, by refocusing its lenses, so that the text can be used to legitimize existential experience which aims to change actual behavior.

---

[27] For more on her status as "*niddah*" (menstrually impure), see below.

[28] On the creation and invention of rituals by committees in Israel, see, e.g., Azaryahu, 1995: 39–68. For an anthropological interpretation of Israel's Memorial Day and Independence Day, see Handelman, 1990: 191–201. There has been a public consensus on these rituals since the establishment of the State of Israel. Recently, certain circles conduct alternative ceremonies for Independence Day and Holocaust Heroes and Martyrs Remembrance Day, out of a sense that the common rituals no longer represent the social experience of these circles.

[29] Douglas, 1973: 173–88.

Birth and Female Identity

Male Identity and Female Identity

The above demonstrates the difference between the basic identities of men and women. Men have a stable and ongoing identity, while women lack such a self-identity. At birth boys and girls receive the identity of father's lineage. While sons bear this identity their entire lives and bequeath it to their offspring, girls, upon their marriage, leave their father's lineage and assume the identity of the husband's line. If a woman was widowed or divorced and remarried a second or third time, her identity changes, in accordance with her new husband's lineage. If she does not remarry, she returns to her father's lineage and her original identity; while her children, in contrast, bear the identity of their father's lineage. That is to say, women have no independent standing, and their standing is established in accordance with the determining man in their lives: their father (and in his absence, their brothers) or their husband. Although children born to a non-Jewish father and a Jewish mother draw their status as Jews from their mother ("for R. Simeon ben Judah said in the name of R. Simeon: If a non-Jew or slave had relations with an Israelite woman, the child is fit"),[30] this does not compensate for her general social standing. On the contrary, this halakhah is an expression of her problematic status: in a society ruled by men, the male enjoys mobility, while woman is bound to her father's or her husband's household. A man might abandon his wife and her children and make a new life for himself elsewhere, but desertion is not an option for his wife, since she does not have the possibility of an independent existence. If children's descent were determined in accordance with their father's affiliation, the children from a non-Jewish father who were abandoned together with their mother, would be of doubtful status. Moreover, in a well structured community, a Jewish man cannot bring into his home a non-Jewess who has not undergone conversion, and therefore the children will necessarily be Jewish; but a woman can bear a child, either as a result of rape or willingly, out of wedlock, to a non-Jewish man, who might very well disappear. In such a case, if the descent followed the father, then the children born from these relations would be non-Jewish, and would be a burden to the community.

Menstrual Ritual Impurity

This social instability is joined by biological instability: during their menstrual period, women oscillate between fertility and infertility, and are in a constant

---

[30]   JT Yevamot 4:15, 6d; cf. BT Yevamot 23a; 45b; Bekhorot 47a.

passage between "culture" and "nature." While menstruating she is impure and temporarily removed from the domain of culture to a domain which is controlled by nature. During this period, when she is not fertile and cannot conceive, she is of no "benefit" to her husband's household, and therefore she is removed from her home, both symbolically and practically. Once the menstruation period has passed she may return to her home and community, after purification in a ritual bath. During the time, when a woman is pure and fertile and is capable of conceiving, she is "inside," within her husband's household. The woman therefore experiences a cycle of separation and incorporation. The laws of *niddah* are an expression of her unstable social status in her community, one that does not offer stable boundaries, since she crosses the lines inside and outside every month. As one who crosses boundaries, she is perceived as threatening the social order, and therefore must be controlled, lest she stray. This control is conducted by men, who are the authorities who rule on the halakhic matters relating to the ritual bath and *niddah*. Her standing is also indirectly influenced by her births, with more sons enhancing her status. In the future, her sons will protect her in her husband's household, and they will take especial care to protect her rights, if her husband is married to more than one wife. In this case, her sons are a subgroup within the father's household that guards their mother's rights, vis-a-vis both her husband and his other wives. This social control separates between the worlds of women and men. Women lack social power, and therefore cannot influence the social agenda. This background enables us to understand some additional issues relating to the new mother and to marriage.

The Ritual Purity of the New Mother:
The Birth of a Male and the Birth of a Female

Torah law specifies different periods of impurity for a woman who has given birth to a male and one who has borne a female. It states, for the birth of a male: "Speak to the Israelite people thus: When a woman at childbirth bears a male, she shall be unclean seven days; she shall be unclean as at the time of her menstrual infirmity. On the eighth day the flesh of his foreskin shall be circumcised" (Lev. 12:2-3). The mother and her infant are isolated from their surroundings for seven days, because the mother acquired the uncleanness of birth, and because the infant, who must nurse from his mother, has not yet been officially accepted into the male community. On the eighth day after his birth he is permanently received into their community by the irrevocable act of the removal of his foreskin.[31] The mother casts off her impurity that same day and returns to her community, for by giving birth to a male she contributed to the continuity of the male descent line of her husband's lineage. The mother's return, however, is not complete: she enters an interim period, a liminal state. As the following verse prescribes: "She shall remain in a state of blood purification for thirty-three days: she shall not touch any consecrated thing, nor enter the sanctuary until her period of purification is completed" (Lev. 12:4). Her liminal state is expressed, on the one hand, by her remaining in her "state of blood purification," that is, the blood she sees from now on is pure, but, on the other hand, she may not come into contact with sanctified objects nor enter the Temple. She left the state of impurity, and may be in the nonsacred domain, but she cannot enter the sacred domain. Consequently, she is precluded from fully participating in social life. The blood of the liminal days of purification does not impart uncleanness, unlike the blood of menstruation or of birth, that attest to a natural process that cannot be controlled and therefore impart impurity; it rather is like the blood from a wound or circumcision, that does not impart impurity, since it can be controlled or supervised (since pregnancy can be avoided).[32] The mother of a son remains an additional thirty-three days in the liminal sphere—that is, she is not really "inside," because a nursing mother generally cannot yet conceive. (In societies that have no knowledge of contraceptives, it is a known phenomenon that menstruation does not return as long as the mother continues to nurse, because of the elevated level of prolactin that stimulates milk production.)[33]

The liminal period concludes with a ritual. The new mother leaves the interim realm and temporarily returns (until her next period) as a full member to her husband's householed: "On the completion of her period of purification, for either son or daughter, she shall bring to the priest, at the

---

[31] See above, n. 17, for the possibility of leaving the society by drawing down the prepuce.

[32] In principle, bodily excretions do not impart ritual impurity, as tears, blood from a wound, urine, and faeces do not impart impurity. In contrast, menstrual blood, an effusion of semen, and the blood of those suffering from gonorreea do impart such impurity. The basic rule is that the secretions that do not impart impurity are those that the individual can control or, in other words, that can be managed. The blood of menstruation and of those suffering from gonorreea comes from an uncontrollable natural process; consequently, anyone coming into contact with them is unclean for seven days (Lev. 11:13). An individual who comes into contact with an effusion of semen is unclean for only a single day (Lev. 15:16), since it can be partially controlled. See Eilberg-Schwartz, 1990: 187; see also Rubin (1995: 17–19).

[33] See the detailed discussion and literature in Rubin (1995: 22–25).

entrance of the Tent of Meeting, a lamb in its first year for a burnt offering, and a pigeon or turtledove for a sin offering. He shall offer it before the Lord and make expiation on her behalf; she shall then be clean from her flow of blood" (Lev. 12:6–7). The woman's "correction" from her uncleanness and her return to society are effected by means of a sacrifice; this correction can be understood in accordance with Levi-Strauss's principle that a ritual corrects something by its reciprocal.[34] Since birth-blood causes impurity because it is like menstrual blood, which cannot be controlled, the situation is corrected by the blood of a sacrifice, which can be managed. It is noteworthy that the mother's reacceptance into society is fundamentally different from the acceptance of the infant: the infant is received by the irrevocable ritual of circumcision, following which he receives an immutable status; his mother is received by means of birth sacrifice, which must be repeated after every birth, symbolizing the woman's reversible situation.

Matters are different for the birth of a girl. The infant does not undergo a rite of passage, nor does her mother return to her place after seven days. The impurity of her birth continues for two weeks: "If she bears a female, she shall be unclean two weeks as during her menstruation, and she shall remain in a state of blood purification for sixty-six days" (Lev. 12:5). The mother of a girl is seemingly punished, and she must remain in her state of uncleanness for two weeks, and in a liminal state for sixty-six days, twice the period of impurity and purification for the birth of a son. This difference is probably because she did not fulfil her husband's families' expectations that she would give birth to a son and thereby contribute to the descent line of her husband's lineage. This idea is supported by the exegesis of Num. 12:14: "If her father spat in her face, would she not bear her shame for seven days? Let her be shut out of the camp for seven days, and then let her be readmitted." The exegete states: "And certainly so regarding the Divine Presence—fourteen days."[35] This means that the impurity of the mother of a son (one week) bears the same relation to that of a woman who gave birth to a girl (two weeks) as the quarantine after the father's censure (one week) to censure by the Divine Presence (two weeks).

Patently, the definition of purity/impurity is social, and not biological, for two reasons: first, even though, in terms of the biological processes, there is no difference between the birth of a male and the birth of a female, behavioral rules differ. Second, even though intensive nursing usually retards the recurrence of the monthly period after birth, its return is a possibility. The

---

[34]   Levi-Strauss, 1978: 332–39; see Eilberg-Schwartz, 1990: 188.

[35]   *Gen. Rabbah* 92 (ed. Theodor-Albeck, p. 1146); *Sifrei* on Numbers, 105, s.v. "*Vayomer*" (ed. Horovitz, p. 104); 138, s.v. "*Vayedaber*" (p. 184).

probability of the period's return during her period of purification is greater for the mother of a girl, since her purification period continues until the eightieth day after the birth, in comparison with the fortieth day following the birth of a boy. Despite this, by Torah law the woman who sees menstrual blood during this period is not deemed impure. The social definition that places her in a liminal state is therefore stronger than the biological definition.

Sacrifice and Immersion

A new mother could bring a sacrifice to conclude the birth period only during the time of the Temple. This raises the question: did a substitute ritual come into being following the destruction of the Temple? Immersion in a ritual bath seems to be this substitute. The Torah makes no mention of an obligatory purification immersion after giving birth, but the early halakhah already required this of the new mother, deducing this need from Lev. 14:19–30, that contains the laws requiring immersion of the woman suffering from a discharge. The Schools of Shammai and Hillel were in agreement on the woman's obligation to immerse following the period of her uncleanness (one week after the birth of a male, and two weeks after the birth of a female), but they disagree regarding her need to immerse following the period of her purification. The School of Hillel exempted her from this immersion, while the School of Shammai required it (M Niddah 10:7). Regardless of this disagreement, all concur that leaving the impurity of giving birth requires immersion. In the absence of a sacrifice, immersion is a significant ritual.

Immersion, like the sacrifice, is a corrective ritual by a reciprocal rite. The impurity that was caused by birth that cannot be controlled (the woman is in the domain of "nature"), is corrected by the controllable immersion ritual (the woman passes to the domain of "culture"), for the time of the immersion, the fitness of the ritual bath, and everything that this entails are under male control and regulation. The immersion is in "fresh water" (Lev. 15:13),[36] in its natural state, through which the impure seeking purification pass, including males with a discharge or males with an emission of semen (Lev. 15:1–18). Immersion, unlike circumcision, is singular in that it is a reversible rite of passage. The person who immerses and is cleansed may become impure once again, and be purified once again by immersion. The nature of water is that it

---

[36] The verse originally refers to one suffering from an issue who comes to be purified, but the rabbis understood it as meaning that all that is impure, whether man or vessel, requires immersion in water in contact with the ground. See *Sifra, Metzora-Zavim* 3:5 (ed. Weiss, p. 79); BT Eruvin 4b.

flows and is not static, and therefore is symbolically capable of transforming from one impermanent state to another. The female immerser leaves "nature" ("fresh water"), returns to "culture," and in the future will return to the former.

A menstruating woman, a woman with a discharge, and a new mother; a male with a discharge, a male with an emission of semen, and any reversible impurity, are cleansed by immersion in water, through which one may cyclically pass. Circumcision, breaking of the glass at a wedding, and the rending of the mourner's garment, in contrast, are irreversible ritual acts. The birth of a girl is not marked by any ritual, not even a reversible one. This is because a girl is not destined to remain in her father's household in which she was born and she will not undergo this cyclical process there; she will go from her father's household to that of her husband, possibly even more than once.

Birth rituals demonstrate the perception of woman's place in a society in which the resources of property, prestige, and power are controlled by males. In such a social structure, the birth of boys will be preferred to that of girls (a position accepted by women, as well), and this determines the status of women. A woman, who changes her identity and her family commitments during the course of her life cycle, has only a single opportunity to attain standing in her husband's lineage: by giving birth to males (bearing only females is liable to weaken her standing even more).[37]

Marriage and Female Identity

The Bridal Procession: Bringing the Bride to the Groom's House

After the betrothal, the bride remains in her father's house until her wedding, after which she moves to her husband's house. The wedding ritual begins with escorting the bride from her father's house to husband's house. The bridal procession came to be known as "hakhnasat kallah," literally, "bringing the bride into [the husband's house]" (this expression is absent from the Mishnah, the Tosefta, the Jerusalem Talmud, and midrashei ha-halakhah, but appears in the Babylonian Talmud and midrashei ha-aggadah).[38] Among all the betrothal

---

[37] See the statement by Bar Kappara: "Happy is the one whose children are males, woe to the one whose children are females" (BT Bava Batra 16b; Pesahim 65a; Sanhedrin 100b).

[38] In the BT, it usually appears in proximity to "hotza'at ha-met" (the funeral procession). See BT Sukkah 49b; Megillah 3b; 29a; Ketubot 17a. Rashi (Megillah 29a, s.v. "Le-Hakhnasat Kallah") interprets this as "accompaniment from her father's house to the house of her husband." R. Eliezer ben Nathan of Mainz (Ketubot 17a [New York, 1958, fol. 258a]), however, states that this term refers to the ceremony of reciting

and marriage rituals, the bridal procession is an independent phase that includes a series of rituals that bridge between betrothal and marriage. The rituals begin with the departure from the parent's house, which makes the bride's separation from her parents' household tangible. She leaves her house for a temporary stay in a neutral realm: the way from one house to the other, which is a public realm belonging to neither her father's lineage nor that of her husband. The transferral ritual takes place in this neutral realm: the bride is carried from her house in a palanquin, which is a sort of a closed and protected bubble within the foreign space, a bubble that is entirely hers. Within it, she no longer belongs to her father's lineage, but is not yet part of her husband's. She is borne on a palanquin on people's shoulders, with makeup and bedecked with "twenty-four ornaments," surrounded by numerous escorts from both lineages; hymns are sung before her, with music by the flute players; those accompanying her dance and call out before her; ears of corn and nuts are tossed before her; and a "cup of tidings" is passed before her. Finally, upon leaving the palanquin, she is integrated within the groom's lineage by means of the wedding canopy, the symbolic structure erected in the house of the groom's father that constitutes the private realm that she shares with her husband.[39]

We must resolve a question concerning the wealth of symbols connected with this festive occasion. How can we explain the major disparity between her legal and social standing in this patriarchal society, where women were excluded of the public realm, and were not allowed to be conspicuous in public, and the considerable resources invested by her father's lineage in empowering her position? Even poor families made efforts to expend resources on this display. Following the seven days of feasting the bride immediately returned to her former status. In the words of the exegete: "Oh! a bride, once the days of her bridal ceremony are over, returns to her [domestic] tasks."[40]

Let us examine some items in the ritual that exemplify this situation.

Jewelry and Ornaments

When the bride is prepared for her meeting with the groom, makeup is applied, and she is dressed specially, and adorned with jewelry. In the Rabbinic literature the term "*takhshitim*," or "*takhshitei nashim*" (respectively, "jewelry" and "women's jewelry") also includes the makeup, cosmetics, and perfumes

---

the marriage blessings. His interpretation apparently follows *Lev. Rabbah* 23:4 (ed. Margulies, p. 530): "for ten who gathered to enter (*le-hakhnis*) the bride, but did not know how to recite the wedding blessing."

[39] For the complete details of the ritual, see Rubin (2004: 216–25).

[40] *Pesikta de-Rav Kahana*, Appendix 6 (ed. Mandelbaum, p. 470).

used by women.[41] The Rabbis used two words: *kishutim* (decorations) and *takhshitim* to refer to "jewelry."

The Rabbis placed great importance of a woman's fine appearance, which they ascribed to one of the eleven regulations enacted by Ezra, "that peddlers be allowed to travel about in the towns [...] because [they sell] women's *takhshitim*, so that they shall not be repulsive to their husband."[42] In this context, we should recall the dicta by R. Hiyya: "A wife is only for beauty, a wife is only for children; and R. Hiyya further taught: A wife is only for [the wearing of] a woman's finery" (BT Ketubot 59b). This presumably is an expression of sincere concern for the woman. Between the lines, however, we can discern a paternalistic stance that regards the wife as an object of her husband: she is only for "beauty," "children," and "a woman's finery," but is not a personality in her own right. Her beauty is not independently important, but only so that she would not be repulsive to her husband.[43] This position is not surprising, in light of what we know from other sources of the Rabbis' patriarchal conception of the wife's place in the family. According to this notion: "does not a wife adorn

---

[41] According to the following midrash, "to adorn oneself" (*le-hitkashet*) means to apply perfume. The midrash begins with the words "Nard and cinnamon" (Cant. 4;14), lists various Land of Israel spices, and then continues: "And where did Israelite women [find the means] to apply perfumes [*mitkashtot*] and gladden their husbands all the forty years that Israel remained in the wilderness? R. Johanan said: From the well [...] R. Abbahu said: From the manna [...] from which the modest and proper Israelite women would adorn themselves and gladden their husbands all the forty years that Israel was in the wilderness." That is, they bedecked, or perfumed, themselves with the water or with the manna (*Cant. Rabbah* 4:29 [ed. Donsky, p. 124]). See also BT Yoma 39b: "The women in Jericho did not have to perfume themselves [*le-hitbasem*] because of the smell of the incense. A bride in Jerusalem did not have to perfume herself [*le-hitkashet*] because of the smell of the incense." Abbaye declared (BT Ketubot 71b: "A prominent woman enjoys the scent of her cosmetics [*kishuteha*] for thirty days"; see also *Avot de-Rabbi Nathan*, Version B, chap. 9 (ed. Schechter, pp. 24–25). The Mishnah (Ketubot 7:3): "If a man vowed to abstain from his wife should she put on a certain kind of adornment [*titkashet*]" means that he prevented her from applying some kind of perfume. See also T Ketubot 7:3 (ed. Lieberman, p. 79).

[42] BT Bava Kamma 82a-b. See also BT Bava Batra 22a: "Ezra enacted for Israel that peddlers should go about from town to town, so that Israelite women would be able to obtain finery."

[43] See also BT Shabbat 64b. The importance that the rabbis ascribed to the woman's beauty and finery is expressed, e.g., in the halakhah that a husband who prohibited his wife by vow from adorning herself must grant her a divorce and pay her the amount of her *ketubah* (marriage contract). See M Ketubot 7:3; T Ketubot 7:3 (ed. Lieberman, p. 79); JT Ketubot 7:3, 31b. In the aggadah, see *Cant. Rabbah* 1:25 (ed. Donsky, p. 25); 5:1 (p. 126).

herself solely for her husband?"[44] The Tosefta brings a parable in the name of R. Gamaliel according to which a married woman, whether she adorns herself or not, "is not gazed upon by any [other] man." That is, no one may look at her, for it is forbidden to court married women. But "if [she is married and] does not adorn herself [for her husband], a curse shall fall upon her," since she will eventually be repulsive to her husband.[45]

The bride is made beautiful with jewelry, which were a clear indicator for the public of her status as a bride. The Mishnah (Yevamot 13:2) states that a minor who was given in marriage by her mother or her brother with her knowledge is allowed to exercise her right of refusal; the JT explains: "What is the meaning of 'with her knowledge'? A canopy is made for her, she is bedecked in *kosmidin* [jewelry],[46] and the name of the man is mentioned before her" (JT Yevamot 13:2, 13c). That is, the jewelry symbolizes that the minor is a bride. According to the expositions in the aggadic literature, brides would bedeck themselves with twenty-four ornaments, in accordance with the list of jewelry types in Isa. 3:18–24.[47] R. Simeon ben Lakish deduces from this: "Just as this bride is adorned with twenty-four ornaments, and if one of them is missing, she is accounted as nothing; so, too, if a Torah scholar who is versed in the twenty-four books [of Scripture] is deficient in one of them, he is accounted as nothing."[48] How can erudition in twenty-three books of the Bible be regarded as "nothing"? The exegete apparently meant to indicate the need for perfection. According to this exposition, we may presume that there was an accepted set of jewelry for a bride, and if this set lacked a single item of jewelry, this defect would be immediately recognized, and "she is accounted as nothing." Otherwise, it would be difficult to understand the nature of the

---

44   *Cant. Rabbah* 1:25 (ed. Donsky, p. 25).

45   T Kiddushin 1:11; see also BT Taanit 23a, the narrative regarding Abba Hilkiah, the grandson of Honi the Circle Drawer: despite his poverty, his wife would greet him bedecked "so that he would not cast his eyes upon another woman."

46   Kosmidin (and not kosmirin, as in the printed edition) are jewelry in Greek (κοσμιδια, kosmidia). See Kosovsky, 1999, vol. 7: 196, s.v. "*Kosmidia-Kosmidin*"; see also Jastrow, 1950: 1325, s.v. "*Kosmidya.*"

47   As is the wording in Isaiah (3:18–25): "In that day, my Lord will strip off the finery of the anklets, the fillets, and the crescents; of the eardrops, the bracelets, and the veils; the turbans, the armlets, and the sashes; of the talismans and the amulets; the signet rings and the nose rings; of the festive robes, the mantles, and the shawls; the purses, the lace gowns, and the linen vests; and the kerchiefs and the capes. And then—instead of perfume, there shall be rot; and instead of an apron, a rope; instead of a diadem of beaten-work, a shorn head; instead of a rich robe, a girding of sackcloth; a burn instead of beauty."

48   *Cant. Rabbah* 4:22 (ed. Donsky, p. 119).

defect in a bride bedecked in "only" twenty-three types of jewelry. We might further hypothesize that such a set was not affordable for every nuclear family; there might have been such a complement in the extended family, which was passed down from generation to generation, and was loaned to the family's brides. If this hypothesis is correct, then this set of jewelry could be regarded as a means that defined the boundaries of the family in the social space. We might further suggest that families not possessing such a set could borrow one.[49] Support for this hypothesis is provided by Nitza Druyan's study of Jewish Yemenite women in Yemen and in Israel. Druyan argues that jewelry was a status symbol of the Jewish woman in Yemen, "but not every bride was able to purchase a bridal gown and jewelry. Such a set was possessed by a wealthy member of the community who would rent out the ritual trappings."[50]

A poor bride, for whom even a borrowed wedding set was beyond her means, looked pitiful. It is said that when R. Tarfon saw a poor bride being led to her wedding, he ordered that she be brought into his house, to be bathed, ornamented, and led to her wedding ceremony.[51] The midrash gives the bride's ornaments the imprimatur of an ancient custom, since it is related that Eve was "bedecked as a bride" by the Holy One, blessed be He, when He brought her to Adam,"[52] and He adorned them with "twenty-four ornaments."[53] Based on this, the exegetes went so far as to claim that "the Holy One, blessed be He, blesses grooms and bedecks brides" in general,[54] and did not do so solely for Eve. We do not know if, in actuality, brides were decorated with twenty-four types of jewelry, but we may assume that every bride was bedecked, in accordance with her family's means, with the accepted set of jewelry, and possibly additional jewelry, as well, depending on the family's wealth. The exegete, who was familiar with the harsh economic situation of many brides, knew that this fine time for the bride was very short, and after it the new wife could usually expect hard times and, as mentioned above, he says sorrow-

---

49   *Num. Rabbah* 3:17 presents a parable: "To what may this be compared? To a king who married a woman, and he brought his paper and scribe, his crown, and he brought her in to his house." According to this midrash, it was expected that the bride would come with her own crown; the king, however, married a poor woman who did not have one, and he gave it to her.

50   Druyan, 1992: 77.

51   *Avot de-Rabbi Nathan*, Version A, chap. 41 (ed. Schechter, p. 133).

52   *Gen. Rabbah* 18:2 (ed. Theodor-Albeck, p. 161); *Avot de-Rabbi Nathan*, Version A, chap. 4 (ed. Schechter, p. 18); *Ex. Rabbah, Tisa*, 41:5.

53   *Tanhuma, Hayyei Sarah*, 2 (ed. Buber, fol. 58b).

54   *Gen. Rabbah* 8:13 (ed. Theodor-Albeck, p. 67); see also *Midrash Tehillim* 25:11 (ed. Buber, p. 107).

fully: "Ho! a bride, once the days of her bridal ceremony are over, returns to her [domestic] tasks." We therefore return to the question, why the bride was set forth so finely and was the center of the bridal procession, while nothing parallel was performed for the groom. While this ritual was performed for the bride, the groom merely sat in his home and awaited her arrival.

The Cup of Tidings and the Sheet of Virginity

An additional question that arises from the study of marriage customs regards the social and symbolic significance of virginity The loss of virginity was regarded as something terrible; a woman who had lost her virginity was entitled to only half the sum in the wedding contract afforded the virgin.

According to the Mishnah (Ketubot 2:1) the signs of a wedding of a virgin were the hymns that were sang while escorting the bride from her father's household to her husband's, and the throwing of ears of corn before her palanquin along the bridal procesion These were meant to show that the woman was a virgin at the time of her wedding, which enabled her to demand the sum of two hundred *zuz* as her wedding contract, and not the sum of one hundred *zuz* given to a nonvirgin bride. The sources teach that in the Second Temple period, and until the Bar Kokhba revolt, the bridal procession contained an additional element, the "cup of tidings," the nature of which has not been determined. Abba Saul, a fourth-generation Tanna (who possessed reports from the time of the Temple), stated that another sign of virginity in the bridal procession was that "they carried before her a cask of tidings" (JT Ketubot 2:1, 26b). The JT does not specify the nature of this cask, perhaps because this was common knowledge when the Tanna made this statement. The Babylonian Talmud (Ketubot 16b), in contrast, was incapable of explaining it. The BT also cites an additional *baraita* (external mishnah) that lists the signs of the wedding of a virgin: "If she lost her wedding contract document, or she hid it, or it was burnt [and she demands the wedding contract sum for a virgin of two hundred *zuz*, then if there are witnesses that] they danced before her, played before her, passed before her a cup of tidings or a sheet of virginity—if she has witnesses regarding one of these, the sum of her wedding contract is two hundred." The BT then asks: "What is the cup [the BT uses the word "*kos*," instead of "*havit*" (cask) in the JT] of tidings?" R. Ada bar Ahavah (a fourth-generation Babylonian Amora) replies: "A cup of wine of *terumah* [the heave-offering] is passed before her, as if to say: This one [i.e., a virgin] is worthy to eat of *terumah* [if married to a priest, without any suspicion of her having engaged in licentious behavior]." This is a strange answer: The bride who is about to enter under the wedding canopy is told that she is fit for another groom? R. Papa (a fifth-generation Babylonian Amora) asks a halakhic question: "Does not a widow [who had been married to a regular priest] not eat of *terumah* [and therefore this cup would not exclusively signify her virginity]? Rather, R. Papa said: This [bride] is first [= a virgin], just as *terumah* is first." Thus, the Babylonian Amoraim offered a symbolic interpretation of the past practice. It is, however, quite evident from their interpretation that they were not familiar with the custom. Nor does this interpretation even hint as to how the word "*besorah*" (tidings) can be understood as referring to the word "*terumah*."

In the continuation of this discursive unit, the BT presents another *baraita*, in the name of R. Judah, a contemporary of Abba Saul: "It has been taught: R. Judah says: A cask of wine was passed before her." Is this "cask of wine" the same "cask of tidings" of Abba Saul, which was so called because its passing was meant to allude to good tidings? Or, perhaps, a cask of wine, too, was passed before the bride? Or, possibly, these were two different customs, from different localities? In any event, R. Ada bar Ahavah thought them to be two different matters: before, he explained that the "cup of tidings" was a cup of *terumah*, and his explanation was rejected by R. Papa; now, he explains how the "cask of wine" could attest to the bride's virginity: "If a virgin, a closed cask of wine is passed before her; and if she has had intercourse with a man—an open one is passed before her." If the public remembered that a "closed" cask had been passed before her, this means that she was a virgin. The Talmud then asks: "Why? Let us pass a cask only before a virgin, and pass nothing before one who has had intercourse?" The answer is that "sometimes, she might have seized the two hundred [*zuz*], and declared: 'I was a virgin, but they did not pass [a cask of wine] before me because they were prevented by an accident [i.e., they were too intoxicated to do so]'" (BT Ketubot 16b). This intriguing discussion actually proves that these practices were no longer current, and it seems to be an attempt to explain an element of a folkloristic story from the past, that we are not certain was ever performed in the manner depicted by R. Ada bar Ahavah.

The associative connection between the closed cask and virginity apparently followed in the wake of the story told of R. Gamaliel [III], the son of R. Judah ha-Nasi:

> Someone came before R. Gamaliel the son of Rabbi [= R. Judah ha-Nasi] and said to him: "My master, I had intercourse [with my new wife], but I did not find any blood." She [the wife] said to him [R. Gamaliel]: "My master, I am still a virgin." He told them: "Bring me two handmaidens, one who is a virgin, and one who has engaged in intercourse." They brought him, and he placed them on a cask of wine. Its smell went through the one who had engaged in

intercourse; but its smell did not go through the virgin. And so, too, with this one: she was placed on it, and its smell did not go through. He [R. Gamaliel] said to him [the husband]: "Go, be happy with your acquisition [= his wife]." (BT Ketubot 10b)

Abba Saul's terminology of the "cask of tidings" apparently paralleled, or was identical to R. Judah's "cask of wine." The nature (essence) of this cask might be understood by its contrast with another term, the *ketzatzah* (or *ketzizah*) ritual, which a family conducted for someone who married a woman "who is unworthy of him."

The Tosefta (Ketubot 3:3) is occupied with the question of a person's fitness to testify as an adult to matters that he saw or heard while a minor. It states: "A person is reliable to say [...] for we ate at the *ketzizah* of so-and-so." The JT (Ketubot 2:6, 26d) uses another, complementary *baraita* to explain the meaning of this concept:

> It is taught: "For we ate at the *ketzitzah* of so-and-so." What is "at the *ketzitzah* of"? When a person would sell his land-inheritance, his relatives would fill casks with ears of corn and nuts and break [the casks] before children. The children would gather [the corn and nuts], and say, "So-and-so has been cut off [*nikatzetz*] from his land-inheritance!" And when it returned to him, they would do so to him and say: "So-and-so has returned to his land-inheritance!"

The BT portrays a different *ketzatzah* ritual:

> What is *ketzatzah*? Our masters taught: How does *ketzatzah* take place? If one of the brothers had married a woman who is unworthy of him, the family members would bring a cask full of fruit, and they would break it in the middle of the open space. They would say: "Our brothers of the House of Israel, hear. Our brother, so-and-so, has married a woman who is unworthy of him, and we fear lest his descendants will be mingled with our descendants. Come and take for yourselves a token for [future] generations, that his descendants shall not be mixed with our descendants." This is the *ketzatzah* regarding which a child is believed to testify (BT Ketubot 28b).

In the continuation of the passage in the JT a third-generation Land of Israel Amora incidentally tells, in the context of the *ketzatzah* ritual for the sale of a field, of such a ceremony for one who married a woman "who is unworthy," in a version different from that in the BT:

> R. Yose the son of R. Bun said: Also, one who married a wife who is unworthy of him—his relatives fill casks with ears of corn and nuts and break [them] before children. The children would gather [the corn and nuts], and say,

"So-and-so has been cut off [*nekatzetz*] from his land-inheritance!" And when he divorced her, they would do so to him and say: "So-and-so has returned to his family!" (JT Ketubot 2:6, 26d).

We may assume that the tradition in the *baraita* is apparently from an early period when farmers would dwell on their land as independent landowners. In such a society, it was accepted that when a father died and his sons inherited his holding, they would join together and continue the shared ownership of the plot of land, in order to ensure that the extended family structure would not dissolve after the division of the inheritance. The sale of lands from the family holding was regarded as a reprehensible act, for the land gave the family its identity, and its sale harmed the patrimonial identity. Furthermore, the sale of land from the family holding weakened the family's strength relative to the neighboring families, since its status was determined in relation to the size of the holding, the size of the family, and, mainly, by the number of its males capable of defending it.[55] In such a structure, the *ketzatzah* ritual was logical, since it was meant to threaten anyone who dared to violate this order.

I am inclined to think that the primary symbolism of the *ketzatzah* ritual, of the sale of land, evolved into the secondary symbolism of the *ketzatzah* ritual for an unworthy wife. The extended family gradually vanished in the Land of Israel in the wake of the Roman conquest and the economic crisis in the land. In the absence of patrimony, the importance of genealogy rose.[56] The preservation of genealogy by "worthy" marriages maintained the family's integrity and identity. The *ketzatzah* ritual, performed for one who took a wife "who was not worthy of him," was included in this. The *baraita* does not include a definition of a "not worthy" wife; the brothers determine this for their brother. She might have been "not worthy" morally, but this could also have referred to her family's lineage, her political power, or her economic standing The brother's marriage to such a woman might have interfered with the other brothers' plans or harmed their standing. The *ketzatzah* ritual symbolizes that,

---

55 This was the practice in the agricultural Arab society in Palestine until the modernization brought about by the British Mandate following WWI. The inheriting sons continued to possess their inheritance jointly after their father's death, until internal family tensions forced them to split up. See Rosenfeld, 1964: 86–90.

56 The Bedouin nomadic society, that is landless, has no family identity based on land holdings, it buries its dead in the desert in the course of its wanderings, without tombstones. It zealously maintains its family identity by means of the family genealogy. See, e.g., Rubin, 1994. On the economic crisis and its impact on family structure see: Rubin, 1997: 92–93; Safrai, 1994.

by this marriage, the brother caused the dissolution of the family bond. The extended family, when united, resembles a cask containing an abundance of fruits or nuts and corn, and its breaking symbolizes the family's dissolution. The "cup of tidings" might be tertiary-level symbolism. After a certain period, when the original significance had waned, the cask turned into a cup, when it received the new meaning that it was given by R. Ada bar Ahavah, who regarded it as a "cup of wine of *terumah.*"

The BT version seems superior to that of the JT, because it is cited as an independent *baraita*, and not as an Amoraitic tradition. The dramatic Babylonian version demonstrates the degree to which this act harmed the public order. It was conducted in the "open space," the public square, and addressed the community: "Our brothers of the House of Israel," as was common in eulogies delivered in public that began with this same wording. Addressing the public with the family term "our brothers" and the ethnic term "House of Israel," as an extended family term, expressed the fear of the dissolution of the sense of social unity caused by this crisis;[57] moreover, the ritual, as portrayed in the JT, is an internal family ceremony that seemed like an amusement for children, without any public message. The corrective ritual in the JT, after the restoration of the land holding or the divorce of the wife, does not sound authentic, since how could a ritual of exclusion also have the opposite meaning, of inclusion?

We will now return to the "cup of tidings" (which might have been filled with fruits or corn and nuts) or the "cask of wine." The cask, whether "of wine" or "of tidings," symbolizes an extended and united family, as is clearly indicated by the *ketzatzah* ritual. Every virgin who joins a family unites two different families of origin, for her offspring will trace their descent from her husband's lineage, which she joined. The crowd throws ears of corn and nuts, and also other items of food, such as strings of fish and dried meat (*Semahot* 8:3), into the bridal procession, in which, among other symbols, the cask is borne. Now, the symbolic message of the cask of tidings ritual and the *ketzatzah* ritual is clear: while, in the wedding ritual, the audience **gives** gifts to the bride and groom by throwing food at them, thereby bringing them into their ranks, in the *ketzatzah* ritual the audience **takes** food from the family, thereby symbolizing the latter's collapse.[58] When the extended family began to disintegrate, and with it its ability to influence the choice of a spouse, the *ketzatzah* ritual would disappear, along with the cask of tidings.

---

[57] On the "open Space" and address: "our brothers, of the House of Israel" in eulogies, see Rubin, 1997: 207, 224–225.

[58] Büchler, 1927: 106.

An additional symbol in this procession, that does not require complex interpretation, is the "sheet of virginity." The Babylonian Talmud (Ketubot 16b) relates that if "they passed before her the cup of tidings, or the sheet of virginity," then these are signs of the wedding ceremony of a virgin. Patently, a bride who preserved her virginity also maintained her family's honor. This fact is demonstrated by "passing" before her, as she sits in the palanquin, the clean (and apparently white) sheet. This sheet was to be presented a second time, after the bride and groom were together, now bloodstained, thus teaching retrospectively of the bride's virginity. It is noteworthy that a virginity blessing was recited after the first act of sexual relations and the presentation of the sheet.

What, then, is the significance of the cask and the sheet? They obviously symbolize virginity, since they attest to the pristine state of the woman in whose bridal procession they were present. Their symbolism, however, exceeds this physical fact: they are important for the standing of the bride's entire family. They are a sign of the family's ability to exert control over its children, and especially its daughters. The symbols attest that the bride is from a "good family"—a home with discipline; that the family is strong and of proper social status.

To conclude our discussion, I must resolve the first question that I posed: how are we to explain the gap between the woman's social status and the considerable investment in the bride, both in money and in honor? I showed mainly the investment in makeup and in jewelry; I did not mention the expenses entailed in the preparation or rental of the palanquin, and at times also of the hiring of its bearers. There were also additional expenses: the hiring of the flute players, the need for food stands along the way, when the distance between the house of the bride's family and that of the groom was great, and other costs. Additionally, much honor was shown the bride by the worthies of the public as they danced before her.[59]

The answer is that the bride's family presented itself to the family of the groom by the bride and the rich rituals accompanying her. The truth be told, the bride was not important in her own right, and she served merely as a symbol representing her family's honor. Her family did not transfer her to the groom's family as a conscious individual, but as a precious family resource, due to the merits accruing from her fertility. The magnificently bedecked bride represents the family's power and wealth, and not necessarily herself.

---

[59] A presentation of the sources relating to the bridal palanquin, the flute-players, the food, and the dancing would exceed the purview of the current article. See Rubin (2004: 187–206).

Thus, a balance between the families is created: between the family of the groom, that represents the power of its male line, and the bride's family, that represents respectability, wealth, and social power with the bride as her icon. In the meantime, until the conclusions of the wedding celebrations, the bride enjoys special attention, that is not usually given a woman.

It should be stressed that this description does not relate to the attitude toward a woman as an individual within her family. Honor and respect to women is mentioned in many Rabbinic dicta, which would exceed the purview of this article. Here, we are concerned with how the culture uses rituals to resolve its internal constructed conflicts. A collective desirous of maintaining its position and to amass power and resources must do it, inter alia, by means of marital ties that invite conflicts. By means of rituals, the culture both expresses and conceals conflicts.

As for our second question, concerning the importance of virginity: it is known that in most simple societies (gatherers, hunters, and nomads) premarital sexual relations are not banned; only a few demand that a woman remain a virgin before her marriage, or at least not become pregnant to any man other than the one to whom she is supposed to marry. In contrast, in agricultural societies, in which social stratification is more rigid, where matters of property, political and family status, are of paramount importance, more emphasis is placed on bridal virginity. A young age at marriage for women is a likely protective mechanism for their virginity. For men, there is no matching emphasis on the ban against premarital and extramarital sexual relations, and therefore prostitution might acquire somewhat legitimate standing.[60]

The unmarried woman's virginity is her and her father's household prime asset. The bride's lineage transfers to the husband's lineage exclusive rights to the bride's procreative ability. This exclusivity is expressed in the bride's virginity: if she is still a virgin, this means that her childbearing rights had not been given to another in the past, for virginity is not only a matter between the bride and groom, it is of interest to the two lineages: as, on the one hand, the exclusive right of the groom's lineage; and, on the other, a matter of the family honor of the bride's lineage. A nonvirgin bride is perceived as one who has given away the "family property"—its rights of fertility—without receiving anything in return. In principle, the marital ties between the two lineages are to be irrevocable.[61] The bride's virginity symbolizes the finality of the bond, since it confirms the granting of her fertility rights to her husband's lineage.

---

[60] See Keesing, 1975.

[61] Even when society permitted divorce, this was rare, because the dissolution of the family had broad repercussions on the property and power relations of the lineages.

The irreversibility of virginity resembles the symbols of the irrevocability of other rites of passage: in circumcision—the cutting and drawing down of the foreskin; in mourning—the tearing of the garment. Just as circumcision cannot be revoked and the torn garment may not be mended, so, too, the girl's virginity cannot return, and the deed is done. Without her virginity, she cannot be married to a proper groom, if anyone was desirous of marrying her. She has defamed the honor of her father's lineage: not only has her innocence been violated, this act proves the lineage's lack of control and powerlessness. Because of her, her brothers' chances of marrying a worthy wife have severely decreased. Accordingly, due to the loss of virginity of one of its daughters, the lineage itself will likely decline. The marriage of a virgin accordingly is afforded special symbols, and the bride receives expressions of esteem for her innocence, even though her virginity should have been taken for granted.

The importance of virginity is also expressed in the procession in which a virgin bride is transferred from her father's house to that of her husband, which is not the case for a widow bride. The clean sheet that was unfurled and carried before the bride is a sign of her unsullied state, the assumption being that her innocence will become public knowledge after this sheet is stained with her virginal blood. The Babylonian Talmud tells of incidents in which grooms came to the Patriarchs, from R. Gamaliel the Elder to R. Gamaliel III, and complained: "I did not find blood." In all these instances, the Patriarchs discovered that the complainants had erred.[62] Regardless of the historical veracity of the narratives, what is essential here is the message that the reader receives regarding the importance of virginity, while, at the same time, learning that one should strive to act moderately and find any possible opening to refute the husband's claim of his wife's lack of innocence, a claim that was often raised due to ignorance in sexual matters.

Shushvinim

I will conclude the discussion of woman's status with an examination of the standing of the bride's *shushvin* (literally, "friend"), whose task differed, so I maintain, from that of the groom's "friend," due to the former's special duty to protect the bride in her husband's household after the wedding. According to the sources, the *shushvin* was the closest friend of the groom, whom he accompanied during the entire betrothal period until the wedding. The sources

---

[62]   BT Ketubot 10a-b. For the narratives of grooms who claimed that their wives were not virgins, see Valler, 1999: 29–50.

indicate that the bride also had such *shushvinim*.[63] There were localities in Judea in which one *shushvin* was appointed on behalf of the groom's lineage, and another from that of the bride, to ensure that no fraud would be perpetrated by either the groom or the bride regarding a complaint about virginity. The groom could act deceitfully by bringing forth a clean sheet that he had already prepared beforehand. The bride could be untruthful, by using a stained sheet that she already had ready. The Tosefta attests: "In former times in Judea two *shushvinim* were appointed, one from the side of the groom, and one from the side of the bride. And even so, they were appointed only for the marriage. [...] In former times in Judah the *shushvinim* would sleep in the place where the bride and groom would sleep."[64] According to the version in the JT (Ketubot 1:1, 25a): "In former times in Judea the *shushvinim* would investigate the place of the groom and the place of the bride."[65] None of this was practiced in Galilee, and anyone in Judea who did not act in this manner could not claim that the bride was not a virgin.[66]

In light of the above, the reason for maintaining this system of control is clear. We already mentioned that in a patriarchal system, the lineage of the bride's father transfers to the groom's lineage the exclusive rights to the bride's fertility, and this exclusivity is symbolized in the bride's virginity. In order to ensure that there is no deceit, both sides exercise supervision by means of the *shushvinim*. Even if the groom and the bride would agree to overlook her lack

---

63   Below I will mention that the bride or groom did not have female *shushvinot* who accompanied them during the wedding. The female form of this term, however, appears in BT Kiddushin 81a, telling of an incident that occurred in the third generation of Babylonian Amoraim: "R. Bibi visited R. Joseph. Once they had eaten, he said to them: 'Remove the ladder from under Bibi.' Rabbah, however, asked: 'If her husband is in town, [is it not so that] we have no fear on account of their being together? R. Bibi, [however,] is different, because she is his *shushvinah* and is intimate with him.'" R. Joseph, who was blind, feared that R. Bibi, who was his guest and dined with him, would descend from the upper chamber and be intimate with his wife; he therefore requested that the ladder be removed from this chamber. In response to the Talmud's question, according to Rabbah, if her husband is in the city, we do not fear such intimacy, the answer is given that R. Joseph's wife was his *shushvinah*, and therefore he was familiar with her. Tur-Sinai, 1953: 316, correctly observes: "The word might be used here in the general sense of close friend, and not in that of the groom's *shushvinah*."

64   T Ketubot 1:4 (ed. Lieberman, pp. 57–58).

65   The Tosefta mentions that the groom and the bride were examined three days before the wedding ceremony, but it does not specify that the *shushvinim* did this. See also the BT version, Ketubot 12a.

66   On the *shushvinim*, see Rubin (2004: 225–33), where I discussed the role of the *shushvin* as intermediary, friend, and confidant, and this institution as a mutual-aid system.

of virginity and feign the blood of virginity, the structure of the ritual would not allow this.

It is noteworthy that the *shushvin* of the groom or the bride is male, and not female. From the functional perspective, these individuals play an important role in supporting the couple during the process of their transition from unmarried to married. They act as intermediaries and as "advocates" in dealings with the other side and against the claims it is liable to raise, and help to make this transition a success. We may presume that in a patriarchal society the *shushvin* of the bride has a greater supportive role than that of the groom, since the bride leaves her parent's household and goes over to that of her husband, which is a foreign place for her, while the groom remains within the framework of his family. In her new and strange place, without the proximity of her relatives, the *shushvinim* are her protectors. This brings us back to our question: why do we not hear of female *shushvinim*? In a society that took such care to separate the sexes, would it not be more reasonable to prefer female confidants and escorts for the bride? And just what did a male *shushvin* do in the company of the bride?

Based on an understanding of the social structure, the answer is clear: In a society in which males are dominant, only they are capable of defending women. Only a male representative of the wife's lineage could protect her rights in her husband's household.[67] No woman could openly speak on her own behalf.[68] The *shushvinim* cannot be kindred spirits and confidants of the woman, because this type of society does not allow such closeness between a woman and a man not her husband. Most likely, women had close women friends who supported them, but such a girlfriend could not fill the official role of her *shushvin*. If this analysis is correct, it would explain why the motif of the bride's *shushvinim* frequently appears in Rabbinic aggadot in King Parables on the subject of weddings, while the groom's *shushvinim* appear in only a single tale.

---

[67] I surmise that the *shushvin* was important for the woman, at least until her eldest son was old enough to protect her.

[68] In traditional Arab society, for example, the woman's brothers are her protectors and defend her honor, without the woman's involvement. On the role of the brothers in traditional Arab society in the Land of Israel, see Rosenfeld, 1964: 74–92, 144–47. According to Islamic law, daughters inherit equally with sons, but they waive their portion of the inheritance on behalf of their brothers, so that they will serve as their sister's protectors. Protection of the sister is extremely complicated in a society in which the bride-price is customary, because in the event of a serious conflict between the wife and her husband, her divorce would require the return of the bride-price by the brothers, and they do not always have the money, or are desirous of repaying it.

In her essay on the wedding in such fables, Ofra Meir found that of the sixty wedding parables that she examined, nine relate to *shushvinim*, and in only one of these are the *shushvinim* those of the groom.[69] Actually, Meir erred in her count, because the parable in *Pesikta Rabbati* 96b that she cited as an example of *shushvinim* of the groom, states that the king "gave his daughter to the *shushvinim*," but these are not the *shushvinim* of the king (since he is not the groom), but of his daughter. In, however, another parable (from *Tanhuma*)[70] that she cites as an example of the bride's *shushvinim*, they are actually those of the groom: instead of "he heard *shushvinah* [her *shushvin*]," it should read "he heard *shushvino* [his *shushvin*]," as it appears in the parallel in *Deut. Rabbah*. In any event, we are left with only a single parable. My examination of twenty-four *shushvinim* parables in the aggadic literature, as well, yielded only this single one. In this parable, however, the *shushvin* is occupied with a matter relating to the wedding itself, as in the other sources referring to the groom's *shushvinim*.[71] All the other parables speak of the bride's *shushvinim*, who are active mainly in the postwedding period, which supports my hypothesis of the supportive role filled by the bride's *shushvin*, specifically, after the wedding. I will present several of these parables to exemplify the argument I advanced.

> A parable, to what may this be compared? To a king who gave his daughter in marriage. He wrote a large *ketubah* for her, and warned her not to act immorally. Eventually, she acted immorally. Her *shushvin* would reproach her […], but she did not repent. Finally, she mended her ways. When her *shushvin* saw that she had mended her ways, he began to chastise her for the actions she had committed. She heard, was silent, and was ashamed, and she did not respond. When her father saw that his daughter had been chastised

---

69   Meir, 1974.

70   *Tanhuma, Ve'ethanan*, 2 (ed. Buber, pp. 8–9).

71   The following is the parable in *Deut. Rabbah, Ve'ethanan*, 1 (ed. Leiberman, p. 35): A parable, to what is this comparable? To a king who wished to marry a woman. He sent his agents to determine if she was comely or not. They went and saw her, and they returned and told him: "We saw her, and there is none uglier than she." His *shushvin* heard [, and said to the king]: "Not so, my master, there is none in the world more comely than she." He [the king] came to marry her. The girl's father said to the king's agents: "I swear that not one of you will enter here, for you shamed her before the king." The *shushvin* came to enter, but he [the girl's father] said to him: "You, too, shall not enter." The *shushvin* said to him: "I did not see her, and I told the king that there was none more comely than her in the world, while they said that there was none as ugly in the world as she. Now I shall see whether it is as I said, or as they said."

and was ashamed and accepted the reproof, he told her *shushvin* to double her *ketubah*.[72]

In this parable, the woman had already been married for some time, and the *shushvin* was not her actual "friend," but someone who supervised her on behalf of her father's household. Incidentally, it should be noted that the "*ketubah*" that her father gave her is not the *ketubah* (= marriage contract) known to us from the world of Rabbinic halakhah, since this is given by a husband to his wife, and not by a father to his daughter. The intent here is to the dowry.

The following two parables demonstrate the role of the woman's *shushvin* as her protector and intermediary after the wedding.

A parable, to what may this be compared? To a king who married a woman, and she had a *shushvin*. Whenever the king was angry with his wife, the *shushvin* would placate him, and the king would be pleased with her. The *shushvin* was about to die. He began to request of the king: "I ask of you, consider your wife." The king replied: "If you command me regarding my wife, command my wife regarding me, that she take care regarding my honor."[73]

R. Judah ben R. Simon said: A parable, to what may this be compared? To a king who became angry with his wife, sent her from him, and removed her from his house. The *shushvinim* heard of this. They went to the king and said to him: "Oh, my lord, is this how a man acts with his wife? What did she do to you?" They went to her and told her: "How long shall you provoke him? Is this the first time you act thus, or the second?"[74]

In both these parables, the *shushvinim* are those of the wife, and not of the husband.[75] He does not need an "advocate" in his house, because he is the ruler, while the woman is powerless and needs the support of a male *shushvin*. In the last parable, the *shushvinim* make no attempt to justify the wife, and merely try to mediate.

Following these parables, we may surmise that in a social structure with an extended-family household, in which the wife lived in the household of her husband's parents, an important role was filled by her *shushvin*. As, however, this social structure was undermined and couples went to live as a nuclear

---

[72]   *Midrash Tannaim*, Deuteronomy, 1:11 (ed. Hoffmann, pp. 6–7).

[73]   *Num. Rabbah* 21:2.

[74]   *Deut. Rabbah* 1:2.

[75]   The following is a partial list of *shushvinim* parables: *Num. Rabbah* 1:5; 2:15; 18:12; *Deut. Rabbah* 3:17; *Lam. Rabbah* 1:1; *Pesikta de-Rav Kahana* 14:3 (ed. Mandelbaum, p. 242); 15:6 (p. 256).

family, apart from the parents, the role of the *shushvin* would disappear. When the *shushvinim* parables were drawn, extended-family households most likely no longer existed in the Jewish society in the Land of Israel. The role of *shushvin* was no more, and its memory remained only in the parables of the *shushvinim* of the royal families.

Summary

Women's social and legal standing in the Rabbinic sources was already extensively discussed by the researchers of the period. A contemporary scholar who examines gender issues may fall into the trap of making moral judgments and presume to speak for an egalitarian approach that exposes women's nonegalitarian standing. I did not seek to make such a judgment in this article, but, aided by a structural analysis, I point out that society adopts ideologies or cosmologies in accordance with its existential conditions. We have seen that when social and economic structure is patriarchal, egalitarian standing for women is inconceivable. Within this constrained structure the Rabbis enacted regulations that enabled a relatively respectable existence for the woman who was subject to a patriarchal regime. I further sought to show that symbols do not exist by chance; rather, their meaning, at times open, and in other instances implicit, emerge from within social structure.

Using a structural analysis I analyzed the position of women as it emerged from the explication of the meaning of the symbols inlaid in birth and marriage rituals. I showed that the woman's identity is usually not continuous or stable, and is derived from the identity of her father's or husband's lineage. Within her husband's household, her status is conditional on her "ability" to continue his descent line by giving birth to males. The instability of her standing is symbolized by the laws of *niddah* that enable her to participate in the life of the society when she is pure and fit for reproduction, but remove her from society when she is in a state of menstrual uncleanness and incapable of conception. For this reason, the mother giving birth to a son is preferable to one who has just borne a daughter: the former returns to society from the impurity of birth after a week, and the latter, after two weeks. The social definitions that create differentiation in the standing of the women are stronger than the biological ones, which do not distinguish between the birth of a male and that of a female.

Woman's social standing is determined also by the absence, for a female birth, of any ritual that would denote the newborn's acceptance into the society, in contrast with the birth of a male, who is received with the irrevocable circumcision ritual. The woman's unstable standing is symbolized in her husband's household by the cyclical and reversible immersion ritual, which alternately includes and excludes her from active social life.

Woman's standing is also indicated by the ritual of the transferral of the bride to the groom's household. Paradoxically (in light of her social standing), the virgin bride is given a very rich "bridal procession" ritual, accompanied by symbols attesting to her virginity. I explained that the magnificence of the ritual is not on account of the bride herself, but is for what she represents. In her marriage, the bride is an icon representing her father's lineage and its standing in the competition between families. These ritual expressions are absent in the wedding of a widow (who is not a virgin). Virginity is the representation of the premier asset of the bride and her lineage: her reproductive capability, which she transfers to her husband's lineage. A girl who did not guard her virginity casts a stain over her family, for this attests to the family's inability to impose its authority on her. The possibilities of matches for her siblings, as well, will likely be impaired as a result of this blemish.

Finally, the role of the wife's *shushvin* is derived from the standing of women. I showed that the role of the husband's *shushvin* comes to an end upon the wedding, while the woman's *shushvin* continues to occupy an important place in this framework. The *shushvin* is not the wife's "friend," but a person who protects her interests in her husband's household following the wedding, as long as she is in need of this defense. By means of this role, the social structure provided a certain degree of protection for the woman, who had been severed from her father's household.

PART FOUR  DEATH

Chapter 6. THE SAGES' CONCEPTION OF THE BODY AND SOUL

In the generations of the early Tannaitic scholars, we find that the Sages maintained a monistic view of the body-soul relationship. According to Urbach (1975: 214–216), man was defined as a singular psycho-physical organism. This represents a continuation of the monistic conception of the body and soul found in the Bible and Apocrypha. The turning point toward a dualistic ideal of body and soul in the Sage's world view began in the first half of the second century CE, following the end of the Second Rebellion and Hadrian's Decree. We must emphasize that when using the term dualism, we do not mean theological dualism, but rather anthropological dualism, meaning the body and soul are considered two different entities.[1]

Parallel to the existence of the Tannaitic monistic view during the first century CE, there were extreme dualistic trends in the Jewish world. The dualistic conception was expanded in the apocalyptic writings in the Apocrypha, the writings of the Judean Desert Sects, Christians, and other groups to whom Philo of Alexandria refers in his writings. The Sages that tended toward the dualistic world view never reached extreme dualism, but rather a variation of moderated dualism, whose nature will be discussed in this paper.

The question remains, how to explain the Sages' transition from monism to dualism? How can we explain the fact that parallel to the period when the

---

This is an English version of an article published in *Daat* 23: 33–63 (1989).

[1] Dualistic view conceives of a reality composed of two basic principles such as good and evil, matter and spirit. In religion it means the belief in the existence of two opposing divine powers which rule the world. Monism does not necessarily parallel monotheism, nor dualism (or pluralism)—polytheism. Even in monotheistic religions it is possible to find dualistic views. Below we will deal with anthropological dualism which perceives of man as composite of two elements: spiritual and corporeal.

Tannaitic scholars maintained a monistic world view, that extreme dualism emerged within the same natural habitat of Eretz Yisrael?

In order to show this transition from monism to dualism, we will isolate certain factors that indicate this transition, and attempt to link them to changes in the social structure. We will see that the individual's position in the social order led to the formation of a cosmology that helped define the meaning of his existence.

Body and Soul in the Apocrypha and Writings of the Judean Desert Sects

The Biblical world view is monistic.[2] Man is represented as one entity composed of body and soul. There are no Biblical references to the belief in the soul's pre-birth existence, nor are there clear statements referring to its existence after death. The term for death, *sheol*, does not reflect the belief in a separate netherworld, but rather represents death in poetic terms. In Isaiah 26:19 there is a reference to the revival of the dead, and this is even more explicit in Daniel 12:2, however, these are not directly linked to a general conception of another world.

The Biblical monistic view is also expressed in the fact that there is no distinction between rewards of the body and soul. There is no sentence in the Bible referring to the soul after death. Reward and punishment are only a matter of this world, not the world to come (Urbach, 1975: 216). In the Bible we do not find a structured theology that deals with death and life after death. There are only a few subtle hints about the survival of the soul. The general orientation is of worldly existence with reward and punishment in this world.

The lack of a clear Biblical conception of the fate of the soul after death, allowed for the simultaneous existence of different theories during the post-Biblical period. These interpretations were based on the same Biblical sources, and still remained more or less within the limits of Jewish society. In the early Apocryphal texts, there are limited references to body and soul; however there are no real differences between the ideas expressed in them and in the Bible. In the books Tobit, Judith and Ben Sira, considered by many scholars to be from the Persian or Hellenistic Period, there are no signs of sectarianism, and

---

[2]   The biblical conception will be described in brief because it is not the focus of this article; for a more in depth study of this idea see Rubin (1977:68–79).

the beliefs regarding death do not differ from the Bible.[3] In 2 Maccabees, we first find a clear belief in afterlife and future rewards for those who die in battle: "He (Judah Maccabee) acted quite rightly and properly, bearing in mind the resurrection... and having regard to the splendour of the gracious reward which is reserved for those who have fallen sleep in goodliness—a holy and pious consideration..." (2 Maccabees 12: 43–45).[4]

It is possible that the turning point can be found in The Wisdom of Solomon, which scholars link to the Ptolemaic Period. In this text, the Biblical fundamentals are present, but it is also possible to identify elements of Greek thought, which makes the distinction between matter and spirit. Flusser (1958)[5] found that the author of The Wisdom of Solomon (9:15) incorporated the dualistic concept in the verse, "for a corruptible body weigheth down the soul, and the earthly form lieth heavy on the mind that is full of cares." We find similar ideas with Plato in Phaedo: "And, my friend, we must believe that the corporeal is burdensome and heavy and earthly and visible. And such a soul is weighed down by this and dragged back into the visible world..." (81c).

In the late Apocrypha, and especially the apocalyptic literature, and the writings of the Judean Desert Sects we find the primary turning point. From the first century BCE to the first century CE, the Judean Desert Sects adopted the view that the course of history was predetermined and will be completed with the end of days. In the End of Days the "reign of wickedness" will be destroyed, and the People of Israel will be freed from the yoke of the Gentiles. Before the end of days, God will choose a special group that will be saved from the tribulation, and become the nucleus of the future society (Licht, 1970). Constant preparedness for the end of days explains the way of life and organization of the Judean Desert Sects, their attitude toward the body, stringent observance of Jewish Law, abstinence from worldly possessions, and rigid social solidarity. In some sects there was even celibacy and a rigid ascetic way of life.

In the Book of Enoch (1:8–9:22), we find the belief in a world of souls in the far West, where souls in limbo await the Day of Judgment.[6] A later text 2 Enoch, which was written around the time of the destruction of the Second

---

3   See for example Tobit 3:1–16; 4:3–5; Judith 16:17; Ben Sira 41:4; 31:16–17; 35:17–18; 41:11.

4   See also 2 Macabees 7:13–14 about the belief in resurrection of the dead, and Albeck (1959: 21–22).

5   In Wisdom of Solomon (3:5, 4:6) we find the belief in reward and punishment in the world to come: the evil will be destroyed and the righteous will have eternal happiness. This is the opinion of Zeligmann (1958). However, Urbach (1975: 204) thinks that the author is more Jewish than Platonic.

6   See Grintz (1953).

Temple, refers to a paradise "for the righteous, who suffer offense in their life," and Gehenna "for the dishonest that work godless things on earth." In this way, reward and punishment are transferred from this world to the next. According to this conception, the soul does not return to the body in the world to come. Instead, the soul remains in a state of eternity (2 Enoch, 8:1–2; 9:1; 10:1–6; 40:12; 42:1–3). This text also introduces the idea of the soul's preexistence, which means that the soul exists separate from the body (10:7–8).[7]

4 Ezra, a Pharisaic text, describes the "treasures" where all the souls of the righteous are gathered after the death of their bodies, while the souls of the evil wander in affliction (70:80–88). The text also describes the process of resurrection and the way the souls return from the Heavenly "treasure" to their body (4 Ezra 4:41–42). Despite the fact that the body is supposed to rise and be revived, the attitude towards this in the text is negative. The author of this text (4:36) and the author of 2 Baruch (21–22) believe that Adam's sin led to the *a priori* determination of how many human's would be born. When this number will be completed, the end of days will arrive, and the time will come for renewal in the world to come. 2 Baruch adds that between this world and the world to come, the Messiah will come and the dead will be revived, the righteous will get their reward, and the evil their punishment.

Body and Soul in the Writings of Philo and Josephus Flavius

Upon a different backdrop, dualistic ideas can also be found in the writings of Philo of Alexandria, whose origins are Stoic-Platonic (Dodds, 1964: 208). These ideas were held among educated Jews in Alexandria. Philo maintained that there was a complete separation between body and soul (e.g. *De Specialbus Legibus* 1:18). Similar to Plato, he distinguishes between three components of man: the physical body; the animal soul, which is tied to the body; and the intellect, which is the divine part of the soul. The body is mortal, but the soul is immortal.[8] The intellect in the soul is an independent entity linked to pure intellect, and part of the Platonic world of ideas. Its ability to acquire ideas is proof of its divine origins, and a sign of the soul's preexistence. The status of

---

[7]   Urbach (1975: 242) maintains that the idea of preexistence in Enoch is different from the Greek philosophical concept. In his opinion, the idea in Enoch does not come from the concept of the opposition between matter and spirit because the spirit that descends to the body does not lose its status. Urbach, more than other scholars, usually finds similarities between the Sages' views and Apocryphal writings.

[8]   See: Plato, *Timaeus* 90. Compare to Philo, *De Opificio Mundi* 134–135. See also Plato's *Phaedo*, and compare to Philo, *De Gigantibus* 12–13.

man's soul is the status of the Supreme Power in the cosmos, by which man passes from the material world to the intellectual world (*De Opificio Mundi* 67, 122, 136, 141, and Urbach, 1975: 234; 248–250).

According to Philo, man's body is not created by God. Rather, man's creation is attributed to someone else ("Let us make man..." Genesis 1:26), because God is a source of good, and nothing bad, like man's body, can come from Him. The soul strives to be released from the body where it dwells. It has no interest in living in this world, but rather in what preceded this life, and what will proceed it (Wolfson, 1970: vol. 1, 231–270).

According to this dualistic conception, there is no complete reward or punishment in this world. Physical external good is not true goodness, because real good cannot dwell in the body. The reward in this world, guaranteed by the Torah to one that does good, is interpreted by Philo to be promises of spiritual goodness in this world, or eternal life (*De Virtutigus* 35, 187; *De Praemiis et Poenis* 1, 2; 1, 7; 4, 22; and Wolfson, 1970: vol. 2, 185–186).

The writings of Josephus Flavius also reflect the views of his period, which include both moderated dualism and extreme dualism. A position of moderate dualism is expressed in his speech at Jotapata, where he explains why he refuses to commit suicide. This position does not degrade the body, nor see a need to separate the body from soul (*Wars* 3. 8:5). However, when he describes Eleazer Ben Yair's speech on Massada, in which he attempts to convince the besieged to commit suicide, he quotes an extreme dualistic position:

> that is life, that is calamity to men, and not death; for this last affords our souls their liberty, and sends them by a removal into their own place of purity... for while souls are tied down to a mortal body... they are themselves dead; for the union of what is divine to what is mortal is disagreeable... Only after the soul leaves the body, it continues invisible, indeed, to the eye of man, as... does God himself... they then go everywhere and foretell many futures beforehand (*Wars*, 7. 8:7).

This position is similar to that of Philo and the apocalyptic literature, which despite their inexplicit statements about the negation of the body, relate to the soul with great importance, and implicitly negate the body.

Josephus Flavius discusses the views of the Essenes, Pharisees, and Sadducees, which we will briefly review for the purpose of our discourse. Flavius associates the Essenes with the views of the apocalyptic writings: The Essenes believed that bodies deteriorate, but souls live forever. Souls are forced into bodies, and leave them gladly. However, the writings of the Essenes deviate from the ideas of the apocalyptic writings (except for 2 Enoch) and the Judean Desert Sects. According to the Essenes, though the soul lives forever, the dead are not revived and there is no Messianic belief (*Antiquities* 18. 1:5; *Wars* 2. 8:10–11).

The Sadducees, according to Josephus Flavius, believed that the soul disappears with the body. They reject the immortality of the soul, and future reward and punishment (*Antiquities* 18. 1:4; *Wars* 2. 8:14). The Pharisees, in contrast, believed in the soul's immortality, the revival of the righteous dead, and also that evil souls "are sentenced to eternal suffering." The soul comes from the highest source and returns to it after death (*Antiquities* 18. 1:3; *Wars* 2. 8:14). The concept of the afterlife was apparently accepted by the Pharisees during the Hasmonean Period (Moore, 1927, vol. 2: 314). Baer (1955: 53–55) maintains that the theory of requital was formulated during the early Hasmonean Period, but he tends to precede it to the pre-Hasmonean Period.

Body and Soul in Talmudic Literature

The Sages never developed a single unified methodological tractate regarding the nature of the soul and life after death. The absence of a dogmatic theology allowed for the existence of a variety of views. Below we survey the Sages' views, and the evolution of their ideas from the early Tannaitic generations to the last Amoraic generations. We will emphasize the social reasons that led to changes in ideology. We begin our discussion by clarifying the term "soul" and its synonyms. We will continue with a discussion on the Sages' conception of the body-soul relationship, in dualistic or monistic terms, and will see how their views of body and soul reflect changes in their attitudes toward the soul's preexistence, postexistence, and reward and punishment in this world or the world to come. In essence, when the body and soul are considered a single entity, there is no preexistence or postexistence of the soul, and thus no reward or punishment after death. However, the more dualistic a view of the body-soul relationship, we will find a belief in the soul's preexistence and postexistence, and in reward and punishment in the world to come.

The Soul

The Sages employ the words *nefesh, ruah, and neshamah* as separate terms for the soul as found in the Bible. Sometimes they also use the terms *hayyah*, and *yehidah*.[9] Below are distinctions between these terms:

---

9   On the biblical distinction between these terms see: Rubin (1977: 69–73). See also Licht (1968), and Seligson (1951).

It has five names: *nefesh, neshamah, hayyah, yehidah. Nefesh* is the blood:
'For the blood is the *nefesh*'—(E.V. 'life') (Deut. 12:23). *Ruah* is so called
because it ascends and descends: thus it is written, 'Who knoweth the
ruah (E.V. 'spirit') of man wither it goeth upwards, and the ruah of the
beast wither it goeth downwards to the earth' (Eccl. 3:21)? *Neshamah* is the
breath, as people say, his breathing is good. *Hayyah* (lit. 'living): because
all the limbs are mortal, whereas this is immortal in the body. *Yehidah* (lit.
unique): because all the limbs are duplicated whereas this is unique in the
body (Genesis Rabbah 14:9).

The term *nefesh* represents the physical living side of man ("blood"). The
ruah is the element of vitality in man. *Neshamah* is the element that operates
man's breathing. The meaning of the terms, according to the Sages, is parallel to
their use in the Bible. The other terms, *hayyah*, and *yehidah* are rarely used.

In the JT Kilayim (8:4, 31c) the components of creating a fetus are discussed: "The white is from the man, from whence come the brains, bones,
and tendons. The red is from the woman, from whence come the skin, flesh,
and blood. The *ruah, nefesh* and *neshamah* come from the Holy One, Blessed
be He, and all three together are partners in making man."[10] This Midrash is
structured on a triangle: each of the partners contributes three elements. The
contribution of God is *ruah, nefesh, and neshamah*. It is implicitly assumed
that there is a difference between the three elements that God contributed.

In the continuation of the above Genesis Rabbah 14:9, Amoraic scholars
state in the name of R. Meir that "the *neshamah* fills the body, and when
man sleeps, it ascends and draws life for him from above." In this source and
others[11] it appears that the role of the *neshamah*, or *ruah*, are to operate the

---

[10] This is apparently an early version of this Baraita, because two other versions, which
seem to be much later, changed the meaning of this triangle. See: BT Niddah 31a, and
Ecclesiastes Rabbah, 5:10. The beginning of the Baraita is also found in the BT Kiddushin 30b. Other cultures possess similar traditions of the parents' "contribution" to
the child. The man is typified as provider of the "seed," whereas the woman provides the
vessel or "the earth." The man plants his seed in the symbolic earth. He also contributes
the bones (white, like the seed) and the woman the flesh (red, like blood) see Keesing
(1975: 12). In a later source, from a Midrash on Psalms 11:6, there is a statement made
in the name of R. Levi, who asks what is the difference between *ruah* and *neshamah*?
The answer is very unclear regarding *neshamah*, which is "a winged grasshopper, it is
attached to the man's spine"; or "a kind of reed filled with blood." However, in this text,
there is no definition for *ruah*. Despite the fact that this source does not provide a clear
answer, the Sages were aware that a difference exists between these terms. From this
response, we can conclude that the *neshamah* is something that operates the body, so
that if the Angel of Death removed it one would "immediately die."
[11] For example, BT Berakhot 10a, the words of R. Shimeon ben Pazzi.

body. It becomes clear that despite the theoretical distinction between these terms, they are interchangeable. R. Akiba uses the term *neshamah* to mean the man[12] and the Sages frequently interchange the terms *neshamah* and *nefesh*. For example: "To whom did David refer in the five verses beginning with 'Bless the Lord, O my soul (*nefesh*)?' He was alluding only to the Holy One Blessed be He and to the *neshamah* (soul). Just as the Holy One, Blessed be He fills the whole world, so the *neshamah* (soul) fills the entire body..." (BT Berakhot 10a) The comparisons continue in this vain throughout the Midrash. The commentator compares the term *nefesh* in the Bible with *neshamah*.[13] In a parallel source, the Midrash has the term *nefesh* instead of *neshamah*: "This *nefesh* fills the body, and the Holy One, Blessed be He fills the entire world." (Leviticus Rabbah 4:8)

Despite the fact that there is usually not a clear distinction between the use of *ruah, neshamah, and nefesh*, it still seems that *ruah* is used in the context of an entity separate from the body, for example, before it enters the body. R. Eliezer, the son of R. Yossi the Galilean, says that "all of the *ruhot* [pl. of *ruah*] are not conceived but before Him," and during man's lifetime "his *nefesh* is in God's hand." (Sifrei, Numbers, 139) This means that before it enters the body the soul is called *ruah*, and afterwards it is called *nefesh*. We also see this usage in the case of a pious man that walks in the cemetery and hears "two *ruhot* (spirits) conversing with one another." (BT Berakhot 18a)

These sources give the impression that the Sages considered the *neshamah* in service to the body and responsible for it. We also find this in the following source: "the gullet is for food, and the wind-pipe is for the voice, the liver is for anger the lungs... are for drinking... and soul is above them all. The Holy One Blessed be He said, I have made thee superior of all of them and yet thou goest forth and committest robbery and violence and sinnest!" (Leviticus Rabbah 4:4)[14] Despite the wording, there is no polarization here between the body and soul, the soul is not supreme rather it is responsible, and operates for the sake of the body even in sleep. This is in contrast to the words of Eleazar Ben Yair, as quoted by Josephus Flavius, that the soul wanders in its

---

12 "A person who deposits (money) with his friend does not want another *neshamah* (= person) to know about it, but rather the third (the Holy One, Blessed be He) that is among them," stated by R. Akiba, Sifra, Tractate Hova, 22:4.

13 See additional places where the Sages use the term *neshamah* in place of *nefesh* in the Bible: BT Shabbat 152b, and parallel sources: BT Hagigah 12b; Ecclesiastes Rabbah, 3:21; 12:7.

14 Saul Leiberman in p. 871 in the Margulies edition of Leviticus Rabbah points out regarding this midrash, that it is basically an ancient Baraita found in the Testament of the Twelve Patriarchs, The Testament of Naftali 2:8.

sleep; is in contact with God; can foresee the future; and aspires to leave the worldly suffering (Urbach, 1975: 249). This introduces us to the question of the relationship between body and soul, which we discuss below.

We can concede that the Sages theoretically distinguished between the different terms for soul, but were not strict in their usage, because in parallel sources the terms are interchangeable. From this we learn that they were not particular about distinguishing between these terms on a day to day basis, since the distinction had no practical application.

The Relationship between Body and Soul

In the discussion on the relationship between body and soul, we will see how the conception of this relationship changed from a monistic view during the early Tannaitic Period, to a moderated dualism during the Amoraic Period.

In the Tannaitic generations before the destruction of the Temple, we do not hear of any opposition between the body and soul. We find this in Leviticus Rabbah 34:3 about Hillel the Elder, who, once when concluding his studies with his disciples, walked along with them in discussion:

> His disciples asked him: "Master whither are you bound?" He answered them: "To perform a religious duty." "What," they asked, "is this religious duty?" He said to them: "To wash in the bath-house." Said they: "Is this a religious duty?" "Yes," he replied: "if the statues of Kings, which are erected in theatres and circuses, are scoured and washed by the man who is appointed to look after them, and who thereby obtains his maintenance through them... how much more I, who have been created in the Image and the Likeness, as it is written: "For in the image of God made He Man" (Gen. 9:6).

This source is not a deification of the body, rather it humbles man, who believes that his body as well as his image were created by God and both are equal (Urbach, 1975: 227).[15] Hence, we find a belief that body and soul are joined and judged together in the afterlife:

---

[15] Regarding the importance of man, who was created in God's image, see T Yevamot 8:7 see the discussion between R. Akiba and R. Eleazar ben Azariah. In the Mekhilta de R. Shimeon ben Ishmael, Tractate Bahodesh 8, a human being is compared to a human king who "entered a country and set up images of himself." In the words of Akavia ben Mahalaleel, "Whence you cameth? From a fetid drop" (Leviticus Rabbah 18.1), we do not see a rejection of the body and its subjugation to the soul, rather an expression of humility before God, because this man that comes from a "fetid drop" stands before him. See Urbach (1975: 224).

Beit Shammai say: [On the Day of Judgment] there will be three groups: one for eternal life; one for eternal shame and suffering—these are the evil people. Those who are equally good and evil, go down to Gehenna and are punished, and then ascend and are healed... And Beit Hillel say: 'Great in mercy' (Ex. 34:6)—He inclines the decision toward mercy... The Israelites who sinned and gentiles who sinned... with their bodies go down to Gehenna and are judged there for twelve months. And after twelve months their souls perish, their bodies are burned, Gehenna absorbs them, and they are turned into dirt. And the wind blows them and scatters them under the feet of the righteous... But heretics, apostates, traitors, Epicureans, those who deny the Torah, those who separate from the ways of the community... Gehenna is locked behind them, and they are judged therein for all generations... (T Sanhedrin 13:3–5).[16]

It is clear from this Baraita that body and soul is a single inseparable unit even after death. They are judged together as one entity.[17]

No real change occurred in this idea, even after the destruction of the Temple, until the second and third generation of Tannaitic scholars. In response to the question of whether immature sons of evil men have a part in the world to come (T Sanhedrin 13:1–2), there is one opinion in line with Raban Gamliel, that "neither the soul nor the body of the young are revived [in the revival of the dead], nor are they judged." This means that the body and soul were of equal status.

A source which contains a latent controversy with the *minim* (heretics) states:

It once happened to Ben Dama the son of R. Ishmael's sister that he was bitten by a serpent, and Jacob (who was a *min*), a native of Kefar Sekaniah, came to heal him, but R. Ishmael did not let him, whereupon Ben Dama said, "My

---

[16] See also *Avot de-R. Nathan* (Shechter ed.) (A) ch. 41; BT Rosh Hashana 16b. Baer (1955: 53–55) maintains that this is an ancient baraita from the early Hellenistic Period; even if the houses of Hillel and Shammai added their own versions, the basis is very ancient. Not all scholars agree with this claim. See: Avi Yona (1952: 94) and Urbach (1967: 133–141).

[17] "The Day of Judgment," whose time is not defined in this baraita, during the time of the Amoraic scholars, apparently became the day that comes at the beginning of every year. In the name of R. Yohanan it was said: "Three books are open [in heaven] on New Year, one for the thoroughly wicked, one for the thoroughly righteous and one for the intermediate. The thoroughly righteous are forthwith inscribed definitely in the book of life. The thoroughly wicked are forthwith inscribed definitely in the book of death. The doom of the intermediate is suspended from New Year till the Day of Atonement: if they deserve well they are inscribed in the book of life; if they do not deserve well they are inscribed in the book of death" (BT Rosh Hashana 16b).

brother R. Ishmael, let him, so that I may be healed by him: I will even cite
a verse from the Torah that he is to be permitted"; but he did not manage
to complete his saying, when his soul departed and he died. Whereupon
R. Ishmael exclaimed, "Happy art thou Ben Dama for thou wert pure in body
and thy soul likewise left thee in purity." (BT Avodah Zara 27b)[18]

The body is termed pure in the same way the soul is termed pure, and there
is no attempt to belittle the body. It is a fact that during this period, we do
not find any negative expressions about the body, nor do we find attempts
to place guilt on the body for sins, so as to remove sin from the soul. This
equality between body and soul is also demonstrated further in the following
well known parable in Leviticus Rabbah (4:5):

> R. Ishmael taught: This may be compared to the case of the king who had an
> orchard containing excellent early figs, and he placed there two watchmen,
> one lame and the other blind, he said to them: "Be careful with these fine
> early figs." After some days the lame man said to the blind one: "I see fine
> early figs in the orchard." Said the blind man to him: "Come let us eat them."
> "Am I then able to walk?" said the lame man. "Can I then see?" retorted the
> blind man. The lame man got astride the blind man, and thus they ate the
> early figs and sat down again each in his place. After some days the king
> came into the vineyard, and said to them: "Where are the fine early figs?" The
> blind man replied: "My lord the king can I then see?" The lame man replied:
> "My lord, the king, can I then walk?" What did the king, who was a man of
> insight, do with them? He placed the lame man astride the blind man, and
> they began to move about. Said the king to them: "Thus have you done, and
> eaten the early figs." Even so will the Holy One, Blessed be He, in the time to
> come, say to the soul: "Why hast thou sinned before Me?" and the soul will
> answer: "O Master of the Universe, it is not I that sinned, but the body it is
> that sinned. Why, since leaving it, I am like a clean bird flying through the
> air. As for me, how have I sinned?" God will also say to the body: "Why hast
> thou sinned before Me?" and the body will reply: "O Master of the universe,
> not I have sinned, the soul it is that has sinned. Why, since it left me, I am cast
> about like a stone thrown upon the ground. Have I then sinned before Thee?"
> What will the Holy one Blessed be He do to them? He will bring the soul and
> force it into the body, and judge both as one.[19]

<hr>

[18] See alternative readings in Dikdukei Sofrim, cf. T Hullin 2:22–23 and JT Avodah Zara
2:2, 40d–41a.

[19] Compare a shortened version in Mekhilta de-R. Shimeon Bar Yohai, Tractate Beshalah,
and in the Mekhilta de-R. Ishmael, Tractate Shirata 5. See also the BT Sanhedrin 91a-b.
In Midrash Tanaim on Numbers (Hoffman edition, p. 183) there is a similar tradition:
"on the Day of Judgment, the Holy One Blessed be He calls to the spirit (*ruah*) from
the heavens and raises the body from the earth, and they are judged as one."

Here we have a continuation of the same Biblical concept of body and soul as one psycho-physical entity.[20]

A sense of dualism increasingly develops after the period of Bar Kokhva's rebellion, and especially during the fifth generation of Tannaitic scholars. During this period, the soul gains in importance over the body. According to sources, apparently Amoraic in origin, the body and soul of man were not created simultaneously as one unit, rather; "at the first hour it was conceived... In the fourth-formed, in the fifth-filled with the soul."[21] The fact that there are three partners in man,[22] his father and mother, who give him his body, and God, who gives the soul, does not necessarily imply that the soul is of higher importance than the body. However, this distinction creates a basis for the importance of the soul over the body. In Ecclesiastes Rabbah (5:10) we read:

> When its time comes to die, the Hole One, Blessed be He removes his portion, and leaves the portion contributed by father and mother before them, and they weep. The Holy One, Blessed be He says to them: "Why do you weep? Have I taken anything of yours? I have only taken what belongs to me!" They say before Him: "Lord of the Universe, so long as your portion was mingled with ours, our portion was preserved from the maggots and worms; but now that Thou hast taken away Thy portion from ours, behold our portion is cast away and given to maggot and worm."

It is clear from this passage that the soul, which is from a divine source, is of a higher order. In the same source R. Judah the Patriarch presents a parable and ends with similar words: "so long as the soul is within the human being he is preserved; but when he dies he is for the maggot and worm."

This deep change in values, that began in the attitude towards the body-soul relationship, can also be found in the Mekhilta de-R. Ishmael (Tractate

---

[20]   The positive relationship to the body reflected by Hillel the Elder is also found in the later generations of Tanaitic scholars. Sarai says to Hagar: "Happy art thou to be united to so a holy body" (Genesis Rabbah, 45:3). R. Yossi ben Halaphta was named "the Holy Body" (JT Yoma 8:1, 44d; Taanit 1:6, 64d). A discussion on the Sages' attitudes toward the body and the Zoroastrian religious attitudes, as they appear in the sources during the Sasanid Period, see Urbach (1975: 249–252).

[21]   *Avot de-R. Nathan* (B), ch. 42, and compare Genesis Rabbah 14:8 and Pirkei de-R. Eliezer, Ch. 12. See also Genesis Rabbah 8:1; BT Sanhedrin 38b, about a similar Amoraic tradition of Rav Aha bar Hanina (third Amoraic generation in Palestine). In the printed versions BT it is written R. Yohanan bar Hanina.

[22]   See note 10. Urbach (1975: 220).

Shirata).[23] In this source, there is a new interpretation of R. Ishmael's parable on the lame and blind men, which awards the soul a higher status:

> Antoninus asked our Teacher, the Saint (R. Judah the Patriarch): "After a man has died and his body ceased to be, does God then make him stand trial?" He answered him: "Rather than ask about the body which is impure, ask me about the soul that is pure." To give a parable for this, to what is this like? To the following: A king of flesh and blood had a beautiful orchard. The King placed in it two guards, one of who was lame and the other blind..."

It is the same parable, but R. Judah the Patriarch, two generations after R. Ishmael, relates to the body as impure and the soul as pure. From this context, it is evident that the body gained a negative value and the soul a positive one. This is to say, each is clearly separate from and opposed to the other. R. Hiyya, from R. Judah the Patriarch's generation, places full responsibility on the soul, unlike R. Ishmael, who placed equal responsibility on the body and soul.

We read in Leviticus Rabbah 4:5:

> R. Hiyya taught: This may be compared to the priest who had two wives, one the daughter of a priest, and the other the daughter of an Israelite, and handed to them dough of terumah, and they rendered it unclean. Said he to them: "Who made the dough unclean?" Each said that the other had made it unclean. What did the priest do? He let the daughter of the Israelite alone, and began taking to task the daughter of the priestly family. Said she to him: "My lord priest, why are you letting the daughter of the Israelite alone, and taking me to task? Have you not handed it (i.e. the dough) to both of us alike?" Said he to her: "She is the daughter of an Israelite, and is not trained (in the laws appertaining to terumah) from her father's house; but you are so trained from your father's house, and for that reason I am leaving her alone, and taking you to task." Even so will it be in the Time to Come. The soul and the body will be standing for judgment, what will the Holy One, Blessed be He do? He will let the body alone, and take the soul to task. The latter will say before Him: "O Lord of the Universe, we have sinned both of us as one; why dost Thou let the body alone, and take me to task?" He will answer her: "The body is from the lower (earthly) regions, from a place where they sin, but thou art from the upper (celestial) regions, from a place where they do not sin. Therefore do I let the body alone, and take you to task."[24]

---

[23]   See in note 19 the parallel sources to the Mekhilta. In BT Sanhedrin 91a-b, Antoninus calls the body and soul "impure body" and "pure soul."

[24]   Urbach (1975: 793, n.91) says that in two manuscripts, the statement was not made in the name of R. Hiyya, but rather in the name of R. Levi, from the third Amoraic generation. Cf. also the Midrash Hagadol on Leviticus (Rabinowitz edition p. 86). However, the same idea could also have been stated by R. Hiyya according to the

There is a vast expanse between the views "He will bring the soul and force it into the body and judge both as one," (R. Ishmael) and "let the body alone and take you (the soul) to task." (R. Hiyya). The former, we define as monism. It treats the body and soul as one entity. The latter views the body and soul as two separate entities and can be defined as dualism. Our question remains, what led to this change in values? We will discuss this later.

Despite the supremacy of the soul, we do not find statements that degrade the body, nor demand its mortification. Rather, we find the position that the soul has a higher status and is obligated to care for the body, because it draws vitality from above for man, according to R. Meir (Genesis Rabbah 14:9). Or, as R. Judah said to Antoninus: "The soul serves the body as salt on meat, preventing it from becoming rancid" (BT Sanhedrin 91b), and other similar obligations that come from its status (Leviticus Rabbah, 4:4).

A distinct turn toward more extreme dualism was taken in the second century CE (third generation of Amoraim). The soul was no longer considered the servant of the body, rather the body the servant of the soul. The body is responsible for man's evil deeds, and he is responsible for the soul's purity.

> R. Shmuel Ben Nahman taught it in the name of R. Abdimi of Haifa: ...The Holy One, Blessed be He said to man: "See, I am pure and My abode is pure and My ministers are pure and the soul I have given you is pure. If you return it to Me as I am giving it to you, it will be well, but if not, I shall throw it away." (Leviticus Rabbah 18:1)[25]

That is to say, the body is responsible for returning the soul in a state of purity, and if the body sins then it defiles the soul.[26] It is explicitly stated in an Amoraic passage that in the world to come man's soul will testify against him (BT Hagigah 16a), while from R. Ishmael's parable we learned that God will not receive testimony of body or soul against one another. Here, however, we witness a turning point. This reflects a tension that is perceived between body and soul that they have grown apart and are in opposition.

Nevertheless, the soul does not strive to leave the body after death. In the name of R. Levi it was said that the soul hovers over the body for three days, and maintains that it will return to it (JT Moed Katan 3:5, 82b; JT Yevamot 16:1, 15b; BT Shabbat 151b).

---

change in view concerning the body soul relationship, which was introduced by R. Judah the Patriarch during his discussion with Antoninus.

[25] Cf. BT Niddah 30b, the passage is in the name of the school of R. Ishmael. Compare also to the parable in BT Menachot 99b, about the man who gave a bird to his servant.

[26] See BT Berakhot 60b regarding the purity of the soul: "the soul you gave me is pure," and also Leviticus Rabbah 4:8.

The problem of the body-soul relationship intensifies with the discourse on the status of the soul before birth, and after death. The scholars asked whether there is preexistence and postexistence of the soul. If the soul exists before birth and after death, what is the nature of its independent existence?

The Status of the Soul before Birth[27]

An additional index of the move from monism to dualism in the views of the Sages can be measured in the changes in attitude regarding the status of the soul before birth and after death. The first Tannaitic scholars do not grant the soul any separate existence before birth. However, by the generation of the Amoraic scholars, there is an acceptance of the soul's preexistence. This ideological transformation occurred simultaneously with the change in the conception of the body-soul relationship.

The Sages dealt with the issue of man, who was made in "God's image." He [R. Akiba] used to say: "Beloved [of God] is man for he was created in the image of God." (M Avot 3:14) This saying represents the essence of Rabbinic thinking.[28] The words of Akaviah ben Mahalaleel allow us to conclude that man, who was created in God's image, was created as one entity, body and soul. Reflect upon three things and thou wilt not come within the power of transgression: know whence thou art come, and whither thou art going, and before whom thou wilt in future render account and reckoning. "Whence thou art come"—from a fetid drop; "and whither thou art going"—to a place of dust worms and maggots, "and before Whom thou wilt in future render account and reckoning"—before the supreme King of kings, the Holy One, Blessed be He (M Avot 3:1). According to Urbach, this Tanna does not refer to body and soul, but speaks of a whole person, without any dualism, who is responsible, and is judged for his actions, and this is the same man who comes from a fetid drop (even though he is created in God's image), and goes to the place of maggots and worms. God himself designed the form of man, both his body and soul, and this is what is written in a Tannaitic Midrash: "out of a drop of fluid he gives to a man a son who is the image of his father." (Mekhilta de-R. Ishmael, Tractate Shirata [Ch. 8]) This conception is the polar opposite of Philo, who maintained that God did not participate in the creation of the body, and transferred it to others, because God is good and could not possibly make something evil." (De Opificio Mundi 67, 134–141)

---

[27]   This is based on Urbach (1975: 253–254).
[28]   Cf. Ben Azzai's words in Sifra, Kedoshim 4:12, and JT Nedarim 9:4, 41c.

Urbach (1975: 242–243) systematically proves that among the Tannaitic scholars, there was not one who held that the embryo is an independent physical entity, with an independent soul. Since it is not considered as having an independent soul, it is not a separate being. In the terminology of later Amoraic scholars we would say that according to the Tannaitic scholars, the embryo is regarded as a "thigh of its mother." This conception is expressed in the Tannaitic halakha. For example:

> If a woman suffers hard labor in travail, the child must be cut up in her womb and brought out piecemeal, for her life take precedence over its life; if its greater part has [already] come forth, it must not be touched, for the (claim of one) life can not supersede [that of another] life (M Ohalot 7:6).[29]

> If a [pregnant] woman were sentenced to death, they do not wait for her until she shall have given birth, [but] if she were sitting on the birth-stool, they must wait for her till she shall have given birth (M Arachin 1:4).[30]

We understand these texts to mean that the fetus is an essential part of its mother, and until it is born it does not posses its own soul.

However, during the end of the Tannaitic period, the issue arises of when the soul is joined with the body. In a discourse between Antoninus and R. Judah the Patriarch, Antoninus asks R. Judah:

> "When is the soul planted in man?" "When he leaves his mothers womb," replied he. "Leave meat without salt for three days" said he, "will it not putrefy?"—"rather, when it is conceived," our teacher (R. Judah) agreed with him…" (Genesis Rabbah, 34:10)[31]

R. Judah the Patriarch presents the traditional position of the Sages, as expressed in the Tannaitic halakha, whereas Antoninus presents another position, by which a soul is given to the embryo at conception. This idea is increasingly accepted along with the trend toward dualistic ideologies that presume the preexistence of the soul. This discussion between R. Judah and Antonimus represents a specific aspect of the polarity between monism and dualism in the body-soul relationship.

---

[29] See also T Gittin 4:7; T Makkot 2:5.
[30] See also T Arachin 1:4 Sifrei Zuta 35:22 and M Hullin 4:3.
[31] Cf. BT Sanhedrin 91a-b, and an alternative reading in Dikdukei Sofrim.

According to the Amoraic scholars, a separate world of souls exists, which consists of souls before birth waiting to be put into the body. The soul enters the body at the moment of conception and functions independently in the body. This is what we learn from "a tractate on the formation of the child," according to the school of R. Yohanan, which is dealt with at length in the Midrash Tanhuma.[32] The text tells that at the time of conception,

> the Holy One, Blessed be He hints to an angel responsible for pregnancy and his name is Laila (night), and the Holy One, Blessed be He, says to him: "Know that this is the night that a man was created from [such a] seed and be careful with that drop and put it in your hand, and scatter it on the threshing floor into three hundred sixty-five parts... Immediately, the Holy One, Blessed be He, told the angel responsible for souls and said to him: "bring me [such a] soul from the Garden of Eden... at this time the Holy One, Blessed be He says to the soul [enter] into this drop in which is in this certain hand... (Tanhuma Pekudei, ch. 3)[33]

It is clear from this that the spirit is given to man from the moment of conception, and not at birth. However, as the "completion" of the embryo is only after forty days, because after forty days he has "form"—as stated by R. Yohanan ben Zakkai (Genesis Rabbah 32:5)—so the soul is only completed after forty days, because R. Yohanan and R. Eleazar maintain that "Torah was given in forty days, and the soul is formed in forty (days)." (BT Menahot 99b)[34] R. Yohanan should have stated that a soul is created in forty days, because according to the Tannaitic scholars, a woman who has a miscarriage on the fortieth day is not unclean from a birth (M Niddah 3:7), only a miscarriage from the forty-first day makes her unclean from a birth, while according to R. Yohanan, the soul of an embryo exists at the time of conception. Therefore, according to R. Yohanan, the soul enters at the time of conception, but it is

---

[32] The source is quoted here with many omissions. See a similar version in Yellinek's "Beit Hamidrash," Part 1, pp. 153–155, and a different version on pp. 155–158. These sources are relatively late, but they reflect the opinion of R. Yohanan and members of his generation. See Urbach (1975: 245).

[33] This is also the opinion of R. Hanina bar Papa (Third Amoraic generation in Palestine) BT Niddah 16b. See also his opinion in Niddah 31a. In BT Sanhedrin 96a, R. Yohanan speaks of an angel by the name of Laila (night). See also R. Yohanan and Reish Lakish on the creation of man in Leviticus Rabbah 14:6.

[34] The opinion of Rav becomes clear on the background of R. Yohanan ben Zakkai, Rav says: "forty days before the creation of an embryo, a divine voice comes out and says: 'daughter of so and so, go to so and so.'" (BT Sota 2a, and BT Sanhedrin 22a) This means at the time of conception a declaration is made, because forty days before the "formation" is the conception.

"completed," i.e., achieves a form, by the fortieth day.[35] This idea that the embryo is an independent entity is also expressed by R. Yohanan in his halakha. He maintains that "the embryo is not regarded as part of the thigh of his mother," (BT Temurah 19a and 25a) meaning the embryo is an independent body and not considered part of its mother's body.

In R. Yohanan's approach we find a balanced relationship between the body and soul: both receive equal care in the hands of God. This is moderated dualism, which is very different from the extreme dualism of Plato or Philo. Perhaps this moderated dualism emerged from a discourse with these approaches. This balanced attitude is even more clear in the continuation of the same midrash. At first the soul refuses to enter the body. It maintains: "Why do you want to put me into that sinful drop, after all I am holy and pure and I am cut from your honored image?" Immediately the Holy One, Blessed be He answers the soul: "the place where I will put you will be more beautiful than the place you live in, and from the moment I created you, you were intended for that drop." According to this passage, mankind exists by maintaining the image of God within man. The soul does not strive to be freed from the sinful human body, because this world is more beautiful than the world from where the soul came.

In the spirit of moderated dualism, this idea enables the development of the conception that the ideal world is one in which the embryo is in his mother's womb. Upon the entry of the soul into the "drop," begins the Golden Age, which ends with birth. R. Simlai (second Amoraic generation in Palestine) delivered the following discourse:

> A light burns above its (embryo's) head and it looks and sees from one end of the world to the other... and there is no time in which a man enjoys greater happiness than in those days... It is also taught all the Torah from the beginning to end... as soon as it sees the light, an angel approaches, slaps it on its mouth and causes it to forget all the Torah completely... (BT Niddah 30b).

Neither the former world, nor the world into which man will be born, nor the world to come, is as idealized as the beginning of life. While still an embryo the soul is not abstract and disembodied, yet it is not part of an active body that might sin. This period is forgotten by man. Why is this so? Because according

---

[35]   According to R. Yohanan, the Torah was given in "the fortieth day" (BT Menachot 97b), which means all the forty days that Moses went up to the heavens, the Torah existed, however, it was just given on the fortieth day. So also the soul exists with the embryo all forty days but is only "formed" on the fortieth day.

to the Sages, man must act in this world according to his choice. If he would remember what he learned, he would not have free choice.

The ideas of R. Yohanan and his generation on the creation of the child existed alongside their perception regarding preexistence of the soul. We have seen according to Urbach, that among the Tannaitic scholars there was no idea of the soul's preexistence, and that this idea appeared first among the Amoraic scholars (Urbach, 1975: 232–242). However, the Amoraic scholars' view of this idea is very different from the Greek philosophers. According to the Amoraic scholars, the soul does not lower itself from a higher place when it enters the body. Nevertheless, their evaluation of the body-soul relationship also differs from the Tannaitic scholars, because in their estimation greater responsibility was placed on the soul. According to Urbach, during the second Amoraic generation (in the second half of the third century), for the first time there is a clear conception of the soul's preexistence. This occurred at the same time as the development of the dualistic idea and parallel to the theory of R. Yohanan concerning the creation of the child's body separately from the giving of his soul. Perhaps in opposition to Urbach, we can say that the buds of these ideas already appeared during the last Tannaitic generation parallel to the turning point that began with the opinion of R. Judah the Patriarch in his argument with Antoninus.[36] At any rate, R. Yohanan stated in the same Midrash Tanhuma: "You should know that all of the souls that have come into existence since Adam, and which will be till the end of the world, were created in the six days of creation, all were in the Garden of Eden and at the giving of the Torah." R. Shimeon ben Lakish, one of R. Yohanan's contemporaries, discusses seven heavens. The seventh heaven is called "Araboth" in which there are "right and Judgment and Righteousness the treasures of life… peace, and…blessing, the souls of the righteous and the spirits (*ruhot*) and souls (*neshamot*), which are yet to be born and the dew wherewith the Holy One, Blessed be He, will hereafter revive the dead." (BT Hagigah 12b)

These ideas are well known in the third Amoraic generation and are heard, for example, in the words of R. Yehoshua of Siknin in the name of R. Levi (Genesis Rabbah, 8:7) and in the words of Abbahu in the name of

---

[36] In *Avot de-Rabbi Nathan* (A), ch. 34, R. Nehemia (4th Tannaitic generation) said that God showed Adam "all the generations destined to come forth from him standing and rejoicing before him as it were." The Tanah R. Joshua ben Korhah said that God showed Adam "every generation and its teachers… every generation and its leaders… every generation and its heroes, every generation and its sinners… (and he told him that) in this generation so and so was destined to be king, in that generation so and so was destined to be a sage."

R. Shmuel bar Nahman (Midrash Tanhuma, Nizavim (ch. 3).[37] This approach places great responsibility for man's behavior on the soul, because it is above all of the body organs, while in the parable of the blind and lame of R. Ishmael, the responsibility was equally divided between the body and soul.

The Status of the Soul after Death

One of the principle beliefs of the Sages is the continued existence of the soul after death. In the period of the first Tannaitic scholars, we find that the concept of life after death possesses elements of a quasi worldly life where the body and soul are united. However, in the later Tannaitic generations, the idea emerges of a special spiritual existence for the soul.

"After death" in the ideology of the Sages is a complex concept that lacks any defined time frame. The ideas that are tied to this concept relate to the fate of the body and soul in the short run, beginning at the moment of death, until the long run, the "End of Days." Incorporated in this are ideas of "Garden of Eden" and "Gehenna," "The Hereafter," "The Days of the Messiah," "The World to Come," and "Revival of the Dead." It is difficult to formulate a single clear picture for the words of the Sages, and connect these concepts into one eschatology. We will attempt, at first, to ascertain the ideas related to the fate of the body and soul immediately after death.

One of the ancient sources that refer to the concepts Garden of Eden and Gehenna is the statement by R. Yohanan ben Zakkai, who was crying at the time of his death. He explained to his disciples the reason for his tears: "There are two ways before me, one leading to Paradise and the other to Gehenna, and I do not know by which I shall be taken, shall I not weep?" (BT Berakhot 28b)[38] This assumption of two paths was generally accepted, however, it is unclear how man reaches the Garden of Eden or Gehenna, with body and soul or just his soul.

One approach maintains that man arrives with both body and soul. We have already heard the opinion of Akaviah ben Mahalaleel (M Avot 3:1) that the whole man, body and soul, is presented to God after his death. Also, according to the House of Shammai and the House of Hillel (T Sanhedrin 13:3–5),[39] man's body and soul stand together for judgment before God on the Day of Judgment (whenever that may be) and are judged on the basis of man's actions. The evil "go down to Gehenna and are judged there for twelve

---

[37] Cf. Targum Yerushalmi to Deut. 29:14 and Genesis Rabbah 24:4.
[38] See also *Avot de-Rabbi Nathan* (A), ch. 25.
[39] See Finkelstein (1950: 212–238).

month… their souls perish and their bodies are burned," while the righteous are granted "eternal life." Also, R. Akiva (M Eduyyoth 2:10), R. Judah (Genesis Rabbah 6:6), and R. Yitzchak (BT Shabbat 152a), maintain that man's body is judged at the time that his soul stands judgment, and the Amoraic scholars R. Joshua ben Levi and Reish Lakhish agree (BT Eruvin 19a). R. Eleazar says the righteous are received by a band of angels with sayings of peace on their lips, while the evil are greeted by bands of angels with sayings of rebuke (BT Kethuvot 104a).

According to the second approach, the soul is disconnected from the body and rises above, while the body remains below in the grave. This view is described in the following Baraita: Concerning the bodies of the righteous men, He saith: "He shall come in peace; they shall repose on their resting-place;" (Isaiah 57:2) and concerning the souls He saith: "Yet will the soul of my lord be bound in the bond of life with the Lord thy God:" (1 Samuel 25:29) concerning the bodies of the wicked, He saith: "There is no peace, saith the Lord, unto the wicked;" (Isaiah 48:42) and concerning the souls of the wicked, He saith: "And the souls of thy enemies will be hurled away, as out of the middle of the sling." (1 Samuel 25:29) We have learned: R. Eliezer (son of R. Yossi the Galilean) said: the souls of righteous men are deposited underneath the throne of honour and the wicked are crowded together until they are crushed (BT Shabbat 152b).[40]

According to an Amoraic source, the treasure is found in the highest of the heavens that is called "Araboth" (Hagigah 12b).[41] The fate of wicked souls is that they "continue to be imprisoned (lit. muzzled),"[42] according to R. Eliezer (BT Shabbat 152b), or they "descend to Gehenna" according to R. Yossi ben Halaphta (Ecclesiastes Rabbah 3:21). This is also the opinion of some Palestinian Amoraic scholars such as R. Abbahu (BT Shabbat 152b), and Babylonian Amoraic scholars such as R. Yosseph and R. Zeira (BT Bava Metzia 93b). In Babylonia, Rabbah asked R. Nahman:

"How is it with the souls of men who are neither righteous nor wicked?" He answered: in the name of Samuel, "the souls of the ordinary men and of the wicked are given over to the angel whose name is Dumah, the souls of the ordinary men are given rest, the others are not given rest" (BT Shabbat 152b).

---

[40] See Dikdukei Sofrim, and cf. Sifrei Numbers 139 and Sifrei Deut. 344. Compare also to R. Jose ben Halaphta in Ecclesiastes Rabbah 3:21.

[41] The treasure is also called "bundle of life," for example, see BT Shabbat 153b based on the verse from 2 Samuel 25:29, "yet the soul of my Lord shall be bound in the bundle of life with the Lord thy God."

[42] On the imprisonment (zomemot) of the wicked soul see Lieberman (1965: 499–501).

According to the second approach, that the soul leaves the body, when does the soul disengage and rise? In the opinion of R. Abbahu, "for full twelve months the body is in existence and the soul ascends and descends, after twelve months the body ceases to exist and the soul ascends but descends nevermore." (BT Shabbat 152b) R. Levi claims that the soul hovers only three days over the body but when it sees that the body is changed and that it cannot return to it, the soul departs (JT Moed Katan 3:5, 82b).[43] R. Hisda, their contemporary in Babylonia, maintains that "man's soul mourns for him for seven whole days." (BT Shabbat 152a)

The first approach is held by the Tannaitic scholars from the first generations, as well as Sages from later generations. The second approach is accepted by the fourth generation of Tannaitic scholars, the generation that lived during and after the Hadrianic Decrees. One can assume that these two approaches parallel the traditions of monism and dualism. The first, where the body and soul are judged together, reflects the tendency toward monism in the first generations of Tannaitic scholars. The second approach, by which the soul departs the body, parallels the dualism found in the period after the Hadrianic Decrees.

Until now we have generally discussed the different approaches toward the fate of the body and soul after death, but what is the nature of the soul's postexistence? What happens to the soul in the Garden of Eden or Gehenna?

In this context, the ideas are even vaguer. From the period of Ben-Zomma, we hear the distinction between the Days of the Messiah, the World to Come, and the Revival of the Dead, which are not identical nor overlapping periods (M Berakhot 1:5).[44] Moore (1927: vol. 2, 387ff) already has proven that at an early time in history the terms "Days of the Messiah," "the World to Come," and "The Hereafter," were considered one period. At a later stage, there began a split in the terminology, and each term related to a different period: there is "the Days of the Messiah," which is a first stage in the "Golden Age" of Israel; afterwards comes the stage of the general "Revival of the Dead," when mankind stands for judgment before God; and finally comes the "World to Come." Moore says that sometimes the World to Come was before the Revival

---

[43] See also JT Yevamot 16:3, 15b; BT Shabbat 151b; Genesis Rabbah 100; Leviticus Rabbah, 18:1; and Lieberman's note p.875 in Margulies ed.

[44] Compare with the words of the "Tanah R. Yose ben Kisma in M Avot 6:9; Sifrei, Deut. 34, and BT Sota 21a; R. Judah in T Arachin 2:7, and in BT Arachin 13b; see the ancient prayer: "There is none to be compared to the Lord our God in this world, and there is none beside thee, our King in the world to come; there is none but thee our Redeemer in the days of Messiah, and there is none like thee in the revival of the dead." See also BT Shabbat 113b.

of the Dead, when it referred to the transition of the individual from death to redemption. During this period, righteous souls go to the Garden of Eden, and evil souls to Gehenna.

Finkelstein (1951: xxxii; 217–219) does not see a historical progression here. He claims that two schools of thought existed: one that the soul descends to the underworld with the body and waits for redemption. According to this view, the World to Come relates to the period after the Revival of the Dead. The second, the soul ascends to the heavens after man's death, and is judged by God. The World to Come relates to the existence between death and the revival of the dead. In the later literature, Finkelstein states, the Sages used the term "World to Come" in a very vague way, in order not to show preference for either opinion.

Without complicating this terminological problem, we will just focus on what the Sages thought about the period between death and redemption (called the "World to Come," according to both Moore and Finkelstein's methods). As we have stated, the relatively few sources are unclear on this subject. We find a subtle hint about the nature of existence after death in the parable of R. Yohanan ben Zakkai about a king who invited guests to a meal without setting a time for it to begin. The wise men among them prepared themselves and sat near the palace ready to be called for the meal, the fools continued with their work. "Suddenly, the King desired (the presence of) his servants, the wise entered adorned while the fools entered soiled… The king said, those who adorned themselves for the banquet… let them sit and eat and drink. But those who did not adorn themselves for the banquet let them stand and watch." The son-in-law of R. Meir adds in the name of R. Meir that fools do not stand and watch, in order that they will not seem as servants to the wise, rather "both sit, the former eating and the latter hungering, the former drinking and the latter thirsting" (BT Shabbat 153a).[45] This is but a parable, but it creates in the consciousness of those who hear it the image of man called before the Creator in his body and his soul. The world to where he is called possesses corporeal pleasures such as eating and drinking.[46]

Another source tells of R. Hanina ben Dosa (the first Tannaitic generation) whose wife (also an impressive character, of whom it is told that she was "learned in miracles), told him to ask from Heaven that he be given

---

[45]   See R. Judah's alternative version of R. Yohanan ben Zakkai's parable, in Tractate Semahot 2:1.

[46]   See an additional parable by R. Yohanan ben Zakkai, BT Berakhot 28b, and in the source in note 38 above. This source also provides the image of man going to his death in both body and soul.

something from the good that is destined for the righteous in the world to come. He prayed, and he was sent a golden leg of a table. In his dream, R. Hanina saw that the righteous all eat beside a three legged table, and he was beside a table with only two legs. He requested mercy and they took from him the leg of the table (BT Ta'anit 25a). This source also presents a corporeal life for the righteous, however it is clear that the reward for the righteous in this world is on the account of his reward in the world to come.

A similar idea regarding corporeal reward is found in the fifth Tannaitic generation. R. Hiyya the Elder and R. Shimeon ben Halaphta sat and learned in the Academy of Tiberias on Pesach eve (some say it was Yom Kippur eve). R. Shimeon ben Halaphta, who had no money to prepare things for the holiday, prayed in a valley. A Hand held out a pearl to him. He went to R. Judah the Patriarch and asked him to loan him three dinars which he would return after he sold the pearl. The wife of R. Shimeon opposed this and said to him: "Do you then desire that your canopy (under which the righteous will sit in the world to come) should contain one pearl less than that of your fellow in the world to come?" (Ruth Rabbah 3:4).

It is possible that this conception is according to the tradition that after death man stands for judgment in his body and soul, and therefore the reward is also for the body. However, according to the tradition that the soul separates from the body, the souls of the righteous "are deposited underneath the throne of honour," while the souls of the evil "continue to be imprisoned," there is no place for corporeal rewards. R. Eleazar (second Amoraic generation in Palestine) expresses this position, he maintains that between the death and redemption, the righteous sleep and do not receive reward, but "the entire reward of the righteous is kept ready for them for the Hereafter, and the Holy One, Blessed be He, shows them yet in this world, the reward He is to give them in the future, their souls are then satisfied and they fall asleep." (Genesis Rabbah 62:2) They are permitted to see the goodness of their reward for a brief moment before they depart the world.

In the third generation of the Amoraic scholars there is an additional development in the idea of the soul's status after death, as seen in a midrash of R. Levi. According to this, "Dumah (the Angel responsible for spirits) takes the person's soul and leads him to a death courtyard (*Hazarmaveth*) with the other spirits. In front of the courtyard runs a brook, and beyond the brook lies an open field. And every day Dumah lets the spirits out, and they eat from the open field and drink at the brook..." they "eat but do not speak, and when they drink the sound of their drinking is not heard." (Midrash Psalms 11:6) This does not seem to be a dominant and accepted conception up to this time, because the sources usually present an ideal spiritual or physical existence. This source describes a gloomy existence and a deteriorated physical and spiritual state, similar to that of prisoners, who have been remanded to a life of degradation in prison. At any rate, according to this and the previous source, from their death until redemption the souls do not participate in intellectual endeavors.

It is very difficult to distinguish between the rabbinic interpretations of the world to come as a future period, and those that deal with the world to come as after death. It seems that most of the commentaries are from the first type, a few are from the second. From the sources in our discourse, we must assume that there is a link between the conception that stems from monism, and the idea that maintains that the body and soul remain united after death. Consequently, it follows that there is a connection between dualism and the idea that the soul separates from the body and ascends after death.

Reward and Punishment

It is clear from the rabbinic sources we have quoted and from other rabbinic sources that a belief in judgment and reward after death became established. Nevertheless, in the first generations of the Tannaitic scholars we find a continuation of the Biblical belief that man is also judged by his actions during his lifetime. An ancient Mishna in Kiddushin says: If a man performs but a single commandment it shall be well with him and he shall have length of days and shall inherit the Land; but if he neglects a single commandment it shall be ill with him and he shall not have length of days and shall not inherit the Land (M Kiddushin 1:6). In this Mishna there is no mention of reward in the world to come (Urbach 1960; 1967). R. Tarfon also speaks of reward in this world: "If thou hast studied much Torah, they give thee much reward, and faithful is thine employer to pay thee the rewards for your labour." However, he also adds "know that the grant of reward unto the righteous is in the Hereafter." (M Avot 2:16)[47] There are specific sins that are punished in this world. For example, women die in childbirth for failure to do three things: family purity, separating *hallah*, and lighting candles on the Sabbath (M Shabbat 2:6).[48] According to R. Nehemiah, blind hatred

---

[47] The verse "know that the grant of reward unto the righteous is in the time to come" is absent from some manuscripts, including the *Avot de-Rabbi Nathan* (B) ch. 35. Also see M Rosh Hashanna 4:1: "If a man says give this sela to charity in order that my children may live, or in order that I may merit thereby life in the world to come, he is a wholly righteous man."

[48] See also JT Shabbat 2:6, 5b; *Avot de-Rabbi Nathan* (B), ch. 9; T Shabbat 2:10; BT Berakhot 31a; BT Shabbat 32a; according to R. Nathan, women also die due to vows, see T Shabbat 2:10; BT Shabbat 32b.

leads to disputes, miscarriages and death of children (BT Shabbat 32a). The Sages also believed in measure for measure both with regard to reward and punishment.[49]

Obviously, every commentary on reward and punishment in this world leaves room for the example of a righteous man who has bad fortune, and an evil man with good fortune. Thus, in connection with honouring parents it is written, "That thy days may be prolonged, and that it may go well with thee." (Deuteronomy 5:15) In reference to the dismissal of the nest it is written, "That it may be well with thee, and that thou mayest prolong thy days." (Deuteronomy 22:7). "Now, if one's father said to him: 'Ascend to the loft and bring young birds', and he ascends to the loft, dismisses the dam and takes the young, and on his return falls and is killed—where is the man's happiness and where is this man's prolonged days" (BT Kiddushin 39b).[50] These phenomena required explanation. Therefore, in addition to reward and punishment in this world the sages promised reward and punishment in the world to come. The Sadducees that did not believe in reward and punishment in the world to come, laughed at the Pharisees: "It is a tradition among the Pharisees to afflict themselves in this world, yet in the world to come they will have nothing." (Avot de-Rabbi Nathan (A), ch. 5)

As long as the gap between performing commandments and frustrated rewards is not too wide, it is possible to adhere to the standard belief about reward and punishment, i.e., that they are mainly in this world, and partially in the world to come. However, when people are punished because they follow the commandments, then there is danger of a cultural crisis similar to the one during the Hadrianic Decrees. We read in the Mekhilta: R. Nathan says:

> Of them that love Me and keep My commandments," refers to those who dwell in the land of Israel and risk their lives for the sake of the commandments. "Why are you being led out to be decapitated?" "Because I circumcised my son to be an Israelite." "Why are you being led out to be burned?" "Because I read the Torah." "Why are you being let out to be crucified?" "Because I ate the unleavened bread." "Why are you getting a hundred lashes?" "Because I performed the ceremony of the Lulab." (Mekhilta de-R. Ishmael, Tractate Bahodesh, ch. 6)

---

49   For example: Absalom was hung by his hair, because he was proud of it, the same follows for the punishment of sota, and the punishments of Samson and Miriam, see M Sota 1:7–10 (see version in Kaufman MS) and see Urbach (1975: 439). See also Leviticus Rabbah 37:2.

50   See also T Hullin 10:16, and BT Hullin 142a.

We could say that during each period one can find an imbalance between actions and reward and punishment, especially in the case of a suffering individual. The individual and community can continue to maintain their basic belief in reward and punishment in this world along with a belief in reward and punishment in the World to Come. However, when there is an extreme imbalance in this relationship for the entire community, as in times of persecution, war, or other catastrophes, then the usual framework of thought is undermined. When this occurs, it is impossible to continue classifying events as was done in the past, instead it is likely that a change will take place in the basic ideology.

But even during the period of Hadrian's Decrees, there were Sages who still believed in the normative idea of reward and punishment in this world: "At the time when R. Simon and R. Ishmael were led out to be killed," R. Simon said to R. Ishmael: "Master, my heart fails me, for I do not know why I am to be killed." R. Ishmael said to him: "Did it never happen in your life that a man came to you for judgment or with a question and you let him wait until you had sipped your cup, or had tied your sandals, or had put on your cloak?" Whereupon R. Simon said to him: "You have comforted me, master." (Mekhilta de-R. Ishmael, Tractate Nezikim, ch. 18)[51] Execution is a disproportionate punishment for such minor sins. But R. Simon accepted it as an answer and the foundations of his belief were not shaken. R. Akiva, however, did not accept this explanation: "…that if something good had been destined to come upon our generation, R. Simon and R. Ishmael—and none else—would have been the first ones to receive it. Now then it must therefore be that these two men have been taken from our midst only because it is revealed before Him by whose words the world would come into being that great suffering is destined to come upon our generation."

This is a major turning point: instead of seeing death as punishment it is seen as a reward. Death is no longer a sanction, but recompense. From here onward the way is clear for a dichotomy: Reward is not in this world but the next, because R. Akiva and his colleagues fulfilled all of the commandments even where they aggravated the authorities, and accepted endured suffering.[52] Consequently, there is no sense to this suffering if it is seen as punishment

---

[51]   Regarding the identity of these individuals see Urbach (1975: 442; 881 n. 74; 882 n. 75); see also Lieberman 1975: 227–228), who maintains that they are not R. Ishmael ben Elisha and R. Shimeon ben Gamliel II, but rather two unknown sages. Even if it is about other sages, their words represent the principle of reward and punishment which we are discussing. Compare to *Avot de-Rabbi Nathan* (A), ch. 38, and (B) ch. 41 which refer to different "sins."

[52]   Urbach (1975: 443–444). See JT Berakhot 9:7, 14b; JT Sota 5: 7, 23b.

for sin. Therefore, R. Akiva's method is different: there is no element of reward and punishment in afflictions; they should be accepted with love as the highest ideal of loving God ("with all your soul [Deut. 6:4] even should He take away your soul") because an individual cannot make an account for the world. Indeed, "When R. Akiva was executed in Cesarea, and the news reached R. Judah ben Baba and R. Hanina ben Teradion, they arose... and exclaimed... "R. Akiva was not executed for robbery, or because he did not labour for Torah with all his strength. He was only put to death as a sign." (Semahoth 8:9) Martyrdom is the highest form of death because the individual gives his life for the community, and for the sake of the continued existence of society. From this point, death would be measured in comparison to martyrdom, which was made the ideal of dedication to the society. This death is the highest in the hierarchy of deaths, which includes the death of righteous persons, death of average persons, and death of evil persons. None of these people are rewarded in this world, but in the world to come.

The change that began in the relationship between behavior, and reward and punishment, is also expressed in a parallel change that began in the relationship between divine providence and free will. The Sages believed in divine providence, while accepting the existence of free will. During periods of normalcy, the element of choice is emphasized, meaning man's ability to choose his path through free will by accepting responsibility. According to this, there exists an innate balance between reward and punishment in the corporeal world. However, during times of crisis, the link between free will and reward and punishment disappears and the solution tends toward the direction of divine providence. This view emphasizes that the world is directed under the guidance of God, while man's influence in directing the world becomes more limited.

Therefore, it is typical for the ancient Mishna in Kiddushin (1:10) to say: "If a man performs but a single commandment, it shall be well with him and he shall have length of days." The same for Hillel the Elder, that when he heard a voice cry in the city, was certain that it did not come from his house (BT Berakhot 60a). Even R. Akiva, who transferred reward and punishment to the world to come, did not reject in any way the idea of choice: "Everything is foreseen, but the right [of choice] is granted, and the world is judged with goodness and everything is with accordance with the preponderance of [man's] deed[s]." (M Avot 3:15) Or as R. Tarfon said: "...and faithful is thy taskmaster who shall pay thee the reward of thy labour." But, R. Tarfon adds, reward and punishment for actions are not given in thus life (as in Mishnah Kiddushin 1:10), but rather in the hereafter: "...and know that the recompense of the reward of the righteous is for the time to come." (M Avot 2:16)

An extreme statement which rejects the idea of reward in this world is made by ben Azzai, from R. Akiva's generation, and by R. Jacob (fourth-fifth generation of Tannaitic scholars). According to ben Azzai: "One duty draws another duty in its train, and one transgression draws another transgression in its train; for the reward of a duty [done] is a duty [to be done], and the reward of one transgression is [another] transgression." (M Avot 3:2) Fulfilling one's duties is the only reward in this world. However, in this world, man's goodness does not depend on his choice.[53] R. Jacob teaches: "…that thy days may be prolonged" (Deuteronomy 22:7) refers to the world that is wholly long, and "that may go well with thee" refers to the world that is wholly good." His final conclusion is "that there is no reward for precepts in this world." (BT Hullin 142a)[54] One can conclude that: Man's goodness in this world is not a consequence of his choice, because the guidance of God is the determining factor; however, this does not negate the importance of free will, because man's choice influences his fate in the world to come.

This is a response of a society living with a sense of an existential crisis. A similar response would be expected in different groups living under somewhat similar conditions. We hear the emphasis on divine providence and the rejection of the principle of choice in the writings of the Judean Desert Sects. The ideology of these sects is extremely apocalyptic. These are persons anticipating the end of days. In the meantime, there exists a "reign of the wicked," which will be destroyed in the end of days, and Israel will be freed from the yoke of the nations. God will choose a special group that will be saved from the evil and will become the core of the future society. Choice is also denied Israel because the world, of which Israel is a part, is divided between "people of light" and "people of darkness."[55] This idea is closely related to the extreme dualistic ideology of the sect. While the Sages maintained a moderated conception of dualism, they also held a moderated ideology regarding the relationship between providence and free will. However, as there was no unified theory among the Sages throughout history regarding the body soul relationship, the same followed for the question of guidance or choice. We proved that even

---

53 See the words of Ben Azzai: "Once a man desires to hearken by his own will, he is led to hearken both when it is his will to do so and even when it is not his will. And if it be his will to forget, he will be led to forget even when it is not his will." (Mekhilta de-R. Ishmael, Tractate Vayasa 1).

54 See the parallel sources: T Hullin 10:16; BT Kiddushin 39b. Urbach (1975: 270–271) maintains that this refers to one extraordinary individual. However Ben Azzai said it refers to many, "The disciples of Abraham, our father, enjoy [their share] in this world and inherit the world to come (M Avot 5:19).

55 Regarding the views and organization of the sect see Flusser (1954) and Licht (1970).

during the Tannaitic generations, there began changes from the emphasis on choice among the first Tannaitic scholars, to a moderated merging of the ideas of free will and divine providence during the later Tannaitic generations. Alongside this, there was a rejection of the principle of reward and punishment in this world, by transferring them to the world to come.

Until now we have discussed in depth the changes in the Sages' conception of four cosmological questions: 1) the nature of the body-soul relationship; 2) the question of the soul's preexistence; 3) the fate of the body and soul after death (post existence); and 4) the question of reward and punishment. The answer to these questions provide the index by which we can measure monistic or dualist world views. A correlation exists among these indices. It is that the view regarding each of the issues changes simultaneously throughout the historical period under discussion. From the first Tannaitic generations until the Hadrianic Decrees, the tendency was toward monism. Change occurs after the Hadrianic Decrees with a trend toward dualism. This transformation becomes clearer during the Amoraic period, in the form of moderated dualism. A summary of these changes can be seen in Table 1.

Table 1

Sages' Responses to Cosmological Questions in Different Periods

Period / Cosmological Questions	Early Tannaitic (Monistic Tendency)	Hadrian's Decree	Amoraic (Dualistic Tendency)
Body-Soul	Body-soul undifferentiated; both possess equal value and responsibility.	Beginning of differentiation; soul has high value and responsibility; soul serves the body.	Differentiation; high value to soul which is responsible for the body; body serves the soul.
Pre-Existence of the soul	Embryo doesn't possess a soul. Enters at birth.	Beginning of preexistential ideas. Soul enters at conception.	Pre-existence. All souls were created during the Creation.
Post-Existence of the Soul	Body-soul judged to-gether. A quasi-"material" existence after life.	Detachment of soul from body. Righteous souls are gathered in Heaven and evil souls are punished.	Righteous sleep until resurrection. Or: souls are kept by angel Dumma in a degenerated state until resurrection.
Reward and Punishment	Reward and punishment in this world. Free will emphasized.	Separation between behavior and reward. Divine direction is emphasized.	

Social Structure and Cosmology

The trends in cosmology having been defined as leading from an anthropological monism to dualism, we now must discover what caused this change. We already emphasized that it is impossible to ignore the influence of social structure on the formation of world view and its changes. Therefore, we will investigate the nature of social change during this period.

Now, it is already possible to state that in a society with a sense of an existential threat, some individuals or groups will be more conscious of this threat than others, or aware of it sooner. (These social sectors will be discussed later.) One of the possible responses to the crisis is withdrawal from the society out of disappointment. This includes reorganization into a lifestyle of asceticism, through the adoption of a cosmology that claims seclusion from this world, and guarantees eternal life in the future. The Judean Desert Sects are an example of this. Their lifestyle expressed a complete sense of apocalyptic doom. Another possible response is that of the Sages, who adopted a different cosmology by which there is no withdrawal from this world in the daily activities of individuals, however, life in this world is considered only a "corridor" to the World to Come. Life in the corridor requires a special lifestyle, not separation, and the rewards will only be received in the future by those who deserve and follow all the rules.[56]

The Liminal State of the World

These responses represent different attitudes toward the purpose of this world. They transform this world from an end in itself that can be exploited by the will of man, into a means to the world to come. Only the correct "use" of this world can open the gates to the world to come. The first approach, represented by the Judean Desert Sects, forbids the "use" of this world, because it is a false and unimportant world. The second approach, represented by the attitude of the Sages, allows the "use" of this world. It maintains that the quality by which the individual uses this world during his lifetime will be the quality of his reward in the world to come. According to both approaches there is no reward and punishment in this world.

According to Turner (1967; 1979; 1982), individuals who live by this conception of reality live in a borderline, or liminal state. This type of reality

---

[56] "R. Jacob said: the world is like a vestibule before the world to come, prepare thyself in the vestibule so that you mayest enter the banqueting-hall (M Avot 4:16). See note 54.

does not exist independently, but rather only in relation to a state of transition from reality to reality; it is an interval period. Turner deals with liminal reality in the context of a well know distinction made by Van Gennep (1960) regarding three stages in rites of passage. Van Gennep defined rites of passage as rites which accompany changes in place, time, and age of the individual, such as puberty, marriage and death. Rites of passage are also associated with changes in group life, for example, New Years rituals, first fruits, and inauguration rituals. In these rites, Van Gennep discovered three universal stages, the stage of separation, in which the initiate is separated from his former state; the intermediate stage (liminal), the stage between what was before and what is about to be; and the stage of aggregation, in which the initiate moves into his new state, acquiring those rights and obligations associated with it.

Turner's research deals with the intermediate stage, which he has expanded beyond the study of rites of passage. In this stage there is a mixture of characteristics of the previous stage and the stage which is to come. Turner contends that there are people whose entire reality is constructed as if they are between two worlds, the world from whence they have come, and the world to where they are going. They are caught "betwixt and between," neither here nor there, as well as both here and there. This is the monastic world of those who cut themselves off from everyday life. These are the individuals who seek to find a higher spiritual plane for themselves and those around them. Similarly, the liminal state is the state of groups dissatisfied with normal human existence. Turner has found that among these groups, interpersonal relations are based on egalitarian ideology, brotherhood and mutual aid, as well as subjugation to a hierarchy of prophets and seers, elders and leaders, who are said to have found the proper way.

The average man is expected to be passive and submissive. The individual shrinks his identity in order to accept and become strong. He is converted into a vessel able to absorb changes in experience. The liminal state is a present with no continuity, and as such, it is characterized by genderless symbols. The distinction between the sexes implies fertility, continuity and life. Sexlessness implies stasis and lack of differentiation. Therefore, liminal groups generally forbid marriage and sexual activity. This intermediate stage, according to Turner, is a state of "no longer what was before" and "not yet what is to be." Consequently, we find the simultaneous appearance of symbols expressing opposed states. Symbols of denigration of the body, rejection of pleasure, identical simple dress, preventing status distinction (these are symbols of "no-longer"); along with symbols of revitalization and becoming, which include acts of bodily purification, washing and ritual submersion, and wearing white clothes, all of which represent characteristics of what is to be (these are symbols of "not-yet"). The two symbolic systems, appearing simultaneously, emphasize anthropological dualism of the liminal state, which is neither life nor death.

These components of liminal reality (equality, passivity, submission to authority, lack of sexuality, and a state of betwixt and between) are found to various degrees in those groups which perceive themselves as having a temporary existence in the present, and which direct themselves to alternative existence. Some of the Judean Desert Sects lived in a fairly extreme liminal state, expressed by uniform white clothing, and an ideology of modesty, simplicity, a rejection of sexuality, acceptance of the supremacy of the leadership, passivity, egalitarianism, and a sense of brotherhood among equals. This passivity was only for this world, the world of transition. Their ideology spoke of a more active future, a fighting union, whose goal was justice.[57]

At the other extreme, a more moderate liminality is present in the world view of the Sages after the Second Rebellion. This was an ideological liminality, more a state of mind than action. It does not aspire to retreat from this world; rather this ideology teaches one to deal with the real world with care. These Sages profess that their world, and not the one that preceded them, is a world in decline, and that a better world would succeed it. This is expressed in the Mishna: "When R. Meir died there were no more makers of Parables...When Rabban Simeon ben Gamliel died... troubles grew many... When R. Akiva died the glory of the Torah ceased... on whom can we stay ourselves? On our Father in Heaven!" (Sota 9:15)[58]

Behavior, Symbols and Cosmology

Consequently, in the Land of Israel, we have found fundamentally different approaches to the corporeal world. Now we must investigate two issues: firstly, why did a turning point occur in the Sages' conception from the Biblical monism regarding the body-soul relationship to a moderated dualism? Secondly, parallel to the period when the Sages maintained their monistic views, perhaps even before the First Century CE, there emerged movements that bore the ideas of dualism in the body-soul relationship. How can we explain the emergence of these dualistic ideas during this period, when these

---

[57] The Judean Desert Sects can be categorized according to the degree to which they adhered to these principles. The group that lived according to the "Manual of Discipline" was more extreme in comparison to the group of "Damascus Covenanters" that allowed women, children, and private property.

[58] Compare with T Sota 15:3–8.

ideas only appear among the Sages during the Second Century? This issue is intensified by the fact that these trends developed upon the same cultural backdrop.

In order to understand the problem, it seems that we must adopt the assumption that concrete behavior is fostered and influenced by cosmology. Behavior is expressed in symbols; therefore the correct analysis of symbols will provide us with an understanding of the cosmology which they represent. Following Douglas (1973), body symbols are the expression of a world view. The way humans relate to reality is expressed by the body. The successful individual or group expresses that success in their body symbols. Depressives, the degraded, and the losers, also express their status through symbols. Therefore, also the conception of the body-soul relationship, monistic or dualistic, will be expressed in the symbolic system.

It is tempting to explain the tendency towards apocalyptic and millenarian movements in terms of social deprivation, like Wilson (1967), Smelser (1962), and Cohn (1962). Baron (1962: vol. 2, 46–56) also thought that the various apocalyptic sects in the Land of Israel drew their power from the deprived strata of society, who found encouragement in a dualistic eschatology. But other historians are extremely cautious in deciding from which social strata members of the various sects were drawn. It has become clear that there is no necessary link between social protest movements and socioeconomic status. Groups of Hippies and Punks, as well as members of other protest movements which reject the western way of life, do not necessarily draw their support from the economically deprived. The student protest movements in Europe and the United States during the 1960's were not supported by the deprived. We must accept the fact that we have no idea regarding sources of manpower for the various sectarian movements for the period under study; but it is obvious that the symbols of these movements certainly denigrate the dominant social structure.

According to Berger (1973: 340),[59] there is a point in time at which the "objective" world view is no longer valid and no longer explains the "true

---

[59]   Berger means "objectivity" as any accepted reasonable interpretation of the world around us ("objective truth"). For example, we accept the statement "the world is round" as an "objective truth" whether we understand the statement or not. We do not have the intellectual competence to ("subjectively") change the statement. The traditional Chinese believed the world was flat and that China was in the center. A modern man can be certain that in a debate with a traditional Chinese on this subject, the modern viewpoint will prevail. Yet, there are certainly many such modern men, who are unable to prove this claim. However, this does not prevent us from maintaining the opinion that the world is round. We are convinced of our own

conditions." At this point, groups with new subjective world views, try to explain their existential situation in the changing reality. Messianic sects, or groups that are open to other cultures like those that accept the philosophy of Philo, understand and analyze reality in a different way. The ideology of the Sages, which underwent a change towards dualism, is a new interpretation to the changing reality.

The biblical laws, and later the rabbinic commentary on the bible, developed a social system that has clear behavior categories, including a system of rights and obligations known to all members of the society. It provides a uniform world view to each member of the society and creates pressures on the individual to identify with these categories. The Sages were an intellectual elite authority, and thus got power of social control. It was not a formal system of control ratified by the Roman authority. Quite the contrary, during most of this period the Sages had only informal control based on their spiritual authority. In a world defined in this way, individuals are fettered by taboos against heretical thought. If these thoughts were made public it would lead to sanctions of exclusion from society. Should such heretical thought remain private, it would simply prevent the receipt of rewards in the world to come. For example, one who denies the revival of the dead has no part in the world to come. Selfhood is limited to a well defined field if thought. Perception of self is of being part of a social world, having collective responsibility, in which the individual and the collective are indivisible, so that a sense of solidarity and partnership between the individual and the collective is created.

When the individual is subordinate to society, and his liberty is limited to its boundaries, we would expect a monistic world view, according to which the spirit operates as a part of the body. The body is regarded sacred and symbolizes the sacred society. An injury to the body is an injury to society. For example, the Biblical Law forbids injury to the body during mourning (Lev.19:28; Deut. 14:1). The relationship to the personal corpus therefore is a symbol of the social corpus. In such a society, wealth will be valued; happiness will be seen as good without any sense of guilt or waste. This type of

---

truth (just as the traditional Chinese were convinced that the world is flat), because every intellectual authority from schoolteacher to textbook accepts this view. That is to say, the "objective truth" is something which acquires social confirmation from many people who constantly and consistently certify this truth. When this social confirmation is undermined, and statements which have formally received social certification lose their "objective truth," then new views arise which are considered subjective. On Berger and his phenomenonological approach, see Berger and Luckmann (1966).

society would not accept, and perhaps object to monasticism and asceticism (Douglas 1973: Chs. 9–10).[60]

In this type of society, where every individual is guided by a shared set of categories, it is clear that the individual is responsible for his actions. Evil in the world is a result of individual failings. Sin is not considered merely a personal failing, it is sin against society.

This is reflected in bodily symbols. According to Douglas, the relationship to the body encodes the relationship to society. If society requires discipline and obedience, and it is able to control, there will be a similar discipline in relation to the body, because respect for the body is the same as respect for society. This explains the emphasis the Sages placed on dress, appearance, and public behavior.[61] They treat bodily excretions with disgust. Coughing, sneezing, and yawning in public are criticized. An individual is expected to make less noise, not to smack his lips, or chew or laugh uncontrollably, when he is in public.[62] These are behaviors limited to situations of intimacy, not appropriate for the formality of public interaction.

---

[60] On the sages' attitude see BT Nedarim 10a: "R. Eleazar Hakappar Berabbi says: it was taught: 'and he shall make atonement for him, for that he sinned against a soul.' (Numbers 6:11) Against which 'soul' then has he sinned? But it is because he afflicted himself through abstention from wine. Now does not this afford an argument from the minor to the major? If one who afflicted himself only in respect of wine is called a sinner, how much more so one who ascetically refrains from everything. Hence, one who fasts is called a sinner." Compare this to JT Nedarim 9:1, 41a: "R. Dimi in the name of R. Issac: What the Torah has declared prohibited to you is not enough, but you seek to impose upon yourself a prohibition as to other matters too." See also JT Kiddushin 4:12, 66d: "R. Hezekiah... in the name of Rav: It is forbidden to live in a city which there are no physician, no bath... In the future a man is going to have to give an account of himself for everything that his ego saw and did not eat."

[61] A few examples will clarify this: "The glory of man being his garments," Exodus Rabbah 18:5, and see BT Shabbat 104a: "Whence do we learn change of garment in the Torah?," regarding the obligation to change into nice clothes for the Sabbath. Or : "It is a disgrace for a scholar to go out with patched shoes into the marketplace." And also R Yohanan said: "The scholar upon whose garment a (grease) stain is found, is worthy of death."

[62] In the Bible there are clear demands requiring the removal of bodily excretions such as discharge, menstrual blood, and semen (Lev. Ch. 15); removal of excrement (Deut. 18:13–14); the prohibition of flagellation (Deut. 14:1–2); and the prohibition of delaying burial of the dead (Deut. 21: 22–23). From the Talmudic literature we will bring a few examples of controlled behavior: JT Berakhot 9:8, 14b discusses the prohibition of spitting in the synagogue. BT Sanhedrin 11a tells of R. Judah the Patriarch who was teaching and smelled garlic and said "whoever eats garlic must leave." BT Bava Batra 58b: "What is the sign of the bed of a *Talmid Hakam*? That nothing is kept under it save sandals in the summer season and shoes in the rain season."

The world view of the apocalyptic sects at the end of the Second Commonwealth expresses a different existential feeling. This is a sense of disquiet with what exists along with frustration leading to a tendency to rebel. The different existential experience generates new social cosmologies expressed in bodily symbols. The body is denigrated as are existing formal patterns of behavior, existing rituals are rejected, and symbols and rituals are generated expressing a different existential experience.

The "objective" world view is shaken. The shared categories decrease, along with the accepted symbols of communication. Solidarity in the sects and the closing of ranks are imperative for a group sensing itself in the midst of a threatening world. It must defend itself against the threatening forces. Inside the group, demands arise for discipline and obedience to authority, as well as rigid control over behavior. Deviation from the rules brings about exclusion. This is a group lacking a strong central church. The group hierarchy is divorced from any external sources of power. Power is derived from within and it is not formal. Entrance to the group is difficult, connection with it is voluntary, and requires strict conformity to norms. Primary sanctions are of excommunication. Sense of self is not different from the previous case. Society is superior to the obedient self, fettered and unable to think independently. Perception of self in this type of group is a matter of being a part of a larger social entity.[63]

World view in this type of society is dualistic with regard to body and soul, or matter and spirit. Society's rewards are not found in everyday life. There is no clear connection between man's actions in this world, and the rewards he receives. The righteous are not necessarily rewarded in this world.

While in the previous type of society the body was a symbol of life, in the present type the body is degraded and must undergo constant purification. Behavioral codes express the alienation of the sect from society. Under this code, the demands of the body—like demands of society—are not valued.

BT Kiddushin 40b: "He who eats in the marketplace is like a dog." Anyone who is familiar with rabbinical literature will find additional examples of this requirement for restrained public behavior.

63   In Douglas' (1973) terminology, she distinguishes between this type of society of "faction" and one of "ascribed hierarchy." We refer here, in a simplified form, to only two of her types of categorization based on two measures: one, group commitment that is determined by the degree of obligation to social categories; two, group control, that is, the degree to which the individual is subjected to group pressure or free from it. Douglas describes four types of societies based on these measures, in principle intermediate types can also exist. See Douglas (1978 and 1982: Introduction), which are an updated version of Douglas (1973).

Yet there is a preference for non-corporeal demands. The spirit has a separate standing, independent and different from the body. Spiritual experience is of extreme value just as bodily experience is not. The theodicy develops along with a philosophy that rejects reward. In the Judean Desert Sects, the evil existing in the world was immanent. The cosmos was controlled by evil forces, whose influence will be eliminated at the End of Days. The world was guided by an ancient godly decree that determined the course of history. During the period of the ancient decree, humanity was divided a priori into two opposing groups, of light and darkness, with no intermediate.[64]

This type of society rejects the rational order and formal hierarchy of the surrounding society. The corporeal world does deserve attention. Only a proper order of life in this world can create conditions sufficient for entering a better world. Proper order in life includes a new social organization, creating a hierarchy, main leadership, and group, along with brotherhood and sharing among the ranks. The body and external status symbols are not considered important. It is the internal man, the spirit, which engenders respect and status. Uniform special clothing expresses the norms connected to the wider society, and creates a barrier with the outside world over and above the sense of pollution carried by those outside the sect. In addition, uniform clothing expresses the equality and unity of the group.

The body-soul dialectic is a metaphor for the relationship between the individual and society. Spirit and knowledge represent the individual who identifies with the group. The body represents society. When the individual and his group identify with society, there is unity of body and spirit. When they are alien to one another, there is separation, or opposition between body and spirit. Debates on the relationship between body and soul wax and wane, and as we have stated, it is not always possible to find a reason or explanation for their presence at a particular point in time. It appears that these debates become relevant as metaphors during periods in which the relations between the alienated subgroup and society become an acute political problem.

The Sages formulated their world view as a result of debates with such sects. Historical events generated a turning point towards a more dualistic world view. Yet the Sages did not arrive at a radical dualistic ideology in the way of the sects, but rather to a more moderate position. The Sages, as representatives of the national leadership, were unable to destroy structures that would lead to the loss of existing categories. However, they had to refocus cosmologies to align them with the changing reality. The leadership of the Sages, struggling over authority and sources of power with a foreign ruler,

---

64   See Yadin (1975) and Licht (1957; 1965).

was able to establish an intellectual and moral authority, which continued to supply a system of classification. This was a leadership of a subjugated nation, fighting for its identity, that was unable to accept a system of values which rejected, from the outset, the struggle in this world.[65] Difficult conditions required a solution unavailable in the previous cosmology, and moderate dualism arose as a partial solution to the problems facing society. The Sages supplied criteria somewhat different from before, but unopposed to earlier criteria, thus continuity was possible in a world of uncertainty. The real world orientation[66] of the Sages continued to exist, yet a channel was opened to the world beyond.

Conclusion

The point of departure of this discussion is found in phenomenological Sociology, which seeks to understand behavior through it social construction, the perception of members of society, and not through any objective standard. This approach sees a connection between the quality of social structure and social organization, and the response to body-soul relationship. This question is tied to the issues of the individual's responsibility for personal acts, and reward and punishment. We have seen that according to Douglas, the body-soul debate symbolically reflects the way in which people perceive their reality. A society will possess a well defined system of reward and punishment, and every individual will be personally responsible for his actions, if the society has: a system of objective well-defined and shared categories; a means for control over individuals; and a sense of collective identity which supersedes each person's individuality. Any failure of the individual will be a failure for the society. Cosmology of such a society would tend to be monistic, and see in the body a reflection of the spirit. This is symbolically reflected in sacredness of the body, because respect for the body is respect for the society.

When the shared system of classification loses its validity and its "objectivity," because various groups in the society have new existential experiences, the existing cosmology can no long supply an adequate explanation and justification for society. Under such conditions, we expect to find new sects with new cosmologies. These sects accept members on a voluntary basis, under strict conditions. They have a rigid discipline, and require a willingness to accept the authority of a hierarchy lacking formal physical sanctions.

---

[65]   Cf Douglas (1973: ch. 6).
[66]   See Weber (1948).

In such groups, the individual is expected to sacrifice his personal identity for the collective. Yet, since reality does not make clear boundaries possible for reward and punishment in this world, there is no connection between acts and reward, and cosmology must be dualistic. This means that the world, controlled by the forces of evil, has no intrinsic value; it is only of value as a point of departure for another more ideal world. The symbolic expression for this point of view involves the exclusion of the body. The body is rejected and denigrated, as well as the society outside the framework of the sect, which sees its members as chosen. The Biblical world view was monistic, body and soul were one unit, reward was given to man in this world as a result of his acts. There are no signs of the separate existence of the soul before birth. Regarding the existence of the soul after death, there are some literary and poetic references to the grave and the shadowy existence of body and soul in death. The Bible hints at a belief in the remaining of the soul, and the revival of the dead, yet there is no development of a "theory" regarding the nature of this existence, and no real departure from a monistic point of view.

During the Second Commonwealth we find different views pertaining to the nature of the soul. In the early apocryphal writings, from the Persian, and Hellenistic Periods, there was a continuation of Biblical monism. At the end of the Ptolemaic Period, there is a budding dualism especially in the writings of the Judean Desert Sects. We find ideas of the soul's preexistence, and reward and punishment after death. Among the Essenes, the soul was considered as having substance, with a goal of freeing itself from bodily fetters, so that it might return to its heavenly origins. This is the eternal soul, with no belief in a revitalization of the dead. It is clear that if we see spiritual life as the ideal existence, then the eschatology would be of freeing the soul from its fetters. These groups find themselves disappointed with existing social order. This cosmology makes it possible for them to better explain reality with its evil and injustice. We find in Philo of Alexandria and Josephus Flavius, dualism similar to that of the Stoics and Plato. These were certainly influenced by the Greek world view, to which they were very close.

The Sadducees continued a world view of extreme monism, with no belief in the revitalization of the dead and the eternity of the soul. According to Douglas' theory, this suits the world view of aristocracy from whom the Sadducees came.

The Sages' view was transitional, tending towards a dualistic position regarding body and soul, pre and post-existence of the soul, and reward and punishment. Among the first generations of the Tannaic scholars, when there were already dualistic ideas appearing in various Jewish sects, the views of the Sages tended to remain monistic. After the dissipation of the Second

Rebellion, there was a tendency towards dualism. According to this dualistic position, the soul had independence though it was somehow tied to the body. The eschatology was of a soul returning to the body, and the body coming back to life. The body was valued, there were discussions on the fate of the body after death, and of the need to respect it. In their world view, the existence of the soul separate from the body was only temporary, until its return to life. Their dualistic perception was most prominent regarding reward and punishment. Rewards were transferred from this world to the World to Come. At any rate, death is a temporary end, only for the body. Death is not a new life for the soul, but an intermediate stage in the continuing history of the individual.

After the Second Rebellion, the Sages, as responsible leaders, did not tend towards the dualistic solution of denial of this world in the way of the apocalyptic sects generations before them. They continued to use the earlier system of categories that made escape from this world impossible, yet they refocused the cosmological lens toward a solution for the difficult problems of the theodicy with a moderate dualism.

Chapter 7. FROM CORPSE TO CORPUS: THE BODY AS A TEXT IN TALMUDIC LITERATURE

Jewish society in the Talmudic period tended to define clear cut behavioral borders for most human activity with a minimum of transitional situations (Rubin, 1987; Cooper, 1987). Purity and pollution, sacred and profane, as well as permitted and forbidden food are clearly defined (Douglas, 1973, 1966; Cooper, 1987; Eilberg-Schwartz, 1990). It is reasonable to assume that the Talmud would define clear boundaries between life and death with very limited liminal states (Turner, 1967: 94–95), or very limited periods of transition. The Talmud is, after all, a legal text, constructed to exclude vague and undefined states.

I

Both Hertz (1960 [1907]) and Huntington and Metcalf (1970) remark that attitudes about death teach us about society's approach to life. World view about life can be studied through an analysis of death customs. This paper focuses on the world view of Jewish sages as it regards the nature of human life. The world view is addressed through a discussion of the attitude of the sages towards dead human bodies and the rules they promulgated regarding proper treatment of the body after death. The source of these rules is the Talmud and Midrashic literature. In Jewish society, as in other societies, the fact of death breaks boundaries; the deceased crosses the border between the living and the dead, and the living break the boundaries of their social status. They move from married to widowed, from parents to childless, from child to orphan. Van Gennep (1960 [1909]) has said that rites of passage are mechanisms for crossing unseen social boundaries; these are never natural they are determined by society and culture. Even physiological events involving natural passage across clear borders, from life to death, require social and cultural definition.

It is society, not nature, that creates the boundary between life and death. Society may treat the living as already dead, creating a state of "social death," a condition that is reported in modern society as well (Sudnow, 1967:72–89; Mulkay, 1993). Hospital staff may treat terminal patients as if they are already dead, going through the routine for removal of the body before actual death; or when personnel of medical staff speak loudly in front of a comma about his/her situation. In other cases, individuals who are biologically dead are considered living until exhumation and reburial (Hertz, 1960 [1907]; Danforth, 1982).

Torah Law generally fixes the maximum period of defilement at seven days. This is the case with the leper (Lev. ch. 13), as well as menstruating women (Lev. 15:19–30) and a person with chronic discharge (Lev. 15:1–15). The same standard period applies to a person who touched a dead body (Num.19:11). This pattern was adopted when the seven-day mourning period was fixed (JT Moed Katan 3:5, 82C; BT Moed Katan 20a). After the seven days are over the bereaved are reintegrated into society.

Periods of transition are short and well defined. The rules of separation during pollution are clear and create well defined boundaries between states. The following discussion of the approach to dying will help to establish this point.

II

Dying is perceived by some as an intermediate stage between life and death (Sudnow 1969). Where it is perceived as an intermediate stage, dying appears to be a liminal state between life and death. It is not yet death, yet not completely life; it is simultaneously life and death. Yet, the sages did not accept dying as a liminal state. Dying was a part of life. It was recognized that most persons who appeared to approach death did finally die (BT Gittin 28a) nevertheless "a dying man is considered the same as a living man in every respect" (Tractate Mourning 1:1). According to R. Meir it is forbidden to close the eyes of a dying man. "Whoever closes the eyes of a dying man is considered as though he has snuffed out his life" (Tractate Mourning 1:4)[1]. This position reveals the sages' view regarding human life. The fate of each person is in God's hands and no person may intervene in any aspect of life.[2] According to Halakha there is no

---

[1]   M Shabbat 23:5 is more expressive. "It is the same as spilling blood." Closing the eyes just before death makes the body easy to deal with after death since rigor mortis has not set in. See Sudnow (1967: 74).

[2]   See Urbach (1975: Ch. 10) regarding the sages position on the importance of life. This position is reflected in the view regarding reproduction. According to R. Eliezer one who does not attempt to have children is "like one who sheds blood" (BT Yevamot 63b).

process of dying, only a sharp transition between life and death.[3] As a result of this lack of transitional period there is no provision for social death. Thus, it is forbidden to dig a grave and/or to prepare shrouds, or anything society can do for the dead. But it is not forbidden for an individual dying person to prepare himself to his own death.

It is an attractive challenge to employ here a structural theory and to attempt to connect changes in the actual treatment of the dead body with changes in belief, and to connect both changes in belief and treatment of the dead body with changes in social structure. In fact, beliefs do seem to change along with social structure, but practices, at least those connected with the traditional treatment of dead bodies among the Jews, do not (Rubin, 1977: 35–42). This may be because practitioners and experts are a special group within the culture. Their practices are in response to technical and other requirements of their specific reality. Cultures take these practices and combine them with their own dilemmas, rounding them off and reforming them to suit the more general requirements of an entire community or cultural system.

Let us put aside the question of the relationship between practice and social structure for the moment, and address the question of how the boundaries between life and death are reflected in the treatment of the dead body.

The position of the sages regarding dying is parallel to their cosmology. That cosmology is revealed in their attitude toward the body, which has been interpreted to symbolize their attitude toward society (Douglas, 1973). Jewish society in Land of Israel in talmudic times was highly categorized, having a strict system of rules, demanding loyalty and obedience. This is symbolically reflected in the attitude toward the body which is treated with dignity and distance (Rubin, 1990: 84–89) [chapter 6 in this volume]. This approach toward the body is further reflected in the attitude toward the dying. He may not be touched, and not because of pollution; rather the sages feared for the collective welfare because any injury to him would symbolically affect the entire society. The individual is subsumed into society; the collectivistic orientation of the sages gives the individual little weight as an entity separate and distinct from society. Individuals, according to Halakha have no rights in their body or in the bodies of others. The ban on touching the body and the loss of civil rights after successful suicide are means of introducing and maintaining this view in the minds of the members of society.

---

[3]   For example a priest who is not permitted to defile himself by entering the house of the dead, is permitted to enter the house of a dying person without consideration of the possibility of pollution (Goren, 1972; Jakobovitz, 1954: 123–125). There is, therefore considerable emphasis in the law on the definition of death, see: Rosenfeld (1972/3), Levi (1972; 1971; 1969).

In the modern western world view there is a strong tendency towards privatization (Luckman, 1967), individuals demand rights over their bodies, claiming autonomy over the routine of daily life. This includes the right to suicide and the right to shorten life by euthanasia. That means that the period of suffering of terminal patients is perceived as a liminal state which may be shortened.

According to the traditional Jewish orientation, death is determined at the moment of physiological death and dying is not a liminal state. There is indeed a category of dying (*gosses*), but this is meaningful in a physiological and not sociological sense.

In the western world view the borderline between life and death may be moved backward and placed anywhere in the liminal area, eliminating the liminal (dying, but not yet dead) as a category. The western physician tries to prevent death at all costs and does not see himself as participating in a process of dying. The physician determines the moment of death. Under certain circumstances society may accept the right to die by eliminating the process of dying, such as in the case of legitimate euthanasia and suicide.[4]

The Jewish view of the status of the dying person as unconditionally alive has Halakhic consequences:

> He may obligate to Levirate marriage (as long as he alive the widow of his childless brother may marry only him), and he may release from Levirate marriage (if his father died without leaving other children the dying man releases his mother from the obligation to marry his uncle). He may confer the right to eat the heave offering (if his deceased father was a priest he confers upon his mother the right to eat of the heave offering)... He may inherit property and bequeath property (Tractate Mourning 1:1, Zlotnik edition p. 31 and 97).[5]

The entire system presents itself as a mechanism for eliminating structural problems such as fuzzy categories and unclear roles. In the case of the dying, one is alive for as long as one is not dead. The dying person must deal with certain problems that are problems of the living; these prevent the condition of the dying person from creating fuzzy categories and unclear roles for others. Paradoxically, a dying man is asked to divorce his wife, rather than create a situation in which she will have to await a decision regarding levirate marriage. When liminality of the dying can be reduced it is done, but this can not have the result of leaving others in a similar state.

---

[4]   On attitudes toward the dying in western society, see Wong and Swazey (1981).

[5]   See M Ohaloth 1:6 and T Eiruvin 8:3.

III

A mechanism which serves to blur liminality is the principle of *continuity*. The dying are expected to finish off all unfinished business, both of a material and spiritual nature. To enter the world to come with nothing left undone. The dying are questioned about debts and family status; for example, if one is childless and his death may produce a levirate marriage he is asked to divorce his wife. This must be done tactfully: "People visit him and are neither encouraging or discouraging..." they speak to him about the things that must be settled." This discussion should not take place in front of women and children "so as not to break his heart" with their crying. Nor it is held with the ignorant (*am haaretz*) who would not understand the possible Halakhic problems caused by his passing (Tractate Mourning according to R. Hiyyah 1:1–2). Similarly, modern thinkers note that it is very important for dying persons to complete their unfinished business so that they can pass away with peace of mind (Kubler-Ross, 1970; Glaser and Strauss, 1965).

Both traditional Jewish and contemporary Western approaches blur the liminal state. They differ in that the traditional Jewish approach stresses the importance of the deceased's social obligations so that society can maintain clearly defined statuses for the living. The western approach stresses his right as a person to a peaceful end without considering too much the needs of society. In Jewish tradition it is the society which is of major concern, its boundaries and structures must be maintained. In western society the individual is the major concern it is his self which must be clearly defined.

Dying is recognized as a process which exists on a biological level, but is rejected by Jewish tradition as a social category. The Jewish attitude toward confession reflects this as well. Confession of sin is a private matter and a device by which the dying person settles his business with the transcendental world. If the major rewards are in the other world where the soul is destined then confession is a necessary preparation for that world, paying off any remaining spiritual debts before death. Note that not everyone is advised to confess. Confession is not recommended for the *am haaretz*. Those who are asked to confess are told that not all those who confess necessarily die, for "many who confessed (when they were ill) are walking (today) in the marketplace" (Tractate Mourning according to R. Hiyyah 1:2).[6]

---

6   The idea of confession stems at least from the days of the Tannah R. Eliezer ben Hyrcanus (second generation of Tannaim, 90–115 CE) who said "repent one day before you die" (M Avot 2:10). According to a later Tannah, R. Eliezer ben Ya'akov (fourth generation of Tannaim, 135–170 CE), his confession and repentance will serve as his advocates on the day of judgement (M Avot 4:11).

IV

Society does not express the liminal state of dying. It has no need to prepare itself for death. When a member of society dies the transition for society is sharp. It is than followed by a short, intensive, liminal state whose main feature is a gradual separation from the dead, that modulates the abrupt transition from life to death. The strong opposition between life and death is mediated and moderated by a weaker opposition between *continuity* and *separation* bridging the hiatus in the stronger opposition and enabling a smooth transition.

Treatment of the corpse reflects the gradual transition to death, presenting both symbols of separation and symbols of continuity. Upon death, the deceased's son or others close to him close the deceased's eyes. This should take place immediately after death and not a second before, "he who closes the eyes of the corpse the moment the soul goes forth, lo, this one sheds blood" (M Shabbat 23:5). Closing the eyes by a son is a symbolic act that reflects both *continuity* and *separation*. The son declares himself the successor[7] while separating the father from this world.[8] By separating himself from his father the son maintains the continuity of the role of family head.

The deceased undergoes a second series of treatments which reflect *separation*. "They tie the cheeks" (M Shabbat 23:5) if his mouth is open, "and they stop his bowels" (T Shabbat 17:18), "in order that air should not enter" (BT Shabbat 151b) and inflate the corpse (Zlotnik, 1966: 97–8). The corpse is completely sealed and separated from the physical world. There can be no input from outside the body. The only unsealed orifice, the ear can not hear because it is forbidden to speak in the presence of the body (JT Berakhot 3:1, 6b). Furthermore they remove the mattress from under it on [cool] sand, so it will keep" (M Shabbat 23:5). The body can not be mistaken for a living person.

Other symbols and symbolic acts reflect *continuity* as well. These are treatments which though done to the corpse could be easily done to living

---

[7]   On parallels in the Greek and Roman world see Kurtz and Boardman (1971); Toynbee (1971: 41–43) and Zlotnik (1966: 18).

[8]   It is forbidden to close the eyes of the dead on the Sabbath, they are not to be touched (*Muktzeh*) (M Shabbat 23:5). Should the eyes be left open they may remain so due to rigor mortis. The following is the suggestion of one sage for dealing with this problem. R. Shimeon ben Elazar said: "if one desires that a dead man's eyes should be closed let him blow wine into his nostrils and apply oil between his two eyelids and hold his two big toes: then they close of their own accord" (BT Shabbat 151b, also see T Shabbat 17:19 and Lieberman, 1962, Part II: 295).

persons. "They anoint it and rinse it" (M Shabbat 23:5; Tractate Mourning 1:3). It was customary to anoint the corpse with oil and then rinse with water, or vice versa[9] (Note that this act is not to purify the dead; neither biblical law nor the Talmud require the purification of the dead (*tahara*). This obligation appears in later law. Cisterns were excavated in the Kings Tombs in Jerusalem which may have been used for ritual bathing of the dead, but there is no evidence that they were made for this purpose (Kon, 1947: 34).[10] Anointment and washing are treatments done to the living. Since the dead are indifferent to such treatment, these can not be instrumental acts. Yet another thing is done for the dead: "they cut his hair and wash a garment for him" (BT Mo'ed Katan 8b, cf. Dikdukei Sofrim),[11] something altogether unnecessary for a soon-to-be-buried body. Despite the acts of sealing the body, acts which imply separation, the dead is washed and shorn as if he were a living person.

It is clear that symbols of continuity and separation operate simultaneously. The body is separated from worldly contact by closing all of its orifices and finally being removed from the bed and placed on the ground. The body is also treated as an actual living person; it is washed and dressed, these are acts of continuity. We are reminded of the Amoraic sages' conception of the human embryo:

> R. Simlai delivered the following discourse: what does an embryo resemble when it is in the bowels of its mother? Folding writing tables. Its hands rest on its two temples respectively... its mouth is closed and its navel is open... (it) produces no excrement because otherwise it might kill its mother. When it leaves the womb the closed organ opens and the open one closes (BT Niddah 30b).

---

[9]   According to Krauss (1910–12: Vol. I: 234, Vol. II: 55, 427, 474), they would first wash the body with water and then smear with oil and spices as is stated in the New Testament (Matthew 26:12; Mark 14:8; 16:1; Luke 23:56; 24:1; John 12:7; 19:11). Büchler (1936) rejects this position, claiming that the oils were use as a detergent to clean away filth. The use of oils and spices after cleansing was not a Jewish custom. The sources which speak of oiling after washing were influenced by non-Jews or were not written in Israel. According to Rashi (BT Shabbat 40b) "oiling precedes washing." According to Maimonides (Laws of Mourning 4:1) washing precedes oiling.

[10] Gen. Rabbah 37:4. "...the name Shinar reflects that its inhabitants die in anguish without a light and without a bath." This sentence is critical of Babylonia where the dead are not washed; as mentioned in our sources. It should not be concluded that these sources refer to the purification (*taharah*) of the dead.

[11] The washing of clothes relates to the period during which it was customary to bury the dead in their own clothes and not in shrouds. Burial in shrouds was introduced by Rabbi Gamliel II (second generation of Tannaim 90–115 CE). See T Niddah 9:17; BT Moed Katan 27b; BT Ketuboth 8b; Tractate Mourning 14:14.

The treatment which the deceased receives places him symbolically in a position similar to that of the embryo. He is ready for rebirth into the world of souls from which he came.[12]

V

Two other symbols are added to the complex of symbols described above. These are the lighting of lamps and the use of spices. In the Mishnah there is a discussion regarding the lamp and light of *havdalah* (the prayer separating the Sabbath from the week day) at the end of the Sabbath. The Mishnah says that blessings on the light and spices are not said "over a lamp or spices of the dead" (M Berakhot 8:6), because the lamp was not for light but in honor of the dead, and the spices are not for people to smell but to cover the bad smell. Later on in Palestine R. Yossi ben Hanina (second generation of Amoraic scholars, 250–290 CE) teaches us that a lamp in honor of the dead was "placed over [on top of] the coffin" (JT Berakhot 8:7, 12b) while those placed before the coffin were put there for the convenience of the living.[13]

---

[12] Tukachinsky (1960, I:94) sensed the meaning of these symbols and writes; "when he is born he is washed and when he dies he is washed…the body leaving the womb and the soul leaving the body are similar to birth." There are practical reasons for sealing the rectum and the vagina at death, both acts are preformed in modern hospitals as well (Sudnow, 1969: 77), but this does not detract from the symbolic significance. Talmudic sources say nothing about nail cutting, though it would seem that nail cutting has the same symbolic significance as hair cutting. Both Maimonides (Moshe ben Maimon 1927: Laws of Mourning, 4:1) and R. Aaron HaKohen of Lunil (HaKohen 1901: Laws of Mourning, 11) who cites Maimonides do not require nail cutting. The Tur (Jacob ben Asher [1475]: Yoreh De'ah 352) who also cites Maimonides proclaims that "they have to cut the hair and the nails." The Rema (Isserlis [1578–80]: Yoreh De'ah, 352:4) accepts this decision. In this way Rabbinic decisions generally were consistent with the complex of symbols originating in the talmudic period. R. Binyamin ben Mathatyah ([1539] 371b) quotes the will of R. Eliezer Halevi: "I request that they cleanse my body properly… That they wash and comb my hair as if I were alive, that the nails of my hands and feet be cut, so that I may come to rest in the same cleanliness and purity as that in which I went to the synagogue each Sabbath, hair washed and nails trimmed…" The Rabbis considered the departure from this world as if it were in preparation for a meeting in another world, something that must be prepared for, either by cutting hair or washing hair and cutting the nails. Some of the rabbis substituted washing the hair for cutting it.

[13] From the statement of Rav (first generation of Amoraic scholars of Babylonia 220–250 CE), we learn that in Babylonia, in the funeral procession of an important person, it was customary to precede him with candles, even if the funeral was during the day (BT Berakhot 53a).

The lamp on top of the coffin is reminiscent of the embryo. According to R. Simlai, a second generation amoraic scholar (250–290 CE) in Palestine, the embryo lies there and a lamp burns over its head… and it looks from one end of the world to the other" (BT Niddah 30b).[14] After the corpse is placed in an embryonic position a lamp is put "over his head" as it was in his mother womb. (The lamp is also identified with the soul: "a lamp is designated lamp and the soul of a man is called lamp [Proverbs 20:27, 'the soul of man is the lamp of God']" [BT Shabbat 30b].) Fire symbols are polysemic, and it is not surprising to find the lamp flame at the borders of passages like the entrance and exit to the sabbath and the birth and death of a human being, as a symbol of vitality and extinction, each meaning balancing the other.

The same is the case with *havdalah* spices, and the spices of the dead. Generally in rites of passage there are visions of fire and lights and sounds of voices which may mark the borders of the passage for the senses of sight and sound (see Huntington and Metcalf 1979: 49–55). The spices define the boundaries for the sense of smell.

The Mishna (above) relates that the spices of the dead are not used in *havdalah*. This leads to the conclusion that spices were used for the dead. In the name of Tanna R. Nathan (fourth generation of Tannaim 135–170 CE) it is taught that if a community collected money for the burial of the destitute, any surplus may be used to sprinkle perfume on the coffin (JT Shekalim 3:7, 47a). We conclude that liquid perfume was sprayed on all coffins. Another source (JT Berakhot 8:7, 12b) relates that in some places in Palestine the custom with spices was similar to that of the lamp: they placed spices "over the coffin" for the convenience of the living. BT Berakhot 53b states that the function of the spices was to cover the odor of the dead. The above sources deal with liquid perfume.

Floral spices were also used, especially myrtle. Later amoraic sources in Babylonia mention that myrtle branches were placed on the coffin (BT Bezah 6a). There is evidence that in both Palestine and Babylonia myrtle was used at weddings. As for weddings in Palestine, we know that the Tanna R. Judah ben Ilai danced before the bride holding myrtle branches (BT Ketubot 17a) as did the Babylonian Amorah R. Samuel ben Isaac (JT Pe'a 1:1, 17b). In Babylonia the bridal canopy was also decorated with myrtle

---

14   See a similar form in Yelinek (1938: Part I, 153–55). This is a fairly late source, but reflects the position of R. Yohanan and his generation. See Urbach (1975: 245–246) and Rubin (1990: 64–67).

(BT Shabbat 150b; Eiruvin 40a). There is even a case of a marriage contracted with a branch of myrtle (BT Kiddushin 12b).[15]

The above sources confirm the use of myrtle in marriage in both the tannaic and amoraic periods in Palestine and Babylonia, and in death ritual in Babylonia as a symbol of eternity, vitality, and revival. The widespread use of the myrtle in the tannaitic period suggests that it may have been placed on the coffin as well, although there is no concrete evidence of this. The Midrash opposes the willow to the myrtle. The willow withers shortly after being cut from the tree while the myrtle stays green for a long time without water (Lev. Rabbah 30:10). For this reason the myrtle symbolizes vitality and success in marriage.[16] The myrtle is resistant to fire, after being burned it brings forth triple leaves in each cell. According to R. Judah this is the splendid myrtle to be used as one of the four species on the Feast of Tabernacles (BT Sukkah 32b). The myrtle symbolizes resistance to misfortune and fire (Hareuveni 1980: 83). With all these qualities it follows that myrtle would be an appropriate symbol for the future of the dead.

The symbols lamp, spice, and myrtle reflect the principle of continuity and gradation. Against the strong opposition between life and death lie a series of moderate opposition bridging the abrupt gap. These are light (lamp)—darkness, vitality (spices)—putrefaction, and revival (myrtle)—extinction. The moderate and more visible opposition make the crisis of death more palatable.

VI

In the introductory discussion it was contended that the rituals of death as reported in talmudic literature would present a view of the meaning of life. Jewish culture classifies to the extreme and creates clear boundaries between categories; it deals with the human corpse in ways which reflect this degree of classification. The dying person is not perceived to be in a liminal state, but remains a part of the category of the living. The very same attitude of distance and respect which attends the living, and reflects the approach to society as a whole, devolves on the living who deal those taking their last breaths.

---

[15] The Midrash explains that the myrtle was chosen for the four species on the Feast of Tabernacles, "because it has a smell, but no taste" (Lev. Rabbah 30:12, p. 709).

[16] See, for example, "one who sees the myrtle in his dream becomes successful in property" (BT Berakhot 57a). Shops were also decorated with myrtle as a symbol of success see BT Aboda Zara 12b.

Dying is part of living and should not be accelerated, the dying person has all the rights and obligations of any other living human being.

To sum up, the blurring of the liminal stage is expressed in the principles of gradation and continuity. Attempts are made to settle the social affairs of the dying person properly, in order to prevent any social dysfunction after death. Matters of a spiritual nature are settled by confession. Death is an abrupt transition because of the lack of a liminal stage of dying. The sharpness of the transition is dulled by polysemic symbols carrying opposed meanings of continuity and separation. The symbols of separation are, the closing of the eyes, closing of body orifices, tying the cheeks, and placing the body on the ground. The symbols of continuity are the anointing of the body, washing the body, trimming the hair, and washing the clothes in which the body will be buried.

Other symbols from material culture bridge the sharp opposition. These are the lamp, spices and the myrtle. These create an opposition between darkness, putrefaction and extinction—and light, vitality, and rebirth. Thus they bridge the gap between life and death.

The corpse is treated in ways similar to the treatment of the newborn. One is born into this world and born again into the world-to-come. The messages are transmitted symbolically in the language of culture, by symbols and symbolic acts which, when interpreted together, form a consistent system of meaning.

Chapter 8. *BIRKAT AVELIM—* THE BLESSING OF MOURNERS: RITUAL ASPECTS OF SOCIAL CHANGE

I

One of the ancient Talmudic practices of condolence, which has today disappeared from Jewish life, was *Birkat Avelim*, the "Blessing of the Mourners." Although the general meaning of this custom is clear, the sources describing it are complicated and unclear and it is difficult to ascertain all of its details. In order to arrive at a better understanding of the custom, it is necessary to examine the original texts, one by one, as far as possible.

Birkat Avelim was recited in the presence of ten people for every person who died.

In M Megilla 4:3 we read:

> One does not recite *Birkat Avelim* nor *Tanhume Avelim* (the "Comforting of Mourners"),[1] nor the Marriage Blessings, nor the invitation to Grace (*Zimmun*) with God's name, with less than ten.

In the T Megillah 4:14 it is stated:

> One does not recite *Birkat Avelim* with less than ten, the mourners not being counted in this number, and one does not recite the Marriage Blessings with less than ten, and the bridegrooms are counted in this number.

Regarding a suicide, we read:

> One does not rend one's garments nor remove one's shoes nor say eulogies for him, but one does stand in the Row for him and recite *Birkat Avelim* for him, for these are done out of respect for the living." (Tractate Semahot 2:1)

---

[1] In precise versions: "One does not recite the blessing of mourners and of bridegrooms..." See e.g. the edition of the Mishnah of M. S. Kaufman and M. S. Parma. See also Ginzberg (1941, II:69).

Some sources indicate that this blessing was recited in the synagogue. Thus, a *baraita* in the Jerusalem Talmud Pesahim 8:8, 36c states:

> At a gathering of bones (i.e., reinternment) one does not say dirges and lamentations nor *Birkat Avelim* nor *Tanhume Avelim*. What is *Birkat Avelim*? That which they say in the synagogue. What is *Tanhume Avelim*? That which they say in the Row (*Shurah*).[2]

More detailed descriptions are found in Tractate Soferim (19:8):

> *Birkat Avelim* is recited in the evening, after prayers, over a cup of wine and in the presence of the worshippers... On the Sabbath, after the cantor has completed the *Mussaf* prayer, he goes behind the door of the synagogue or to the corner of the synagogue where he finds the mourners and all their relatives, and he says the blessing over them..."[3]

In Pirkei de-Rabbi Eliezer (ed. Horowitz, 1972: ch. 17, p. 65) it is stated that:

> Since the Temple was destroyed, the Sages introduced a rule that bridegrooms and mourners are to go to the synagogue and houses of study. The people see the bridegroom and rejoice with him, and see the mourner and sit on the ground with him. Thus, all of Israel may fulfill the obligation of performing deeds of loving-kindness. It is of this that it is said, "Blessed are You, who rewards those who perform loving-kindness."

It is not explicitly mentioned here that they recite a blessing. On the other hand, other sources would suggest that the blessing was recited in the house of mourning.

In Lev. Rabbah 23:4, Rabbi Johanan of Sepphoris, a third-generation Palestinian *amora*, applied the verse, "Like a rose among the thorns," (Cant. 2:2) to the practice of loving-kindness, mentioning, among other things:

> Ten who entered the house of mourning and did not know how to recite *Birkat Avelim*, and one of them knew...

Further on, it relates that Rabbi Jonah taught his disciples various blessings:

---

2   Cf. TJ Moed Katan 1:5, 80c; JT Sanh. 6:11, 23d and pars. In Semahot 12:4: "One does not stand in the Row for them nor recite *Birkat Avelim* nor *Tanhume Avelim*, but says on them words of comfort for themselves." In MS. Oxford, the words *Birkat Avelim* are missing (see Semahot, ed. D. Zlotnick, 1966: 35).

3   This quotation follows Lieberman's (1967: 49, n. 56) reading in Tosefta ki-Feshuta, Berakhot 3:23 following the version in Mahzor Vitri (p. 715).

Even the Marriage Blessings and the Mourner's Blessing, saying "You should be complete people in every respect."

It is possible that in the house of mourning the blessing was recited at the time of the meal. We learn explicitly of *Birkat Avelim* recited in the Grace after Meals:

In those places where it is customary to recite three blessings within *Birkat Avelim*, one recites three; two, one recites two; one, one recites one. In those places where it is customary to recite three blessings within *Birkat Aveliem*, one combines the first (i.e., blessing of Grace) with that concerning the resurrection of the dead, concluding "[Blessed is He...] who revives the dead." In the second, [one includes the] Condolence of Mourners, concluding "He who comforts His people in his City." In the third [one mentions] the performance of loving-kindness, and does not conclude it. One who recites the parting words (*ha-maftir*[4] in the cemetery does not conclude it. (T Berakhot 3:23–24; Lieberman, 1967).

In the JT Ketubot 1:1, 25a we likewise read:

R Hiyya taught, "One recites *Birkat Avelim* all seven days." Just as one uses [in it] the formula, "He who comforts his people in His city," so too [in the Marriage Blessings] one uses the formula, "He who rejoices His people." Just as [in *Birkat Avelim*] one makes mention of [the deceased], so too [in the Marriage Blessings] one mentions [the bride, and she need not leave her chamber.][5]

Additional evidence that the *Birkat Avelim* was recited following Grace at the meal is found in Tractate Soferim (19:8), from which it follows that in addition to the usual cup of wine filled for Grace after Meals, a second cup was filled for *Birkat Avelim*, following the rule that "One does not recite two sanctifications over one cup." (BT Pesahim 102b) In tannaitic times, ten cups of wine were drunk at the meal of mourners and ten blessings relating to the mourners were recited (see below).

From other sources, we learn of a third view according to which *Birkat Avelim* was recited in the "plaza" in front of the grave.

---

[4] They took leave of the deceased (*petirah*) in the cemetery, reciting texts which contained the same content as the three blessings of *Birkat Avelim*, but lacking the formal endings.

[5] Cf. JT Megillah 4:4, 75a. On the conclusion, "He who comforts His people in His city," see Heinemann (1964: appendix to Ch. 2).

What is *Birkat Avelim*? The blessing of the plaza. R. Yitzhak said in the name of R. Johanan: *Birkat Avelim* is recited in the presence of ten, mourners not being counted in this number; Marriage Blessings are recited in the presence of ten, bridegrooms being counted in this number. (BT Megillah 23b)[6]

This blessing is recited immediately after burial; in the case of two corpses brought for sequential burial, we learn:

If they took out the first one and buried him, they do not stand in the Row nor recite *Birkat Avelim* until after the second one has been taken out... (Semahot 11:3)

The "Blessing of the Plaza" was recited not only after the burial but, under certain circumstances, all seven days.

R. Yitzhak said in the name of R. Johanan: One recites Marriage Blessings in the presence of ten all seven days, the bridegroom being counted in this number; and *Birkat Avelim* in the presence of ten all seven days, the mourners not being counted in this number. But is there a Blessing of the Plaza all seven days? There is, in those cases where "new faces" (i.e., people who had not yet consoled the mourners) came." (BT Ketubot 8a)[7]

Thus, whenever new visitors came during the week of mourning, the mourner and his entourage went out to the cemetery plaza and there, in the presence of ten, recited *Birkat Avelim*.

We may summarize our findings until this point as follows:
1. *Birkat Avelim* is recited only in the presence of ten.
2. The mourners are not counted in this quorum of ten.

---

[6] But cf. Midrash Sekhel Tov to Gen. 50:26 (Ed Buber 1900–1901: 334): "They go up to the mourner's home and fill a cup of wine, and recite *Birkat Avelim*, that is, the Blessing of the Plaza." From this it follows that the Blessing in the Plaza was identical to the blessing in the mourner's house. This midrash is extremely late, so that the Blessing of the Plaza was no longer explained in its original meaning.

[7] Many commentators, including Ha-Meiri, attempted to explain this passage as if the blessing at the meal and that in the plaza were one and the same; that is, that *Birkat Avelim* is the blessing recited at the meal held in the plaza. The blessing recited on the first day after the burial is called the Blessing of the Plaza because of its location. On other days, when "new faces" were present, a meal of condolence would be held at the mourner's home, at which he was comforted with *Birkat Avelim*—i.e., the Blessing of the Plaza. But this interpretation does not match with the plain meaning of the sources.

3. According to various sources, the site of this blessing was either:
    a. The synagogue
    b. The meal in the mourner's house
    c. The cemetery plaza
4. According to the view that it was recited in the synagogue, it was recited every evening over a cup of wine, and on the Sabbath after *Mussaf*.
5. According to the view that it was recited at the mourner's meal, it was formulated in either three, two or one blessing, according to local custom.
6. *Birkat Avelim* was recited at the meal every day of the seven, according to the Jerusalem Tamud.
7. According to the view that it was said at the cemetery plaza, this was done immediately after burial.
8. According to the Babylonian Talmud, the blessing was recited in the cemetery plaza all seven days, whenever "new faces" were present.

II

We still need to establish the character of these blessings and the differences, if any, between those recited in the synagogue, in the house of mourning, and in the plaza. To do so, additional sources must be examined.

> Ten cups of wine are drunk in the house of mourning: two before the meal; five with the meal; and three after the meal. These three are after the meal: one for Grace after Meals; one for deeds of loving-kindness; one for the comforting of mourners (or, according to the version in Tractate Semahot, one for *Birkat Avelim*; one for *Tanhume Avelim*; one for deeds of loving-kindness). When Rabban Gamaliel died, they added an additional three: one for the *hazan* of the congregation; one for the head of the congregation; and one for Rabban Gamaliel. When the Court saw that they drank in excess, they made an enactment against it and restored things as they had been." (JT Berakhot 3:1, 6a; Semahot 14:14)

Somewhat different is the parallel source in BT Ketubot 8b:

> The Sages introduced [the drinking of] ten cups in the house of mourning: three before the meal, to open his [the mourner's] digestive tract; three during the meal, to wash down the food; and four after the meal—one for the blessing "He who feeds the world," one for the Blessing of the Land, one for "He who rebuilds Jerusalem," and one for "He who is good and beneficent."

They added four additional blessings: one for the *hazanim* of the city; one for the leaders (*parnassim*) of the city; one for the Temple; and one for Rabban Gamaliel. People started to drink to excess, so things were restored as they had been.

From these two sources, it would seem that *Birkat Avelim* was recited over cups of wine prior to Rabban Gamaliel's time, but their number and order was not fixed (see below). According to the version in Semahot, *Birkat Avelim* was recited at the meal in the mourner's house, while in the Babylonian Talmud neither *Birkat Avelim* nor *Tanhume Avelim* is mentioned. The major difference between the Babylonian Talmud, on the one hand, and the Semahot, on the other, is in the internal division of the cups within the meal. According to the Babylonian Talmud, there were three before the meal, three during, and four after; according to Semahot and the Jerusalem Talmud, there were two, five and three. One can clearly see that the three blessings after the meal, referred to there, parallel the three blessings in the Tosefta to *Berakhot*, previously quoted:

> In those places where they recited three blessings within *Birkat Avelim*, the first [blessing] is combined with that concerning the resurrection of the dead, and concludes, "He who revives the dead," the second includes the condolence of Mourners, and concludes, "He who comforts His people in His city," the third, the performance of loving-kindness, and has no conclusion.

This parallelism may be illustrated as follows:

Semahot	Tosefta Berakhot
One for *Birkat Aveliem*	One combines the first with that concerning the resurrection of the dead, concluding "[Blessed is He]… who revives the dead."
One for *Tanhume Avelim*	In the second, [one includes the] Condolence of Mourners, concluding "He who comforts His people in his City."
One for loving-kindness	In the third [one mentions] the performance of loving-kindness, and does not conclude it

Ginzberg and Lieberman[8] quite correctly note that the term *Birkat Avelim* as such also includes the blessing of *Tanhume Avelim* and of *Gemilut Hasadim* (deeds of loving-kindness), but when these two blessings are mentioned together with it, then the term refers only to *Birkat Avelim* proper. Thus, *Birkat*

---

[8]   Ginzberg (1941, II:72–73), and Lieberman (1967: 49).

Avelim mentioned in Semahot is identical with that blessing which concludes "He who revives the dead (*Mehayeh ha-metim*)" in the Tosefta.[9]

The meaning of the Tosefta is thus as follows: In those places where it as the custom to recite three blessings of *Birkat Avelim* in the Grace after Meals recited in the house of mourning, these are not recited separately, but the first blessing of *Birkat Avelim* is incorporated within the first blessing of Grace concluding with "*Mehayeh ha-metim*;" the second blessing of *Tanhume Avelim* is incorporated in the second Blessing of Grace, "He who comforts His city;" and the blessing dealing with *Gemilut Hasadim* is incorporated in the third blessing of Grace, but this is not concluded with a special formula relating to *Gemilut Hasadim*, but with the regular concluding formula for that blessing of Grace. The Tosefta continues by saying: "One who takes leave of the deceased (*ha-Maftir*) in the cemetery (see above, n. 4) does not conclude the blessing." Although blessings generally do have formal conclusions, in the cemetery, when leave-taking is said before the burial, it is not concluded because *Birkat Avelim* in its entirety is only recited after the burial. The one who delivers the leave-taking may use the content of those blessings for this purpose, but may not conclude it with the authorized formula of a blessing.[10]

Why was the third blessing of Grace not concluded with a special formula for *Gemilut Hasadim*, as the first two blessings were concluded with their own respective conclusions? It is difficult to find an explanation for this.[11] It

---

[9]   See below the version of *Birkat Avelim* in BT, which concludes "He who revives the dead."

[10] On the possibility of incorporating one blessing within the framework of another, see M Berakhot 5:2. For example: *Havdalah* is a blessing which stands by itself, but in the *Amidah* prayer it is included within the blessing *Honen ha-Da'at*, without a conclusion of its own. Cf. Berakhot 16a: "And they (day labourers) eat their bread and do not say a blessing before it (because that blessing is not from the Torah) but they recite two blessings after it. How? [The say] the first blessing as established, and the second one opens with *Birkat Ha-arez*, and includes *Boneh Yerushalayim* within *Birkat Ha-arez*. Lieberman explains this Tosefta differently. In his view, the first blessing of *Birkat Avelim* is included within *Zimmum* (the introductory blessing calling upon those present to recite Grace), while the second blessing of *Birkat Avelim* is included within the third blessing of Grace, and the third one is incorporated within its fourth blessing. This suggestion is based upon the resemblance of the content of those respective blessings. See Lieberman (1967: 49–53).

[11] Lieberman (1967: 57) believes (see n. 10) that this blessing is incorporated within the fourth blessing of Grace, that of *ha-Tov ve-ha-Metiv*, which has no conclusion. It opens with "Blessed" (i.e., "Blessed are You, Lord... the God, our Father, our King, our Mighty One...") but does not conclude with "Blessed." Ginzberg was astonished at the fact that this blessing has no conclusion, and finds no explanation for this. See Ginzberg (1941, II:69, n. 51).

might be conjectured that the original blessing formula was retained in order to make it clear that these blessings are primarily blessings over food, and so that one unfamiliar with the various formulae of blessing would not think that they had failed to recite Grace at this meal. One could not, on the other hand, conclude the third blessing with two subjects—that of the rebuilding of Jerusalem and that of deeds of loving-kindness—because Rabbi Meir had already ruled that "One does not conclude with two subjects." (Berakhot 49a) It seems reasonable to assume that the blessing of *Gemilut Hasadim* had a concluding formula, used when it is recited by itself, as in the cemetery or the synagogue. Indeed, from the rule not to "conclude it" in Grace, one may infer that it in fact did have such a conclusion. Moreover, in the passage from Pirkei de-Rabbi Eliezer cited above, it is stated that since the destruction of the Temple, the Sages have enacted that one should comfort the mourner in the synagogue, "And of them is it said, 'Blessed are You, who grants a good reward to those who perform loving-kindness,'" which is one version of the formula of conclusion of this blessing.

According to the version of the Babylonian Talmud, four cups of wine were consumed after the meal, corresponding to the four blessings, *Ha-zan, Birkat Ha-arez, Boneh Yerushalayimi*, and *Ha-tov ve-ha-metiv*. We shall now examine the passage (BT Ketubot 8b) concerning the blessing of the plaza. An incident is related there concerning Resh Lakish and Rav Judah bar Nahmani, his interpreter, who recited *Birkat Avelim* on the second day of mourning. Resh Lakish asked Rav Judah bar Nahmani: say something

> In praise of the Holy One, blessed be He. He [Rav Judah] said: "The great God, in His very greatness, mighty and strong, in His great awesomeness, he restores the dead to life with His word and does great deeds beyond measure and miracles beyond number. Blessed are You, O Lord, who revives the dead."...Concerning the mourners, he said: "Our brothers, who are weary and saddened in this mourning, give heart to examine this, for it endures forever, it has been the way since the Six Days of Creation. Many have drunk, many will drink; as the former ones have drunk, so shall the latter ones drink; Our brothers, may the Master of Consolations console you. Blessed is He who consoles the mourners"... Concerning those who comfort the mourners, he said: "Our brothers, who practice kindness, children of those who practiced kindness and hold steadfast to the covenant of Abraham our father. Our brothers, may the Master of Recompense grant you your recompense. Blessed is He who grants recompense." Of all Israel, he said: "Master of the Universe, redeem and save Your people Israel from pestilence, from sword, from captivity, from despoilment, from drought and from blight, and from all kinds of disaster which befall the world. Before we call, You answer us. Blessed is He who stops the plague."

The first three of the four blessings mentioned in the Babylonian Talmud are thus parallel to the three blessings mentioned in the Tosefta, although the conclusion of the second blessing is different in the two sources, while the conclusion of the third blessing is absent in the Tosefta. According to the Tosefta, these are the three blessings which have been incorporated within the three blessings of Grace—*Ha-zan, Birkat Ha-arez,* and *Boneh Yerushalayim*—without the fourth blessing, *Ha-tov ve-ha-metiv.* In our case (following the Talmud's interpretation of the incident involving Resh Lakish and his interpreter), the blessings in the Babylonian Talmud were recited in the plaza, and not during Grace after Meals. However, it would seem that these blessings were incorporated within the blessings of Grace on those occasions that they were recited at a meal. According to the Babylonian version, in which four cups of wine were drunk after the meal, four blessings were recited within which four blessings of *Birkat Avelim* were incorporated into, corresponding to *Ha-zan, Birkat Ha-arez, Boneh Yerushalayim* and *Ha-tov ve-ha-metiv*—one cup for each blessing of Grace, which are also the four *Birkat Avelim* benedictions mentioned in TB Ketubot.

III

From this, it would seem that there were two different customs: that of Babylonia, according to which four blessings were said, and that of Eretz Yisrael, according to which three blessings were recited. However, the solution is not that simple, because this entire passage, in which the Babylonian *amoraim* discuss the problem, relies upon Palestinian *amoraim,* so that it would appear that the four blessings recited by Rav Judah bar Nahmani are in fact Palestinian. Thus, it would seem that in Eretz Israel itself it was customary to recite four blessings or that there were two different traditions there. It may also be that in blessings of the plaza, four blessings were recited, but in Grace only three. It has already been demonstrated[12] that in tannaitic times there was no fixed unified version of the prayers, and thus we have received variant versions of the same blessings which are, in fact, essentially alternatives which existed alongside one another. There were some individuals who spontaneously composed their own versions in the course of praying while others, who were unable to do so, used one or another of the widespread versions. At a later stage, the Sages introduced detailed requirements as to details and phrases which had meanwhile become set formulae, while in the later Amoraic

---

[12] See Heinemann (1964: ch. 2).

period, exact forms were fixed for the opening and closing of each blessing. Finally, texts were set for the central content of the blessings as well, when each blessing received its normative, obligatory formulation.[13]

As far as can be seen, the state of affairs regarding *Birkat Avelim* was no different. There were certainly different versions of the blessings (as has been demonstrated above, in the variant conclusions to the blessing of *Gemilut Hasadim*. "He who grants recompense," and "He who grants a good reward to those who perform loving-kindness," and of *Tanhume Aveiem*: "He who comforts His people in His city," and "He who comforts the mourners,") as well as different customs as to when and how to recite the blessing (the Tosefta speaks of places in which it was customary to recite three, two, etc.). On this basis, the various traditions which have come down to us from Eretz Israel itself can be understood. It is clear that there was no single, universally accepted version or text of *Birkat Avelim*. There is also a source in Semahot which proves that in Eretz Israel there were those who did not recite the fourth blessing of Grace in the house of mourning.

> One who blesses (i.e., Grace) in the house of mourning does not recite the fourth blessing, said R. Jose ha-Galilee. Rabbi Akiva said: "He who is good and does good," while the Sages said: "Blessed is the true judge." (Semahot 14:15)[14]

This *baraita* appears in Semahot immediately after a *baraita* concerning the ten cups drunk in the house of mourning, which states that one drinks "three after the meal." It would appear that the editor of this tractate introduced immediately after this the *halakhah* that in a house of mourning one does not recite the fourth blessing, thereby explaining why there are "three after the meal."[15]

---

[13]   See Heinemann (1964: 36–37).

[14]   There are some manuscripts which end as follows:

> The Sages say: "Blessed is the true judge, who rules in His deeds, that we are all His people and His servants, and in all this we are obligated to praise Him and bless Him." See Semahot (ed. Higger, 1931: 210).

[15]   On the Grace after Meals, the time of its composition, and the difference between the first three blessings and the final blessing, see Finkelstein (1929). Cf. Büchler (1933), and Heinemann (1964: Ch. 2 and appendix to Ch. 2). BT Berakhot 46b (compare *Dikduke Sofrim*) cites this source, inverting the names of the *tannaim*:

> R. Nahman bar Yitzhak said: "Know that *ha-Tov ve-ha-Metiv* is not from the Torah, for it is uprooted in a house of mourning, as the Sages have taught.' What do they say in a house of mourning? 'Ha-tov ve-ha-Metiv.' Raabbi Akiva said, 'Barukh dayan ha-emet.'"

The reason for the difference in the order of cups between the source in the Jerusalem Talmud and Semahot as against that in the Babylonian Talmud can now be understood. By changing the number of blessings, and thereby *ipso facto* the number of cups following the meal, the order of those cups before and during the meal must also change, in order to retain the overall number of ten cups.[16]

IV

We mentioned above that it was customary to incorporate one blessing within another. We also noted that, at least during the Tannaitic period, there were no set formulae for the blessings, and that there were many blessings which were improvised by those who recited them. We have evidence from a relatively late

---

Rav Nahman bar Yitzhak relates here one of the customs of Eretz Yisrael, in which three blessings of Grace are recited in the house of mourning, while in Babylonia four blessings were recited.

[16] Ginzberg explains the difference in the customs relating to the number of cups between Eretz Yisrael and Babylonia, as follows: In Eretz Yisrael it was customary to drink two cups before the meal because "in the West [Eretz Yisrael] they were not particular about pairs," (BT Pesahim 109b–110a) while in Babylonia they were particular on this point and thus differed from the Eretz Yisrael practice, drinking three cups before the meal. As there was need of a total of ten cups, one cup was subtracted from those within the meal and added before the meal. However, as four cups also constitutes "pairs," the number of cups within the meal was set at three, and one was added after the meal, as they were not particular about "pairs" after the meal, because "a cup of blessing does not combine [with others] for evil." (BT Pesahim 109b)
This explanation is hardly acceptable because the total number of cups was not set at the outset (see above), and only after the number had been set were they concerned about the problem of pairs. Yet the Talmud, in fact, sees all ten cups as forming one unit. It is explicitly taught in the name of Ula:

Ten cups do not constitute 'pairs.' Ula gave his reason, as Ula said—and some say it was taught in a *mishna*—"The Sages introduced the ten cups in the house of mourning. Now, if you would suspect that these cups are considered 'pairs,' how could our Rabbis have instituted something that would lead to danger?" (BT Pesahim 110a)

It follows that in the ten cups there is no fear whatsoever of "pairs." Moreover, even if one says that there is no fear of demons, but that the Talmud here does fear magic (BT Pesahim 110b), we have nevertheless seen that all ten cups are considered one unit, and that the Talmud does not relate separately to those cups before, during or after the meal with regard to either "pairs," demons or magic.

source that such was, in fact, the case with regard to Grace after Meals. In one of his *responsa*, Rav Hai Gaon states:

> One may not add anything at all to the prayers or the blessings, but one is to recite the prayers for weekdays on weekdays, and the prayers for Sabbath on Sabbath, for the Sages taught "From this point on it is forbidden to say the praises of God. Therefore, the law is that one may not add even one word from *Birkat Avelim* in any of the four blessings: neither in *Zimmum*, nor in *Ha-Zan*, nor in *Birkat Ha-Eretz*, nor in *Boneh Yerushalayim*, but only in *Ha-tov ve-ha-metiv* exclusively." (*Ozar Ha-Geonim, Ketubot*, p. 31)

From Rav Hai Gaon's emphasis, one may infer that he was struggling for the establishment of a fixed, obligatory version (*nusah*). There is no doubt that earlier, as well as in his own time, improvisations within the text were customary. In the Cairo *genizah*, a number of texts of Grace after Meals for mourners were discovered. In some of these texts, liturgical poems (*piyyutim*) were added to the first three blessings of Grace, while in one text *Birkat Avelim* was added to the formula of *Zimmun*. These texts are instructive examples of the blessings of Grace which "include" and integrate *Birkat Avelim*.[17]

V

It would appear that over a period of time, at least in Babylonia, they ceased to incorporate *Birkat Avelim* within Grace, and instead, one special blessing was introduced for mourners. The source for this can be found in the words of the sixth generation Babylonian *amora*, Mar Zutra.

> Mar Zutra came to the house of Rav Ashi, whose son had died. "He opened and said: 'Blessed... is He who is good and does good, the true judge, who

---

[17]   See Haberman (1939), *piyyutim* #49–52. It is interesting that those versions of Grace designated as #50 and #51 contain only the first three blessings. In #52, a blessing with God's name (but without the formula "King of the Universe") appears within the *Zimmum*. The form of the blessing is:

> Let us bless He who comforts the mourners, of whose [bounty] we have eaten and by whose goodness we live. Blessed is He who comforts the mourners, of whose [bounty] we have eaten and by whose goodness we live. Blessed are You O Lord, who arouses His creatures in compassion, who created man with mercy and justice.

> Here, Grace is combined with that blessing of *Birkat Avelim* concerned with the resurrection of the dead.

judges in righteousness, who takes [souls] in judgment and rules His world to do with as He wills, for all of his ways are justice, for all is His and we are His people and His servants, and in all things we are required to thank Him and to bless Him. May He who repairs breaches in Israel repair this breach.'" (BT Berakhot 46b)[18]

Apparently, this version of the blessing, which was crystallized at the end of the Babylonian *amoraic* period, remained the final and obligatory version.

After the ten cups at the meal were abolished, the accepted custom came to be that at the end of the meal Grace was recited over one cup of wine, and afterwards *Birkat Avelim*, in the form of one blessing similar to that of Mar Zutra, was recited over a second cup. This reconstruction is offered on the basis of Soferim 19:8 quoted above.

The single blessing of *Birkat Avelim* was apparently that of Mar Zutra, or a variant thereof. In *Midrash Sekhel Tov* to Genesis (50:26, ed. Buber, 1900–1901: 335), we find that they recited blessings over two cups. There, they first recited *Birkat Avelim* in a formula similar to that of Mar Zutra,

---

18   See alternative readings in *Dikduke Sofrim*. It is noteworthy that in this blessing the blessings of *haTtov ve-ha-Metiv* and *Dayan ha-Emet*, which were recited by R. Akiva and by the Sages in the house of mourning, are combined. This blessing is identical, in many details, to that found in one of the versions of Semahot 14:15 (see n. 14 above). The idea at the end of the blessing is also found in Palestinian sources. R. Hanina bar Pappa (a third generation Palestinian *amora*) prayed for R. Tanhum bar Hiyya, who was a mourner, and said to him, "May your breach be repaired." See JT Moed Katan 3:7, 83c, and *Genesis Rabbah* 100, p. 1292. We may see how Mar Zutra's version was expanded in comparison with the earlier ones:

According to Semahot:	**According to Mar Zutra:**
Blessed	Blessed is He who is good and does good
The true judge	The true judge, who judges in righteousness and takes souls in judgment
Who rules in His deeds	Who rules in His world, to do with it as He wills, for all His ways are justice
For all of us	For all is His
are His people and servants	For we are His people, and His servants
and in all (this) we are obligated to praise Him and bless Him	and in everything we are obligated to praise Him and bless Him
Rav Hanina's version:	
May your breach be repaired	May He who repairs breaches in Israel repair your breach

189

...and afterwards they gave that cup to the mourners, and poured another cup, and recited over it "*Bore peri ha-gefen*," and drank.

In the Geonic period, there is no reference to the blessing over the cup, as they had evidently already abolished the cups in the meal. Opinions are divided about the inclusion within it of the blessing for comforting of the mourners.[19]

VI

Birkat Avelim needs to be more thoroughly studied. The material covered so far does not tell us during which period and in what places the blessing was made in the cemetery plaza, when the blessing was made at the meal, and when the blessing was made in the synagogue. It is unclear whether the alternative customs were a matter of personal choice or were simultaneously practiced. It is known that the custom of *Birkat Avelim* in the synagogue was practiced in Jerusalem after the destruction of the Temple.

In the source mentioned above from Soferim 19:9 we are told that R. Eliezer b. Hyrcanus spoke of two gates in Jerusalem:

> ...One for bridegrooms and one for mourners and the banished. On the Sabbath, Jerusalemites would gather in order to ascend the Temple mount and sit between these two gates in order to perform acts of kindness for each other (...when one entered by the mourners gate... it became known that he was in mourning and the people would say to him "He who dwells in this House will comfort you"...[20]) When the Temple was destroyed it was decreed that bridegrooms and mourners should attend the synagogue.

The source relates that on weekdays the mourners were blessed after the evening service and on the Sabbath the cantor blessed the mourners after the *Mussaf* service behind the synagogue. This source reports the custom of Jerusalem—there is no source regarding the custom outside Jerusalem. Were they blessed in the synagogue before the destruction of the Temple or was this not common practice at all? The Jerusalem custom was practiced for only a brief period; after the Bar Kokhba revolt Jews were not permitted to live in Jerusalem. Later sources report that in Palestine, mourners did

---

[19]   On the *geonic* versions of the blessings, see *Siddur Rav Amram Gaon* (ed., Davidson, Assaf and Yoel, Jerusalem, 1930: 104–105), Levin (1939: *Ketubot*, p. 34) and *Midrash Sekhel Tov* to Gen. 50:26 (ed. Buber, 1900–1901: 335).

[20]   The text in parentheses is an addition found in *Pirkei de Rabbi Eliezer* Ch. 17.

not attend synagogue during the first week of mourning except for the Sabbath. In Babylonia, mourners attended synagogue during the first week of mourning. (JT Moed Katan 3:5, 82c; BT Moed Katan 53a; Semahot 10:12; Levin, 1943: 37) Therefore, in Palestine, they ceased to practice the custom of *Birkhat Avelim* in the synagogue and there is no information regarding this practice in Babylonia although it is known that the mourners attended synagogue every day.

The other issues concerning the blessing of the mourners remain a puzzle. We can only repeat that in the land of Israel it was customary for some to incorporate three blessings of the mourners in the Grace after Meals. The conclusion of these blessings differed from the standard conclusions for blessings by using a formula for mourning. In some places in Palestine they omitted the fourth blessing from the Grace. Further customs include reciting one or two mourner's blessings within the *Birkat Hamazon*. In Babylonia, four mourners's blessings were incorporated into the four *Birkat Hamazon* blessings, each having the standard conclusion. We lack evidence as to where each custom was practiced.

During the Amoraic period in Babylonia it was accepted to make one mourning blessing on a cup of wine along with the *Birkat Hamazon*. During the Gaonic period a mourner's blessing was incorporated into the fourth blessing of the *Birkat Hamazon*. All the other customs were nullified by the Geonim.

Since further data are lacking concerning the mourner's blessings we can only speculate as to why the blessings were reduced from four or three to one. Anthropologists have shown that when social cohesiveness is strong and social networks are dense, participation in ritual will rise and ritual will become more frequent during times of crisis. (Gluckman 1962; Douglas 1973) In a highly cohesive community, during a crisis of death, mourning rites are practiced by the wider social network and community and not simply the bereaved family (Rubin 1986, 1990a).

In the land of Israel we observe a process of community change which, among other things, led to the passing of the extended family and greater emphasis on the nuclear family. During the period of the Roman High Commissioners, this process of change was at its peak. It became further accelerated after the Bar Kokhba revolt. As a result, gentiles were granted the right to own land in Israel, Judea was emptied of its Jewish population, and the major centers were transferred to the Galilee. (Alon 1954, I: ch. 5) The tendency toward nucleation was further exaggerated during the third and fourth centuries when there was an economic crisis in the Roman Empire. (Alon, 1954, II: 242–262) This decline continued through the Byzantine period at the conclusion of the Amoraic Era. The Jewish agricultural extended family of the mid Second Temple Period was reduced to an urban nuclear family form or to tenant farmer status. (Rubin 1972)

When the family and community are not stable, rites and ceremonies may become less important. This explains the reduced significance of the mourners' meal and the loss of the customs of the ten cups of wine and the blessing of the mourners. Elaborate mourning rites with special meals on each of the days of mourning require an appropriate social setting. Such customs are possible when the community is composed of extended families. The blessing of the mourners required a quorum of ten men, not counting the mourners. That is to say that there was a requirement that at least ten men free themselves from other obligations on each of the seven days of mourning for the blessings to take place. A meal in which ten cups of wine are drunk must have taken time and resources. In an extended family in a cohesive community it may have been possible to find ten non-mourners to participate in the ceremony without interfering with normal economic and social routines. As society becomes less integrated and the families tend more toward a nuclear type it is less likely that the daily meals could be carried out by any but the richest citizens.

As a result, the rites became more and more limited. They were reduced to only one blessing of mourners. It is impossible to say when and where each change took place, but the trend can be identified over time.

BIBLIOGRAPHY

'Abd al-'Al, M. D. (1957). *Comparative Study of the Unedited Work of Abu 'l-Hassan al Suri and Yussuf ibn Salamah.* PhD diss., Leeds University, (2 vols).

Abusch, Ra'anan (2003). "Circumcision and Castration under Roman Law in the Early Empire," in: Elizabeth Wyner Mark (ed.), *The Covenant of Circumcision: New Perspectives on an Ancient Jewish Rite.* Hanover and London: Brandeis University Press, pp. 75–86.

Albeck, Chanokh (1944). "Betrothal and betrothal rites," in: Louis Ginzberg and Avraham Weiss (eds.), *Studies in Memory of Moses Schorr 1874–1941.* New York: Professor Moses Schorr Memorial Committee, pp. 12–24 (Hebrew).

Albeck, Chanokh (1959). *Mavo La Mishnah (Introduction to the Mishnah).* Jerusalem and Tel Aviv: Dvir (Hebrew).

Albeck, Chanokh (1961). "Marriage in Antiquity." *Sinai* 48: 145–151 (Hebrew).

Albeck, Chanokh (1969). *Mavo La-Talmudim (Introduction to the Talmud, bavli and Yerushalmi).* Tel Aviv: Dvir (Hebrew).

Alon, Gedaliahu (1954). *Toldot ha-Yehudim be-Eretz Yisrael bi-Tekufat ha-Mishnah ve-ha-Talmud (History of the Jews in Eretz Yisrael in Mishnaic and Talmudic Age).* Tel aviv: Ha-Kibbutz ha-Meuchad (Hebrew).

Alon, Gedaliahu (1957). "*Le'heker ha'halakhah shel Filon*" ("Toward a Study of the Halakhah of Philo"), *Meh'karim Betoledot Yisrael (Studies in Jewish History).* Tel Aviv: Hakibbutz Hameuhad, vol. 1, pp. 83–114 (Hebrew).

Alon, Gedaliahu (1958). "The Sociological Approach in the Study of the Halakhah," in: *Meh'karim Betoledot Yisrael (Studies in Jewish History).* Tel Aviv: Hakibutz Hameuchad, vol. 2, pp. 181–227 (Hebrew).

Alon, Gedaliahu (1984). *The Jews in Their Land in the Talmudic Age.* Jerusalem: Magnes, 2 vols.

Anderson, Michael (1994). "What is New about the Modern Family?" in: Michael Drake (ed.), *Time, Family, and Community.* Oxford: Milton Keynes, pp. 67–90.

Ashley, Timothy R. (1993). *The Book of Numbers—the New International Commentary of the Old Testament.* Grand Rapids, MI: Eerdmans.

Aune, David E. (1994). "The Synoptic Gospels: Matthew, Mark and Luke," in: Harvey Nimkoff (ed.), *Approaches to the Bible*. Washington, D.C.

Avi-Yonah, Michael (1946). *Bi-yemei Roma U'Bizantion (In the Days of Rome and Byzantine Empire)*. Jerusalem: Bialik Foundation (Hebrew).

Avi-Yonah, Michael (1956). "The Samaritan Revolts against the Byzantine Empire," *Eretz-Israel* 4: 127–132 (Hebrew).

Ayali, Meir (1987). *Poalim ve'omanim: melakhtam u'ma'amadam be'sifrut hazal (Laborers and Craftsmen: their Work and Status in the Rabbinic Literature)*. Givatayim: Yad Latalmud. (Hebrew).

Bacher, Benjamin Zeev (1922). *Aggadot ha-Tannaim (The Legends of the Tannaim)*. Jerusalem: Dvir (Hebrew).

Baer, Yitzhak F. (1955). *Israel Ba-Amim (Israel among the Nations)*. Jerusalem: Bialik Foundation (Hebrew).

Bamberger, Bernard J. (1961). "Qetanah, na'arah, bogereth," *Hebrew Union College Annual, 32*: 281–94.

Baron, Salo W. (1966). *A Social and Religious History of the Jews* (2nd ed.). New York and Philadelphia: Columbia University Press and Jewish Publication Society.

Barthes, Roland (1972). *Mythologies*. (Trans. by A. Lavers). London: Jonathan Cape.

Basser, Herbert W. and Fishbane, Simcha (eds.) (1993). *Approaches to Ancient Judaism*. Atlanta, GA: Scholars Press.

Batten, Loring W. (1913). *A Critical and Exegetical Commentary on the Book of Ezra and Nehemiah*. Edinburgh: Clark.

Ben David Arye (1974). *Talmudische Ökonomie*, I. Hildeshim: Olms.

Bendor, Shunya (1996). *The Social Structure of Ancient Israel: The Institution of the Family (Beit 'Ab) from the Settlement to the End of the Monarchy*. Jerusalem: Simor.

Berger, Peter L. (1973). "Religious Institutions," in: Neil J. Smelser (ed.) *Sociology*, New York: John Wiley.

Berger, Peter L. and Luckmann, Thomas (1966). *The Social Construction of Reality*. Harmondsworth: Penguin Books.

Beyth-Marom, Ruth (1990). *Research Methods in the Social Sciences*. Unit 3. Tel Aviv: Open University (Hebrew).

Bialoblocki, Shmuel (1964). "The Attitude of Judaism towards Proselytes and Proselytism," *Bar-Ilan* 2, Jerusalem: Kiryath Sepher, pp. 44–60 (Hebrew).

Binyamin ben Mathatyah (1539). *Responsa of Binyamin Zeev*. Venice (Rev. ed. Jerusalem: Yad Harav Nissim 1980) (Hebrew).

Blenkinsopp, Joseph (1989). *Ezra-Nehemiah: A commenaery*. London: SCM Press.

Bloch, Maurice (1977). "The Past and Present in the Present," *Man* 12 (ns): 278–283.

Boàs, Franz (1896). *Race, Language and Culture*. New York: Macmillan.

Boyarin, Daniel (1993). *Carnal Israel: Reading Sex in Talmudic Culture*. Berkeley: University of California Press.

Braudel, Fernand (1969). "Histoire et sciences socials, la longue durée," in: *Écrits sur l'histoire*. Paris: Flammarion, vol. 1, pp. 41–83.

Braudel, Fernand (1972–1973). *The Mediterranean and the Mediterranean World in the Age of Phillip II*. New York: Harper and Row.

Braudel, Fernand (1977). *La Méditerranée: L'espace et l'histoire*. Paris: Arts et Metiers Graphiques.

Brin, Gershon (1971). *Ha'bekhor be'yisrael bitekufat ha'mikra* (*The Firstborn in Israel in the Biblical Era*), a Ph.D.dissertation, Tel Aviv: Tel Aviv University. (Hebrew).

Brin, Gershon (1977). *"Dinei bekhorot bamikra"* ("Laws of the Firstborn in the Bible"), *Tarbiz* 46: 1–7 (Hebrew).

Brin, Gershon (1994). *Sugiyot bamikra uva'megilot* (*Issues in the Bible and in the Megillot*), Tel Aviv: Hakibbutz Hameuchad. (Hebrew).

Büchler, Adolph (1927). "The induction of the bride and bridegroom into the *chupa* in the first and second centuries in Palestine," in: A. Freimann et al. (eds.), *Livre d'hommage a la mémoire du Dr Samuel Poznanski*. Warsaw: En comm. chez O. Harrassowitz, pp. 82–132.

Büchler, Adolph (1933). "Toldot Birkat ha-Tov ve-ha-Metiv" in: Avigdor Aptowitzer and Zecharia Schwartz (eds.), *Ma'amarim le-Zikhron Tzvi Peretz Chajes*. Vienna: Alexander Kahut Fund, pp. 137–167.

Büchler, Adolph (1935). "Explanation of Mishnah Shabbath 23:5," in: *Festschrift for Professor Samuel Krauss*. Jerusalem: Rubin Mass, pp. 36–54 (Hebrew).

Burger, Thomas (1976). *Max Weber's Concept Formation: History, Laws, and Ideal Types*. Durham: Duke University Press.

Chadwick, Henry (1953). (tr. and ed.), *Origen: Contra Celsum* Cambridge: Cambridge University Press.

Cheal, David (1992). "Ritual: Communication in action." *Sociological Analysis*. 53: 363–374.

Clines, David J. A. (1984). *Ezra, Nehemiah, Esther*. Grand Rapids, MI: Eerdmans.

Cohn, Norman (1962). "Medieval Millenarism: Its Bearing on the Comparative Study of Millenarian Movements," in: Sylvia L. Thrupp (ed.), *Millenial Dreams in Action*. The Hague: Mouton, pp. 31–43.

Collins, Ronald (1988). *Sociology of Marriage and the Family: Gender, Love and Property*. Chicago: Nelson-Hall.

Cooper, Samuel (1987) "On the Rules of Mixture: An Anthropological Study in *Halakhah*," in: Harvey E. Goldberg (ed.), *Judaism Viewed from Within and from Without: Anthropological Studies*. Albany, NY: State University of New York Press, pp. 55–74.

Cooper, Samuel (ND). "Symmetries in Jewish law and custom," Unpublished manuscript.

Cooper, Samuel (NDa). "The Three Sins for which Women Die in Childbirth," Unpublished manuscript.

Cronbach, Lee J. and Meehl, Paul E. (1955). "Construct Validity in Psychological Tests." *Psychological Bulletin, 52*: 281–302.

Dan, Joseph (1993). "The 'New Aspect': The Regression to 1925." *Haaretz*, (October 22). p. B9 (Hebrew).

Dan, Joseph (ed.) (1986). *Sefer hayashar*. Jerusalem: Mossad Bialik (Hebrew).

Danforth, Loring M. (1982). *The Death Rituals of Rural Greece*. Princeton, NJ: Princeton University Press.

Davidovitch, David (1977). "Some Jewish Marriage Customs that Passed into Disuse," *Yeda-'Am, 43–44*: 105–112 (Hebrew).

Davis, Fred (1992). *Fashion, Culture and Identity*. Chicago: University of Chicago Press.

Dean, James Elmer (ed.) (1935). *The Epiphanius Treatise on Weighs and Measures*. Chicago, ILL: University of Chicago Press.

Denniston, G. Carter (1996). "'Modern' Circumcision: The Escalation of a Ritual." *Circumcision* 1: 3–11.

Deshen, Shlomo (1978). "The 'Kol Nidre' Enigma: An Anthropological View of the Day of Atonement Liturgy." *Ethnology*, 18: 121–133.

Dodds, E. R. (1964). *The Greek and the Irrational*. Berkely: University of California Press.

Douglas, Mary (1966). *Purity and Danger: An Analysis of the Concepts of pollution and Taboo*. London: Routledge and kegan Paul.

Douglas, Mary (1973). *Natural Symbols: Explorations in Cosmology*. New York: Vintage.

Douglas, Mary (1978). *Cultural Bias*, London: Royal anthropological institute.

Douglas, Mary (1987). *How Institution Think*. London: Routledge and Kegan Paul.

Douglas, Mary (ed.) (1982). *Essays in the Sociology of Perception*. London: Routledge and Kegan Paul.

Douglas, Mary and Wildavsky, Aaron (1982). *Risk and Culture: An Essay on the Selection of Technical and Environmental Dangers*. Berkely: University of California Press.

Druyan, Nitza (1992). "Yemenite Jewish Women—Between Tradition and Change," in: Deborah S. Bernstein (ed.), *Pioneers and Homemakers: Jewish Women in Pre-State Israel* Albany: State University of New York Press, pp. 75–93.

Duliere, L. (1967). "La seconde circoncision pratiquée entre Juifs et Samaritains," *L'Antiquité Classique* 36:553–565.

Durkheim, Emile (1938). *The Rules of Sociological Method*. (Trans. by Sarah A. Solovay and John H. Mueller). Chicago: University of Chicago Press.

Durkheim, Emile (1965). *The Elementary Forms of Human Life*. (Trans. by Joseph Ward Swain). New York: Free Press.

Ehrlich, Uri (1994). *The Methods of Prayer and their Significance in the Mishnah and Talmud Eras*. Unpublished Ph.D. dissertation, Jerusalem: Hebrew University (Hebrew).

Eilberg-Schwartz, Howard (1990). *The Savage in Judaism: An Anthropology of the Israelite Religion and Ancient Judaism.* Bloomington, IN: Indiana University Press.

Eisenstein, Judah David (ed.) (1928). *Bibliotheca Midraschica (Otzar Midrashim),* (11 vols.). New York.

Epstein, Louis M. (1927). *The Jewish Marriage Contract: A Study in the Status of the Woman in Jewish Law.* New York: Jewish Theological Seminary of America.

Evans-Pritchard, Edward Evan (1940). *The Nuer.* Oxford: Clarendon.

Fenshman, F. Charles (1982). *The Book of Ezra and Nehemiah—the New International Commentary on the Old Testament.* Grand Rapids, MI: Eerdmans.

Finkelstein, Louis (1929). "The Birchat Hamazon." *Jewish Quarterly Review (NS),* 19:211–262.

Finkelstein, Louis (1936). *Akiba: Scholar, Saint and Martyr.* New York: Covici and Friede.

Finkelstein, Louis (1951). *Mavo le-Massektot Avot ve-Avot de-Rabbi Nathan (Introduction to the Treatises Avot and Avot of Rabbi Nathan).* New York: JPS (Hebrew).

Finkelstein, Louis (1962). "Ancient Tradition about the Beginnings of the Sadducees and the Boethusians," in: Meir Ben-Horin, Bernard D. Weinryb, and Solomon Zeitlin (eds.), *Studies and Essays in Honor of Abraham A. Neuman.* Leiden: Brill. Hebrew section, pp. 622–639.

Firth, Raymond (1973). *Symbols: Public and Private.* Ithaca: Cornell University Press.

Fishbane, Simcha and Lightstone, Jack N. (eds.) (1990). *Essays in the Social Scientific Study of Judaism and Jewish Society* (Vol. 1). Montreal: Dept. of Religion, Concordia University.

Fishbane, Simcha, and Schoenfeld, Stuart (eds.) (1992). *Essays in the Social Scientific Study of Judaism and Jewish Society* (Vol. 2). Hoboken, NJ: Ktav.

Fitzmyer, Joseph A. (1981). *The Gospel According to Luke—the Anchor Bible.* Garden City, NY: Doubleday.

Flusser, David (1954). "The Religious Ideas of Judean Desert Sects." *Zion 19:* 89–103 (Hebrew).

Flusser, David (1958). "The Dualism 'Flesh and Spirit' in the Dead Sea Scrolls and the New Testament." *Tarbiz 27:* 158–165 (Hebrew).

Foucault, Michel (1965). *Madness and Civilization: A History of Insanity in the Age of Reason.* (Trans. by Richard Howard). New York: Vintage.

Foucault, Michel (1972). *The Archaeology of Knowledge.* (Trans. by A. M. S. Smith). London and New York: Tavistock.

Foucault, Michel (1980). *The History of Sexuality.* (Trans. by Robert Hurley). New York: Vintage.

Frankel J. (1956). *The History of the Shekl.* London.

Freimann, Avraham H. (1945). *The Order of Betrothal and Marriage after the Conclusion of the Talmud.* Jerusalem: Mossad Harav Kook (Hebrew).

Frenkel, Yonah (1991). *Darkei ha-Midrash veha-Agaddah*. Givatayim: Yad La'Talmud, (2 vols.).

Friedman, Menachem (1992). "The Lost Kiddush Cup: Challenges in Ashkenazic Haredi Culture—A Tradition in Crisis," in: Jack Wertheimer (ed.), *The Uses of Tradition: Jewish Continuity in the Modern Era*. New York: JTS, pp. 175–190.

Garber-Talmon, Yonina (1952). "Time in the Primitive Myth" *Iyyun* 2: 201–214 (Hebrew).

Geertz, Cliford (1973). *The Interpretation of Cultures*. New York: Basic Books.

Geertz, Hildred (1961). *The Javanese family: A Study of Kinship and Socialization*. New York: Free Press of Glencoe.

Gell, Alfred (1992). *The Anthropology of Time*. Oxford: Berg

Ginzberg, Louis (1941). *Perushim ve-Hidushim ba-Yerushalmi: Berakhot*. New York: Jewish Theological Seminary.

Ginzberg, Louis (1968). *The Legends of the Jews*. (7 vols.). Philadelphia: Jewish Publication Society of America.

Gladstein-Kestenberg, Ruth (1978). "The breaking of a glass at a wedding." *Studies in the History of the Jewish People and the Land of Israel*. 4: 205–208 (Hebrew).

Glaser, Barney G. and Strauss, Anselm L. (1965). *Awareness of Dying*. Chicago: Aldine Publishing.

Glassberg, Ya'akov (1892). *Sichron B'rith la-Rischonim*. Berlin: Itzkowski, [photocopy edition: Jerusalem, (1971)].

Gluckman, Max (1962). *The Ritual of Social Relations*. Manchester: Manchester University Press.

Goldberg, Harvey (ed.) (1987). *Judaism Viewed from Within and from Without*. Albany, NY: State University of New York Press.

Goldberg, Harvey E. (1998). "Breaking the cup at a wedding: An interpretive anthropological view," in: Orit Abuhav et al. (eds.), *Israel: A Local Anthropology: Studies in the Anthropology of Israel* Tel Aviv: Tcherikover, pp. 595–608 (Hebrew).

Goldshmidt, Daniel (ed.) (1965). *Seder ha-selihot*. Jerusalem: Mosad Ha-Rav Kook (Hebrew).

Goode, William J. (1959). "The Theoretical Importance of Love." *American Sociological Review, 24*: 38–47.

Goren, Shlomo (1972). "HaAdam v'Qitzo." *Haaretz* (Oct. 11), p. 12 (Hebrew).

Grintz, Yehoshuah Meir (1953). "Anshei Ha-yahad." *Sinai* 32: 11–43 (Hebrew).

Gruber-Fredman, Ruth (1981). *The Passover Seder: Afikoman in Exile*. Philadelphia: University of Pennsylvania Press.

Gruenwald, Itamar (1993). "A disagreement that is not for heaven's sake." *Haaretz* (October 29), p. B9 (Hebrew).

Haberman, Avraham Meir (1939). *"Birkat Me'en Shalosh u-Me'en Arba."* Yediot haMachon Le-Heker ha-Shirah ha-Ivrit. Berlin-Jerusalem: Schocken.

Hakohen, Aaron of Lunil (1901). *Orkhot Zaddikim*. Berlin (Hebrew).

Halbertal, Moshe (1997). *Interpretative Revolutions in the Making: Values as Interpretative Considerations in Midrashei Halakhah.* Jerusalem: Magnes Press (Hebrew).

Halbertal, Moshe (2001). "David Hartman and the Philosophy of the Halakhah," in: Avi Sagi and Zvi Zohar (eds.), *Renewing Jewish Commitment: The Work and Thought of David Hartman.* Tel Aviv: Hakkibutz Hameuchad and Shalom Hartman Institute, vol. 1, pp. 13–35 (Hebrew).

Halbwachs, Maurice (1941). *La topographie legéndaire des Évangiles en Terre Saint: Étude de mémoire collective.* Paris: Presses universitaires de France.

Halbwachs, Maurice (1980). *The Collective memory,* New York: Harper and Row.

Handelman, Don and Katz, Elihu (1990). "State Ceremonies of Israel—Remembrance Day and Independence Day," in: Don Handelman, *Models and Mirrors: Towards an Anthropology of Public Events.* Cambridge: Cambridge University Press, pp. 191–233.

Handelman, Don (1990). *Models and Mirrors: Towards an Anthropology of Public Affairs.* Cambridge: Cabridge University Press.

Haran, Menachem (1962). "Dress," in: *Encyclopaedia Biblica.* Jerusalem: Bialik Institute, vol. 4, p. 1046.

Hareuveni, Nogah (1980). *Nature in Our Biblical Heritage.* Kiryat Ono: Neot Kedumim (Hebrew).

Hauptman, Judith (2001). "Women read Talmud," in: Renée Levine Melammed (ed.), *"Lift up your voice": Women's Voices and Feminist Interpretation in Jewish Studies* Tel Aviv: Yedioth Ahronoth (Hemed Series), pp. 28–40 (Hebrew).

Haviland, William A. (1975). *Cultural Anthropology.* New York: Holt, Rinehart and Winston.

Heiman, Aharon (1964). *Toledot Tanna'im ve'Amora'im (History of Tanna'im and Amora'im).* Jerusalem: Kirya Ne'emanah (3 vols.).

Heineman, Joseph H. (1954). "The Status of the Labourer in Jewish Law and Society in the Tannaitic Period," *Hebrew Union College Annual,* 25: 263–325.

Heineman, Joseph H. (1964). *Ha-Tefilah bi-Tekufat ha-Tannaim ve-ha-Amoraim (The Liturgy in Tannaic and Amoraic Period).* Jerusalem: Magness Press (Hebrew).

Hempel, Carl G. (1959). "The logic of functional analysis," in: L. Gross (ed.), *Symposium on Sociological Theory.* New York: Harper and Row, pp. 271–307.

Hempel, Carl G. and Oppenheim, P. (1953). "The logic of explanation," in: Herbert Feigel and May Brodbeck (eds.), *Readings in the Philosophy of Science.* New York: Appleton-Century-Crofts, pp. 319–352.

Herr, Moshe David (1977). "The Rabbinic Sages' Perception of History," *Proceedings of the Sixth World Congress for Jewish Sciences.* Jerusalem: The Hebrew University, pp. 129–142 (Hebrew).

Herr, Moshe David (1983). "Continuity in the Chain of the Torah Tradition," in: Haim Beinart et al. (eds.) *Yitzchak Baer Memorial Volume.* Jerusalem: The Historical Society of Israel, pp. 43–56 (Hebrew).

Hertz, Robert (1960 [1907]). Death and the Right Hand. Glencoe: The Free Press.

Hoffman, Lawrence (1996). *The Covenant of Blood: Circumcision and Gender in Rabbinic Judaism*. Chicago: University of Chicago Press.

Hoffman, Lawrence (1987). *Beyond the Text: A Holistic Approach to Liturgy*. Bloomington, IN: Indiana University Press

Hoshen, Dalia (1991). "The Theory of Suffering in the God Perception of R. Akiva." *Da'at*, 51: 5–33.

Huntington, Richard and Metcalf, Peter (1979). *Celebrations of Death: The Anthropology of Mortuary Ritual*. Cambridge: Cambridge University Press.

Idel, Moshe (1993). *Kabbalah: New Perspectives*. (Trans. by Avriel Bar Levav). Tel Aviv: Schocken (Hebrew).

Isserlis, Moses ben Israel (1578–1580). *Mapat Ha-Shulhan on Shulhan Arukh*. Cracow (Hebrew).

Jacob ben Asher (1475). *Tur Yoreh De'ah*. Piove di Socco (Hebrew).

Jacob Son of Aaron (1908). "Circumcision among the Samaritans" in: W. E. Barton (ed.), *Bibliotheca Sacra* 65: 695–696.

Jakobovitz, Immanuel (1959). *Jewish Medical Ethics*. New York: Bloch.

Jastrow, Marcus (1950). *A Dictionary of the Targumim, the Talmud Babli and Yerushalmi, and the Midrashic Literature*. New York: Pardes.

Judd, Robin (2003). "Circumcision and Modern Jewish Life: A German Case Study," in: Elizabeth Wyner Mark (ed.), *The Covenant of Circumcision: New perspectives on an Ancient Jewish Rite*. Hanover and London: Brandeis University Press, pp. 142–155.

Kahana, Yitzhak Zeev (ed.) (1960). *Maharam mi-Rotenburg, Teshuvot, Pesakim, ve-Minhagim*, Jerusalem: Mossad ha-Rav Kook (Hebrew).

Kashani, Reuvrn (1971). "The Samaritans: History, Tradition, and Customs," *Bi-Tefutzot ha-Golah* 13: 202–219 (Hebrew).

Kasher, Menachem Mendel (1992). *Torah Sheleimah*. Jerusalem: Aharon.

Katz, Jacob (1960). "*Hevrah mesoratit ve'hevrah modernit*" ("Traditional Society and Modern Society"), *Megamot* 10: 304–311 (Hebrew).

Katz, Jacob (1961). *Bein Yehudim Le'goyim (Between Jews and Gentiles)*. Jerusalem: Bialik Institute. (Hebrew).

Katz, Jacob (1961). *Exclusiveness and Tolerance*. Oxford: Oxford University Press.

Katz, Jacob (1974). *Tradition and Crisis: Jewish Society at the End of the Middle Ages*. New York: Schocken.

Katz, Jacob (1993). "On Jewish Social History: Epochal and Supra-Epochal Historiography," *Jewish History*, 7: 89–97.

Keesing, Roger M. (1975). *Kin Groups and Social Structure*. New York: Holt, Rinehart and Winston.

Kirchheim, Raphael (1851). *Karmei Shomron*. Frankfurt.

Knohl, Israel (1995). *The Many Facets in the Belief in Monotheism*. Tel Aviv: Ministry of Defence (Hebrew).

Knorr-Cetina, Karin (1981). *The Manufacture of Knowledge*. Oxford: Pergamon.

Knorr-Cetina, Karin (1999). *Epistemic Cultures: How the Sciences Make Knowledge*. Cambridge, MA: Harvard University Press.

Kon, Maximillian (1947). *The Tombs of the Kings*. Tel Aviv: Dvir (Hebrew).

Kosovsky, Moshe (1999). *Concordance to the Talmud Yerushalmi*. Jerusalem: Israel Academy of Sciences and Humanities and Jewish Theological Seminary of America (Hebrew).

Kottak, Conard P. (1974). *Anthropology: The exploration of human diversity*. New York: Random House.

Krauss, Samuel (1910–12). *Talmudishe Archäeologie*. Leipzig: G. Fock, 3 vols.

Krauss, Samuel (1945). *Kadmoniot ha-Talmud (Antiquities of the Talmud)*. Tel Aviv: NP, (4 vols) (Hebrew).

Krausz, Ernest, Miller, Stephen H. and Rubin, Nissan (1983). *Research Methods in the Social Sciences: Strategy, Planning, and Measurement*. Tel Aviv: Dekel (Hebrew).

Kroeber, Alfred Lewis (1919). "On the Principle of Order in Civilization as Exemplified by Changes of Fashion," *The American Anthropologist*, 21: 235–263.

Kübler-Ross, Elizabeth (1970). "The Dying Patient's Point of View," in: Orville G. Brim, H. E. Freeman, S. Levine, N. A. Scotch (eds.), *The Dying Patient*. New York: Russel Sage Foundation. pp. 156–170.

Kuhn, Thomas S. (1970). *The Structure of Scientific Revolutions* (2nd ed.). New York: New American Library.

Kuper, Hilda (1973). "Costume and Identity," *Comparative Studies in Society*, 15: 348–367.

Kurtz, Donna C. and Boardman, John (1971). *Greek Burial Customs*. London: Thames and Hudson.

Latour, Bruno (1993). *We have never been modern*. (Trans. by C. Porter). Cambridge, MA: Harvard University Press.

Latour, Bruno and Woolgar, Steve (1979). *Laboratory Life: The Social Construction of Scientific Facts*. Beverly Hills, CA: Sage.

Lauterbach, Jacob Z. (1925). "The ceremony of breaking a glass in a wedding." *Hebrew Union College Annual*. 2: 351–380.

Leach, Edmund (1976). *Culture and Communication: The Logic by which Symbols are Connected: An Introduction to the Use of Structuralist Analysis in Social Anthropology*. Cambridge: Cambridge University Press.

Leach, Edmund (1981). *Rethinking Anthropology*. London: Athlone.

Lerner, Miron B. (1963). "In Memory of the Destruction." *Mahanayim* 83: 28–33 (Hebrew).

Levy, Jacob (1960). *Studies in Jewish Hellenism*. Jerusalem: Bialik Institute.

Levi, Ya'akov (1969). "Declaration of Death by the Physician." *HaMa'ayan* 9(1):15–18 (Hebrew).

Levi, Ya'akov (1971). "Saving the Neophyte after the Death of the Mother." *HaMa'ayan* 1(4):11–18 (Hebrew).

Levi, Ya'akov (1972). "Brain Death." *HaMa'ayan* 12(3):24–34 (Hebrew).

Levin, Binyamin Menashe (1939). *Ozar ha-Geonim.* Jerusalem: Mossad ha-Rav Kook.

Levi-Strauss, Claude (1962). *La pensée sauvage.* Paris: Plon.

Levi-Strauss, Claude (1966). *The Savage Mind,* London: Weidenfeld and Nicolson.

Levi-Strauss, Claude (1969a). *The Elementary Structure of Kinship.* (Trans. by J. H. Bell, J. R. von Sturmenr, and R. Needham). Boston: Beacon Press.

Levi-Strauss, Claude (1969b). *Structural Anthropology.* (Trans. by Claire Jacobson and Brooke G. Schoepf). London: Allen Lane and Penguin.

Levi-Strauss, Claude (1969c). *The Raw and the Cooked.* (Trans. by John Weightman and Doreen Weightman). New York: Harper and Row.

Levi-Strauss, Claude (1975). "Four Winnebago Myths: A Structural Sketch," in: David H. Spain (ed.), *The Human Experience,* Homewood, ILL: Dorsey, pp. 351–361.

Levi-Strauss, Claude (1978). *The Origin of Table Manners.* (Trans. by John Weightman and Doreen Weightman). New York: Harper and Row.

Licht, Jacob (ed.) (1957). *Megilat Ha-hodayot (The Thanksgiving Scroll).* Jerusalem: Bialik Institute (Hebrew).

Licht, Jacob (1965). *The Rule Scroll.* Jerusalem: Bialik Institute (Hebrew).

Licht, Jacob (1968). "Nephesh," in: *Encylopaedia Biblica,* Jerusalem: Bialik Institute, Vol. 5, pp. 598–904 (Hebrew).

Licht, Jacob (1970). "Midbar Yehudah, Kat U'Migilot" ("The Judean Desert, Cult and Scrolls"), in: *Encyclopaedia Hebraica,* Jerusalem: Encyclopaedia Publishing Company, vol. 22, pp. 195–207 (Hebrew).

Lieberman, Saul (1942). *Greek in Jewish Palestine.* New York: Jewish Theological Seminary of America.

Lieberman, Saul (1950). *Hellenism in Jewish Palestine.* New York: Jewish Theological Seminary of America.

Lieberman, Saul (1962). *Tosefta Ki-Fshutah.* New York: The Jewish Theological Seminary of America.

Lieberman, Saul (1965). "Some Aspects of After Life in Early Rabbinic Literature," in: Saul Lieberman (ed.), *Harry Austryn Wolfson Jubilee Volume,* vol. 2, English Section, pp. 493–532. Jerusalem: American Academy for Jewish Research.

Lieberman, Saul (1967). *Tosephta ki-Feshuta: Berakhot.* New York: Jewish Theological Seminary.

Lieberman, Saul (1975). "Redifat Dat Israel" ("Attacks on Judaism"), in: *Salo W. Baron Jubilee Volume.* Jerusalem: American Academy for Jewish Research. Hebrew Section, pp. 213–245.

Lieberman, Saul (1991). *Studies in Palestinian Talmudic literature*. (Ed. By David Rosenthal). Jerusalem: Magnes Press (Hebrew).

Liebes, Yehuda (1993). "Metaphysics of interpretation." *Haaretz* (October 15), p. B9 (Hebrew).

Lightstone, Jack N. (1988). *Society, the Sacred, and Scripture in Ancient Judaism*. Waterloo, Ont.: Laurier University Press.

Luckman, Thomas (1967). *The Invisible Religion*. New York: Macmillan.

Macionis, John and Plummer, Ken. (1997). *Sociology: A Global Introduction*. New York: Prentice Hall.

Mack, Hananel (1996). "Time, Place and Distribution of Midrash Bamidbar Rabbah," *Tehudah* 11: 91–105 (Hebrew).

Maoz, Azaryahu (1995). *State Cults*. Sedeh Boker: Ben-Gurion Research Center and Ben-Gurion University (Hebrew).

Margoliot, Mordechai (1974). *Hilkhot Eretz Yisrael min Hagenizah (Laws of Eretz Israel from the Genizah)*. Ed. By Yisrael Ta-Shma. Jerusalem: Mosad Harav Kook. (Hebrew).

Martens, John W. (1990). "A Sectarian Analysis of the Damascus Document," in: Simcha Fishbane and Jack N. Lightstone (ed.), *Essays in the Social Scientific Study of Judaism and Jewish History*, Montreal: Concordia University, pp. 27–40.

Mead, George H. (1929). *The Nature of the Past*, in: John Coss (ed.), *Essays in Honor of John Dewey*, New York: Holt, pp. 235–242.

Meir, Ofra (1974). "The Wedding in Kings' Parables (in the Aggada)," in: Issachar Ben-Ami and Dov Noy (eds.), *Studies in Marriage Customs (Folklore Research Center Studies*, 4). Jerusalem: Magnes Press, pp. 9–51 (Hebrew).

Michaelis, Wilhelm (1968). "Proitotokos," *Theological Dictionary of the New Testament*, 6. Grand Rapids, MI: Eerdmans.

Mills, J. (1864). *"Three Month's Residence at Nablus, and an Account of the Modern Samaritans."* London: Murray.

Moore, George Foot (1927). *Judaism*. Cambridge: Harvard University Press (3 vols).

Moore, Sally F. and Myerhoff, Barbara G. (eds.) (1977). *Secular Ritual*. Assen and Amsterdam: Van Gorcum.

Moshe ben Maimon (1927). *Mishneh Torah*. (Tr. by S. Glazer) New York: Maimonides.

Mulkay, Michael (1993). "Social Death in Britain," in: David Clark (ed.), *The Sociology of Death: Theory, Culture and Practice*. Oxford: Blackwell and Sociological Review, pp. 31–49.

Murdock, George P. (1949). *Social Structure*. New York: Macmillan.

Myers, Jacob M. (1965). *Ezra, Nehemiah—The Anchor Bible*. Garden City, NY: Doublday.

Neubauer, Jacob (1994). *The History of Marriage Laws in Bible and Talmud*. Jerusalem: Magnes Press (Hebrew).

Neusner, Jacob (1975). *Between Time and Eternity: The Essentials of Judaism*, Encino, CA: Dickenson.

Neusner, Jacob (1979). *The Talmud as Anthropology*. New York: Jewish Theological Seminary of America.

Nora, Pierre (1988). "Between History and Memory," *Representations*, 28: 7–25.

Nuni-Weiss, Efrat (2006). *The Social Construction of the Scientific Object in the Research Laboratory*. PhD diss. Bar-Ilan University (Hebrew).

Paige, Karen E. and Paige, Jeffery M. (1981). *The Politics of Reproductive Ritual*. Berkeley: University of California Press.

Paine, Robert (1983). "Israel and Totemic Time," *Royal Anthropological Institute Newsletter* 59 (December): pp. 19–22.

Philips, Bernard S. (1976). *Social Research: Strategies and Tactics* (3rd edition). New York & London: Macmillan.

Pickering, William S. F. (1974). "The Persistence of Rites of Passage: Towards an Explanation." *British Journal of Sociology*, 25: 63–78.

Popper, Karl R. (1945). *The Open Society and its Enemies*. London: Routledge.

Popper, Karl R. (1959). *The Logic of Scientific Discovery*. New York: Basic Books.

Potolski, Moshe (1975). "The Principle that One Deduces Nothing before the Giving of the Torah." *Dinei Yisrael* 6: 195–230 (Hebrew).

Pummer, Reinhard (1989). "Samaritan Rituals and Customs," in: Allan D. Crown (ed.), *The Samaritans* Tubingen: Mohr, pp. 650–690.

Ravitsky, Avi and Rosenak, Avinoam (eds.) (2008). *New Approaches to the Philosophy of Halacha*. Jerusalem: Magnes Press (Hebrew).

Roberston-Smith, William (1927). *Lectures on the Religion of the Semites*. New York: Appleton.

Romberg, Henry G. (1982). *Bris Milah*. Jerusalem and New York: Feldheim.

Rosenak, Avinoam (2005). "Aggadah and Halakha: Reflections on Trends in Thought and Study of the Philosophy of the Halakha," in: Amichai Berholz (ed.), *The Quest for Halakha: Interdisciplinary Perspectives on Jewish law*. Tel Aviv: Yedioth Ahronoth, pp. 285–312 (Hebrew).

Rosenak, Avinoam (in press). *The Halakhah as a Generator of Change: Critical Studies in the Philosophy of the Halakhah*. Jerusalem: Magnes Press (Hebrew).

Rosenfeld, Henry (1964). *They Were Peasants: Social Anthropological Studies on the Arab Village in Israel*. Tel Aviv: Hakibbutz Hameuchad (Hebrew).

Rosenfeld, Nachman (1972/3). "Declaring a Person Dead." *Niv HaMidrashia* 9–10: 179–181 (Hebrew).

Rosenthal, Eliezer Shimshon (1963). "*Ha-moreh*." *Proceedings of the American Academy for Jewish Research*, 31: i-lxxi (Hebrew).

Rosen-Zvi, Ishai (2004). *The ritual of suspected adultress (Sotah) in Tannaic literature*. PhD diss. Tel Aviv University (Hebrew).

Ross, Tamar (2005). "Orthodoxy, Women, and Halakhic Change: A Theological Analysis and Interpretive Aspects," in: Amichai Berholz (ed.), *The Quest for Halakha: Interdisciplinary Perspectives on Jewish Law* Tel Aviv: Yedioth Ahronoth, pp. 387–437 (Hebrew).

Rossi, Ino (ed.). (1974). *The Unconscious in Culture: The Structuralism of Claude Levi-Strauss in Perspective*. New York: Dutton.

Rubin, Nissan (1972). "For Whom Does One Mourn? A Sociological Analysis of Talmudic Sources." *Bar Ilan Yearbook* Ramat Gan: Bar Ilan University Press, vol. 10, pp. 111–122.

Rubin, Nissan (1977). *A Sociological Analysis of Jewish Mourning Patterns in the Mishnaic and Talmudic Periods*. Ph.D. Dissertation. Ramat Gan: Bar Ilan University (Hebrew).

Rubin, Nissan (1981). "*La'mashma'ut ha'hevratit shel ha'bekhor bamikra*" ("Concerning the Social Significance of the Firstborn in the Bible"), *Bet Mikra* 33 (113): 155–176 (Hebrew).

Rubin, Nissan (1988). "Historical Time and Liminal Time: A Chapter in Rabbinic Historiosophy," *Jewish History* 2(2): 7–22 (Hebrew).

Rubin, Nissan (1990). "The Sages' Conception of Body and Soul," in: Simchah Fishbane and Jack N. Lightstone (eds.), *Judaism and Jewish Society*. Montreal: Concordia University Press, pp. 47–103.

Rubin, Nissan (1990a). "Social Network and Mourning: A Comparative Approach." *Omega* 21: 113–127.

Rubin, Nissan (1993). "*Birkat Avelim*—The Blessing of Mourners," in: Herbert W. Basser and Simcha Fishbane (eds.), *Approaches to Ancient Judaism*. Atlanta, GA: Scholars Press, pp. 119–141.

Rubin, Nissan (1994). "Secondary Burial in the Mishnaic and Talmudic Periods: A Proposed Model of the Relationships of Social Structure to Burial Practices," in: Itamar Singer (ed.), *Graves and Burial Practices in Israel in the Ancient Period*. Jerusalem: Yad Itzhak Ben-Zvi and Israel Exploration Society, pp. 248–69 (Hebrew).

Rubin, Nissan (1995). *The Beginning of life: Rites of Birth, Circumcision and Redemption of the First-born in the Talmud and Midrash*. Tel-Aviv: Hakibbutz Hameuchad (Hebrew).

Rubin, Nissan (1996). "Coping with the Value of the *pidyon ha'ben* Payment in Rabbinic Literature—An Example of a Social Change Process," *Jewish History* 10: 39–61.

Rubin, Nissan (1997). *The End of Life: Rites of Mourning and Burial in the Talmud and Midrash*. Tel Aviv: Hakkibutz Hameuchad (Hebrew).

Rubin, Nissan (1999). "On drawing down the prepuce and incision of the foreskin (*peri'ah*)." *Zion*. 54: 105–117 (Hebrew).

Rubin, Nissan (2003). "*Brit Milah*: A Study of Change in Customs," in: Elizabeth Wyner Mark (ed.). *The Covenant of Circumcision: New Perspectives on an Ancient Jewish Rite*. Boston: University Press of New England and Brandeis University Press, pp. 87–97.

Rubin, Nissan (2004). *The Joy of life: Rites of Betrothal and Marriage in the Talmud and Midrash*. Tel Aviv: Hakibbutz Hameuchad (Hebrew).

Rubin, Nissan (2008). "Birth and Marriage Ceremonies: A Critical Reading of Women's status," in: Avi Ravitsky and Avinoam Rosenak (eds.), *New Approaches to the Philosophy of Halacha*. Jerusalem: Magnes Press, pp. 491–519 (Hebrew).

Rubin, Nissan, and Peer, Drora (2000). "Army Retirement Rites: Formal and Informal." *Megamot. 40*, 103–40 (Hebrew).

Safrai, Shmuel (1967). "Monetary Development in the Third and Fourth Centuries as Reflected in the Talmudic Literature," in: A. Kindler (ed.), *International Numismatic Convention*. Tel Aviv: Schocken.

Safrai, Zeev (1994). *The Economy of Roman Palestine*. London and New York: Routledge.

Sagi, Avi and Zvi Zohar (1995a). *Conversion to Judaism and the Meaning of Jewish Identity*. Jerusalem: Bialik Institute and Shalom Hartman Institute (Hebrew).

Sagi, Avi and Zvi Zohar (1995b). "The Halakhic Ritual of Giyyur and Its Symbolic Meaning," *Journal of Ritual Studies* 9: 1–13.

Samet, Moshe (1993). "Conversion in the First Centuries C.E.," in: Isaiah Gafni, Aaaron Oppenheimer, and Menachem Stern (eds.), *Jews and Judaism in the Second Temple, Mishna and Talmud Period*. Jerusalem: Yad Izhak Ben-Zvi, pp. 316–343 (Hebrew).

Schwartz, Barry (1991). "Social Change and Collective Memory: The Democratization of George Washington," *American Sociological Review*, 56: 221–236.

Seidler, Meir (2005). "From the 'First Attempt' to the 'Last Accord': Metahalakha in the Teachings of Mendelssohn and Breuer on the Background of the Challenge of Modernity," in: Amichai Berholz (ed.), *The Quest for Halakha: Interdisciplinary Perspectives on Jewish Law*. Tel Aviv: Yedioth Ahronoth, pp. 313–334 (Hebrew).

Seligson, Miriam (1951). "The Meaning of the Word Naefaeљ in the Old Testament Hebrew Language." *Studia Orientala*, Helsinki.

Sellers, Ovid R. (1962). "Weights and Measures," *Interpreter's Dictionary of the Bible*, 4. New York.

Shils, Edward A. (1981). *Tradition*. Chicago, ILL: University of Chicago Press.

Silman, Neomi (2006). *The Symbolic Meaning of Wine in Jewish Culture*. PhD diss. Bar-Ilan University (Hebrew).

Simmel, Georg (1904). "Fashion," *International Quarterly*, 10: 130–155 (reprinted in *American Journal of Sociology*, 62: 541–558, 1957).

Smallwood, E. Mary (1959). "The Legislation of Herodian and Antoninus Pius Against Circumcision," *Latomus* 18: 334–347.

Smallwood E. Mary (1961). "The Legistlation of Herodian and Antoninus Pius Against Circumcision," *Latomus* 20: 93–96.

Smelser, Neil J. (1962). *Theory of Collective Behavior*. London: Routledge and Kegan Paul.

Sperber, Daniel (1966). *"Matbeʿot-Yahasei Arakhim u-Mishkalot bi-Tekufat ha-Geonim"* (Coins—Relative Values and Weights during the Geonic Period"), *Sinai*, 58: 164–168 (Hebrew).

Sperber Daniel (1970). *"Midot u'mishkalot"* ("Measures and Weights"), *Encyclopaedia Hebraica*, vol. 22. Jerusalem: Encyclopaedia Publishing Company, pp. 236–238. (Hebrew).

Sperber, Daniel (1970a). *"Al Erko shel ha-Maneh"* ("Regarding the Value of the Maneh"), *Talpiyot* 9 (3–4): 591–611 (Hebrew).

Sperber, Daniel (1974). *Roman Palestine 200–400: Money and Prices*. Ramat Gan: Bar Ilan University Press.

Sperber, Daniel (1983). "The Custom of Drinking Wine during Circumcision," *Milet* 1: 223–224 (Hebrew).

Stern, Menachem (1976). "The Period of the Second Temple," in: Chaim Hilel Ben-Sasson (ed.), *A History of the Jewish People*, Cambridge, MA.: Harvard University Press, pp. 196–205.

Stollman, Aviad (2005). "Closeness and Openness in the Perception of the Halakha: The Intellectual History of the Halakha and of the Sciences," in: Amichai Berholz (ed.), *The Quest for Halakha: Interdisciplinary Perspectives on Jewish law.* Tel Aviv: Yedioth Ahronoth, pp. 335–353 (Hebrew).

Storey, John (ed.) (1996). *What is cultural studies?: A Reader*. London: Arnold.

Sudnow, David (1969). *Passing On: The Social Organization of Dying.* Englewood Cliffs, NJ: Prentice Hall.

Sussman, Ya'akov (1997). "Professor J. N. Epstein and the Hebrew University," in: Sahaul Katz and Michael Heyd (eds.), *The History of the Hebrew University of Jerusalem: Origins and Beginnings.* Jerusalem: Magnes Press, pp. 476–486 (Hebrew).

Tcherikover, Avigdor (1950). "Syntaxis and Laographia," *Journal of Juristic Papyrology* 4: 179–207.

Tcherikover, Avigdor (1954). "The Decrees of Antiochus and Their Problems," *Eshkolot* 1 :86–109 (Hebrew).

Tcherikover, Avigdor (1959). *Hellenistic Civilization and the Jews.* Philadelphia, PA: Jewish Publication Society.

Tcherikover, Avigdor (1972). "The Hellenistic Movement in Jerusalem and Antiochus' Persecutions," in: Avraham Schalit (ed.), *The World History of the Jewish People*, vol. 6, *The Hellenistic Age*. London: W. H. Allen, pp. 115–144.

Tcherikover, Avigdor and A. Fuks (1957). *Corpus Papyrorum Judicarum.* Cambridge, MA.: Harvard University Press.

Toynbee, Jocelyn M. C. (1971). *Death and Burial in the Roman World.* London: Thames and Hudson.

Tukachinsky, Yechiel Michal (1960). *Gesher HaHayim.* Jerusalem (Hebrew).

Turner, Victor W. (1960). "Social Dramas and Stories about them." *Critical Inquiry.* 7: 141–68.

Turner, Victor W. (1967). *The Forest of Symbols: Aspects of Ndembu Rituals*, Ithaca, NY: Cornell University Press.

Turner, Victor W. (1974). *Dramas, Fields and Metaphors.*, Ithaca, NY and London: Cornell University Press.

Turner, Victor W. (1979). "Variations on a Theme of Liminality," in: Sally E. Moore and Barbara G. Myerhoff (eds.) *Secular Ritual*, pp. 36–51. Assen/Amsterdam: Van Gorcum.

Turner, Victor W. (1982). *Celebrations: Studies in Fertility and Ritual*. Washington, DC: Smithsonian Institution Press.

Tur-Sinai, Naphtali Herz (1953). "*Shushvin*" in: Moshe D. Kassuto, Yosef Klausner and Yehoshuah Guttman (eds.) *Sefer Assaf (Presented to Simha Assaf on His Sixtieth Birthday)*. Jerusalem: Mossad Harav Kook, pp. 316–322 (Hebrew).

Urbach, Epharim E. (1955). *Ba'alei Ha-Tosafot (The Tosaphists)*. Jerusalem: Bialik Institute (Hebrew).

Urbach, Ephraim E. (1960). "Asceticism and Suffering in the Talmudic and Mishnaic Sources," in: Salo E. Barron et al. (eds.), *Yitzchak F. Baer Jubilee Volume*, Jerusalem: Historical Society of Israel, pp. 48–68 (Hebrew).

Urbach, Ephraim E. (1967). "The Laws of Inheritance and Everlasting Life," in: *Proceedings of the Fourth World Congress of Jewish Studies*. Jerusalem: World Union of Jewish Studies, pp. 133–141.

Urbach, Ephraim E. (1975). *The Sages: Their Concepts and Beliefs*. Jerusalem: Magnes Press.

Urbach, Ephraim E. (1978). "Halakhah and History," in: Robert Hamerton-Kelly and Robin Scroggs (ed.), *Jews, Greeks, Christians: Religious Cultures in Late Antiquity— Essays in Honor of William David Davies*, Leiden: Brill, pp. 112–128.

Urbach, Ephraim E. (1998). *Studies in Judaica*, (ed. By Moshe David Herr and Jonah Fraenkel). Jerusalem: Magnes Press, 2 vols. (Hebrew).

Urbach, Ephraim E. (2002). *The World of the Sages: Collected Studies*. Jerusalem: Magnes Press (Hebrew).

Valler, Shulamit (1999). *Women and Womanhood in the Talmud*. (Trans. by Betty S. Rozen Trans.). Providence, RI: Brown Judaic Studies.

Van Gennep, Arnold (1960 [1909]). *The Rites of Passage*. (Trans. by Monika B. Wizdom and Gabrielle L. Caffee). London: Routledge and Kegan Paul.

Villien, Yosef (1996). "The Breaking of a Cup at a Wedding: The Custom and its Source." *Sinai*. 118: 262–266 (Hebrew).

Wallis, Robert (1983). "Ritual," in: M. Mann (ed.), *The Macmillan Student Encyclopedia of Sociology*. London: Macmillan, pp. 334–335.

Weber, Max (1948). "The Social Psychology of World Religions," in: Hans H. Gerth and C.Wright Mills (eds.) *From Max Weber: Essays in Sociology*. London: Oxford University Press, pp. 267–301.

Weber, Max (1949). *The Methodology of Social Sciences*. (Trans. by Edward A. Shils and Henry A. Finch). Glencoe, IL: Free Press.

Weiss, Issac Hirsch (1924). *Dor Dor ve-Dorshav.* New York (Hebrew).

Wenham, Gordon J. (1978). "Leviticus 27:2–8 and the Price of Slaves," *Zeitschrift fur die Alttestamentliche Wissenschaft*, 90: 264–265.

Wenham, Gordon J. (1981). *Numbers: An Introduction and Commentary*: Leicester: Inter-Varsity Press.

Wilson, Bryan R. (ed.) (1962). *Patterns of Sectarianisnm.* London: Heinemann Educational Books.

Wolfson, Harry Austryn (1948). *Philo.* 2 vols. Cambridge: Harvard University Press.

Yadin, Yigael (ed.) (1955). *Megilat Milchemet Bney Or bi-Vney Chosech (The Scroll of the War of the Sons of Light against the Sons of Darkness.* Jerusalem: Bialik Institute. (Hebrew).

Yelinek, Aharon (1938). *Bet Ha-Midrasch.* Jerusalem: Bamberger and Wahrmann, 6 Vols. (Hebrew).

Yerushalmi, Yoseph H. (1982). Zakhor, *Jewish History and Jewish Memory.* Seattle: University of Washington Press.

Zeligmann, I. L. (1958). "Deixai autoi fos." *Tarbiz* 27: 127–141 (Hebrew).

Zlotnik, David (ed. and tr.) (1966). *The Tractate Mourning.* New Haven and London: Yale University Press.

GENERAL INDEX

General Index

AUTHORS INDEX

Authors Index

216

Authors Index

SOURCES INDEX

CPSIA information can be obtained at www.ICGtesting.com
Printed in the USA
BVOW06s1911060815

411975BV00004B/29/P